U0635624

Legal Translation 101

法律翻译 101

杨文峰　著

中国出版集团

中译出版社

图书在版编目（CIP）数据

法律翻译 101：汉文、英文 / 杨文峰著 . -- 北京：
中译出版社 , 2020.9（2022.8 重印）
ISBN 978-7-5001-6201-8

Ⅰ . ①法… Ⅱ . ①杨… Ⅲ . ①法律—英语—翻译
Ⅳ . ① D9

中国版本图书馆 CIP 数据核字（2020）第 141209 号

出版发行 / 中译出版社
地　　址 / 北京市西城区新街口外大街 28 号普天德胜大厦主楼 4 层
电　　话 /（010）68359376，68359827（发行部）　68359719（编辑部）
传　　真 /（010）68357870
邮　　编 / 100044
电子邮箱 / book@ctph.com.cn
网　　址 / http://www.ctph.com.cn

策划编辑 / 刘香玲　　王秋璎
责任编辑 / 张　旭
封面设计 / 潘　峰

排　　版 / 冯　兴
印　　刷 / 北京玺诚印务有限公司
经　　销 / 新华书店

规　　格 / 710 毫米 ×1000 毫米　1/16
印　　张 / 22
字　　数 / 212 千字
版　　次 / 2020 年 9 月第一版
印　　次 / 2022 年 8 月第二次

ISBN 978-7-5001-6201-8　　　　定价：68.00 元

版权所有　侵权必究
中 译 出 版 社

序　言

　　杨文峰老师本非法律专业出身，乃是根红苗正的翻译精英，毕业于北京外国语大学，专攻语言文学，毕业之后进入翻译领域，却对法律翻译情有独钟，在这个领域刻苦精研，十几年如一日，译文已超千余万字，心得体会颇丰。中国对外翻译有限公司一路相伴，深觉杨老师多年心血不能辜负，力劝杨老师将心得体会集结成册，惠及万千在法律翻译领域奋斗的同行。杨老师慨然应允，耗费数年时光，从数千案例中精选材料，搜求务必周全，辨析必求严谨，斟酌权衡，反复修订，终成此书。

　　法律翻译之不易已是众所周知，其中最难的便是对法律概念的理解和翻译。法律概念为社会关系的浓缩提炼，本已纷繁复杂，更兼中外法律体系各有特色，哪怕名义相同的概念，其内涵也不能完全重合。译者既要明了各种法律概念原本的基础意义，了解其在不同法系的微妙区别，熟知其各种习惯搭配用法，还要权衡中外语境，斟酌对等译文，无论是学识不足，经验不够，还是工作态度不严谨，都有可能导致翻译时顾此失彼，带来遗憾甚至损失。

　　此书立篇即在解决这个问题。杨老师治学严谨，广泛梳理法律语料以搜求代表性的常用术语，中外文本并重，不仅涵盖中国法律，还涉足英、美、加等国及欧盟的法律，不仅有严谨的合同文本，也有联合国涉及法律事项的报告，材料多样而宗旨如一，俱是为了辨明同一术语在不同语境下的意义用法。书中共集得法律术语逾千，或意相近而形不同，或形相似而意不同，各有其容易混淆之处。杨老师谋篇周密，对形似但意不同的术语，采取多个术语并列的方式，先叙述共同含义，随后逐加详述，列举其名、动、形、副各种词形，配以精选实例，意在供读者熟悉各术语的常见与特殊用法，从中揣摩把握翻译的尺度；对意同而形不同的术语，则侧重指出其容易混淆之处，同样提供丰富实例，力求详尽周到体现各方面区别，以便读者如观雪洞，对相近词汇的枝蔓了解明白。试举一例，譬如法律文本中司空见惯的 duplicate 一词，书中即举出诸多形近词、义近词、惯用法，援引法律词典、国内法条和美国联邦证据规则予以辨析，且结合翻译实践点评译文，内容丰富，分析有据，一节读罢，令人叹服。

此书取名《法律翻译 101》，101 者，美国法学院一年级课程代码，杨老师用 101 为此书命名，取其为法律翻译初级入门之意，但这实在是杨老师的谦虚，如大家仅将此书视为入门指南，未免会令明珠蒙尘，汗血盐车。在我看来，此书不仅可做翻译教材，为初窥法律翻译门径的译员指点迷津，更可作为简明的法律术语用法词典，为苦于中英文法律写作的人提供用以模仿的经典范本，合两种作用于一身，此书的效用可谓大矣。

此书即将付梓，中国对外翻译有限公司向杨老师表示祝贺，并愿翻译界同行俱能从此书获益。

中国对外翻译有限公司
党委副书记、副总经理
2020 年 8 月

目　录

accountability, duty, liability, obligation & responsibility

汉语中的"责任 / 负责"一词含有多重意思：① 表示对事务、工作等的义务；② 表示对它们的权力（也就是"主管"）；③ 表示不履行这方面的义务或滥用这方面的权力要承担的不利后果。这几个单词在法律文件中都与负责 / 责任 / 义务有关，意思又有区别。

(1)

accountability [əˌkaʊntəˈbiləti] *n.[U]*

accountable [əˈkaʊntəbl] *adj.* responsible

accountable/accountability 侧重"责任"第一和第三义项。它常构成下面的短语：

accountable to sb. for sth. 应当对……负责，应当对……作出解释，应当对……有交代

hold sb. accountable for sth. 要求某人对某事负责

例 1. Each State Party shall, in accordance with the fundamental principles of its legal system, take appropriate measures to promote transparency and accountability in the management of public finances. 各缔约国均应当根据本国法律制度的基本原则采取适当措施，促进公共财政管理的透明度和问责制。

例 2. As the Government extends its authority in those areas, it is committed to eradicating the practice of death by stoning while working towards declaring a moratorium on the death penalty. The perpetrators of such crimes will be held accountable for their actions. 随着政府扩大在这些地区的威信，政府致力于取缔以石刑处决犯人的做法，同时谋求宣告暂缓执行死刑。犯有此类罪行者其行为将被追究责任。

例 3. The Council notes that the *Darfur Peace Agreement* stipulates the principles of enhancing accountability and preventing impunity. It calls on all parties to uphold the principles which are equally applicable to States and non-State actors and to cooperate fully in the implementation of the Agreement. 理事指出,《达尔富尔和平协定》规定了加强问责和防止有罪不罚的原则。理事会呼吁所有各方维护这些同样适用于国家和非国家行为方的原则,并在执行该协定方面充分合作。

例 4. This new vision is fully captured by the proposed SDG 4 *"Ensure inclusive and equitable quality education and promote lifelong learning opportunities for all"* and its corresponding targets. It is transformative and universal, attends to the "unfinished business" of the EFA agenda and the education-related MDGs, and addresses global and national education challenges. It is inspired by a humanistic vision of education and development based on human rights and dignity; social justice; inclusion; protection; cultural, linguistic and ethnic diversity; and shared responsibility and accountability. 这一新愿景完全体现在了拟议的可持续发展目标 4 ("为所有人确保包容、公平的优质教育并促进终身学习机会") 及其相关具体目标之中。新愿景既具有变革性也具有普遍性,致力于全民教育议程和与教育有关的千年发展目标的 "未竟事业" ,应对全球和国家的教育挑战。它脱胎于人文主义的教育和发展观,其基础是人权和尊严,社会正义,包容,保护,文化、语言和民族多样性,共同责任和义务。

例 5. The Director of Portfolio Management, along with the Chief Investment Officer, coordinates all global portfolio management activities and monitors portfolios for compliance with XYZ's internal guidelines. The Director of Research ensures consistent adherence to XYZ's disciplined research methodology. Our team-driven, collaborative environment provides for group oversight of the research and investment process, with analysts, portfolio managers and the Director of Research ultimately accountable for stock recommendations. 投资组合管理总监与首席投资官一起,协调所有全球投资组合管理业务,监督投资组合遵守 XYZ 内部指导准则的情况。研究总监确保 XYZ 严谨的研究方法能够得到始终如一的遵守。我们的团队起带动

作用，充满合作气氛，可以对研究和投资流程进行集体监督，并由分析师、基金经理和研究总监对股票建议承担最终责任。

例 6. With these controls in place, we are confident in our ability to offer a "XYZ portfolio" to all of our clients. The full accountability and oversight of our Director of Portfolio Management-Institutional and Chief Investment Officer, as well as regular peer review of all portfolios, minimizes the risk of "rogue traders" and ensures that every client benefits from our best thinking. Breaches are addressed by the Director of Portfolio Management and dealt with on an individual basis. 有了这些控制机制，我们相信自己能为所有客户提供一款"XYZ 的投资组合"。投资组合管理总监及首席投资官全面负责和督导，再加上对所有投资组合进行的定期同侪审核机制，我们就可以最大限度地减少产生"魔鬼交易员（rogue traders）"的风险，使每一位客户都能从我们公司最佳的投资理念中受益。投资组合管理总监负责处理违反规定的行为，处理措施落实到个人。

(2)

duty ['dju:ti] *n.[C,U]*

duty 也表示义务，侧重于职责，它的另外一个常用义项就是税。

例 7. In conformity with the *General Corporation Law of the State of California*, the Limited Partners will not take part in the management of the business or transact any business for the Fund, and will have no power to sign for or to bind the Partnership. However, the Limited Partners will have rights, powers and duties normally granted to Limited Partners under the *Uniform Limited Partnership Act* and as described in 8 *C.F.R.* 204.6(j)(5)(iii) regarding the requirements for the *EB-5 Program*. 依照《加利福尼亚州通用公司法》，有限合伙人不得参与管理本基金的营业或处理本基金的任何事务，他们也无权签署有利于或约束本合伙组织的契约。但是，有限合伙人将会具有《统一有限合伙法》通常赋予有限合伙人的各种权利、职权和义务，《联邦法规汇编》第 8 编第 204.6（j）（5）（iii）条对《EB-5 方案》规定了若干要求，其中就对上述权利、职权和义务作出了说明。

例 8. In case of misconduct as well as graft or serious dereliction of duty of the Management Personnel, the Board of Directors shall dismiss them at any time without further remuneration to be paid to them and at the same time may claim compensation for damages caused by them to the Company. 如果管理人员出现不法行为和以权谋私或者严重玩忽职守，董事会应当随时解雇他们，无须另行给付报酬，同时可以要求被解雇的管理人员赔偿公司损害。

例 9. CCC shall withhold any amount for the payment of tax and duties in accordance with the Applicable Laws, with respect to the assets entrusted by KKK or any transaction related thereto, in respect of income and capital gains. CCC shall provide KKK with details of calculation of tax and duties in accordance with the Applicable Laws. CCC 应当依照法律适用的规定扣缴与 KKK 委托 CCC 的资产或者与涉及该资产的交易有关的收入和资本收益的应纳税款。CCC 应当向 KKK 提供依照法律适用计算赋税的详细资料。

(3)

obligation [ˌɒbliˈgeiʃən] *n.[C,U]*

obligation 是最严格意义上的义务，也就是上面所说的中文"责任／负责"一词的第一个义项。

例 10. This Agreement and all rights and obligations hereunder are personal to the parties hereto and neither one of the parties hereto shall assign or attempt to assign any such rights or obligations to any third party without the prior written consent of the other. 本协议以及本协议所规定的各项权利和义务与本协议当事人有关；在未获得对方当事人事先书面许可的情况下，各方当事人均不得向第三人转让或者试图转让本协议所规定的任何权利或义务。

例 11. Except as otherwise provided in the Contract, the Engineer shall have no authority to relieve the Contractor of any of his obligations under the Contract nor to order any work involving delay in completion of the Works or any extra payment to the Contractor by the Employer, or to make any variations to the Works. 除非合同另有规定，工程师无权免除承包人依照合同承担的任何义务，也无权命令承包人进行延误工程完工的任何施工，或要求雇主向承包人额外支付款项，或对工程进行任何改动。

例 12. The Office commits itself not to enter into contracts with third parties that would lead to unfair competition for the Company. This Agreement shall not, however, restrict the Office in the fulfillment of its obligations to the public or in the fulfillment of its normal, legal and traditional functions. 贵局承诺不与第三人订立可能导致针对本公司的不公平竞争的合同。但是，本协议不限制贵局履行对公众承担的义务，亦不限制贵局履行正常的、法定的和惯常的职能。

例 13. The obligations set out in this clause shall apply during the term of this Agreement and shall continue for a period of 3 years after termination or expiration hereof. 本条规定的各项义务应当适用于本协议的存续期间，在本协议被终止或者本协议期限届满之后三年内，上述义务依然适用。

例 14. Unless explicitly agreed, there is no obligation to place Purchase Orders and no minimum purchase commitment of ABC and Subsidiaries, and estimates or forecasts furnished by ABC or Subsidiaries to XYZ shall not constitute a Purchase Order or a commitment to purchase. 除非明示约定，ABC 和子公司不承担签发采购订单和作出最低采购承诺的义务，ABC 或者子公司向 XYZ 提供的估算或预测不构成采购订单或采购承诺。

(4)

liability [ˌlaɪəˈbɪləti] *n.[U]*

liability 侧重于"责任"的第三义项，也就是不利后果。我们经常遇到协议中的责任限制条款（Limitation of Liability）：

例 15. Service Provider acts as an independent sub-contractor and undertakes the performance of the Services at its own account and risk. The Parties understand and agree that, unless specifically provided in this Agreement, neither Party grants the other Party any authority to make or give any agreement, statement, representation, or warranty or otherwise incur any liability or obligation on behalf of the other Party. For the avoidance of doubt Service Provider is not an agent or employee of Customer. 服务商作为独立的分包人，自行负担费用和承担风险履行服务。双方当事人理解并且约定，除非本协议明确规定，任何一方当事人均未授权对方订立或者作出任何协议、声明、陈述或保证或者以其他方式代表对方承担任何责任或义务。为避免产生疑问，服务商并非客户的代理人，亦非客户的雇员。

例 16. 1. Limitation of Liability

1.1 Without prejudice to the Security Agent's duties at law, the Security Agent shall not be liable for any losses arising in connection with any action taken or not taken by it under this Assignment or in relation to the Assigned Contracts unless directly caused by its gross negligence or wilful misconduct.

1.2 The Company may not take any proceedings against any director, officer, employee or agent of the Security Agent in respect of any claim it might have against the Security Agent, or in respect of any act or omission of any kind (including gross negligence or wilful misconduct) by that officer, employee or agent in relation to this Assignment or the Assigned Contracts.

1 责任限制

1.1 在不损害担保代理人的法定义务的情况下，担保代理人对于自己根据本转让协议或者对于被转让合同采取或没有采取的行动所造成的任何损失不承担责任，除非该损失是由担保代理人的重大过失或故意的不法行为直接造成的。

1.2 对于公司可能针对担保代理人享有的任何请求权，或者公司对于担保代理人的任何高级职员、雇员或代理人有关本转让协议或被转让合同的各种作为或不作为（包括重大过失或故意的不法行为在内），公司不得针对担保代理人的董事、高级职员、雇员或代理人提起任何诉讼。

注意：liability（责任）是不可数名词，liabilities 的意思是负债。

例 17. XYZ shall indemnify and hold harmless ABC, its Subsidiaries, any Distributors and Customers against any and all costs, expenses, losses, damages and liabilities arising from XYZ's non-compliance with, or breach of, any representation or warranty or obligation under this Article 15 (Warranty). XYZ 应当向 ABC、ABC 的子公司、任何经销商和客户给予赔偿，使之免于承受由于 XYZ 不遵守或者违反本协议第十五条（保证）项下的声明、保证或义务而产生的任何和所有支出、费用、损失、损害以及债务。

(5)

responsibility [riˌspɒnsəˈbiləti] *n.[C,U]*

responsibility 包含了责任的三个义项。相应地，responsible 可以表示有责任心，有担当，管理某种事务，还表示做了错事要承担不利后果。

例 18. It is now time to improve investment in research, policies and programmes to create enabling conditions for youth, including the most vulnerable and marginalized and especially young women, to prosper, exercise rights and engage as responsible citizens and social actors. 现在应加强对研究、政策和计划的投资，为青年人，包括最弱势和最边缘化的青年人，特别是为青年妇女，创造有利条件，使其能够取得成功，行使权利并成为负责任的公民和社会参与者。

例 19. Both Party A and Party B shall monitor the risk profile of the Product's investment portfolio. Party B shall take its monitoring of the risk profile of the Product's investment portfolio into account in making its investment recommendations. Party A shall be responsible for the overall construction of the Product's risk profile and ensuring that the Product is managed on a discretionary basis within it. 甲乙双方应当监测产品投资组合的风险概况。乙方在提出投资建议时应当考虑它对产品的投资组合风险概况的监测。甲方应当负责产品风险概况的综合构建并负责确保在它构建的风险概况范围内全权管理产品。

下面这个例句中，第一个 responsible for 的意思是义务，第二个 responsible for 则表示承担不利后果的责任。

例 20. In all cases where Buyer is responsible for contracting for the supply of services, facilities or equipment based on drawings, specifications or other engineering data prepared by Seller, Seller's liability shall be limited to the supply of correct engineering information and will not be extended to cover the repair, replacement or alteration of any service, facility or equipment except for Co-manufactured Equipment where Seller is responsible for the direct cost to repair or replace the faulty part. 只要买方负责根据卖方准备的图纸、规格说明或者其他工程数据订立提供服务、设施或者设备的合同，卖方的责任即应限于提供正确的工程资料而不包括修理、更换或者改动任何服务、设施或者设备。但是对于共同制成设备，卖方负担修理或者更换有缺陷部件的直接费用。

例 21. The obligations and responsibilities of the Contractor under this Contract shall be suspended to the extent of his inability to perform them and for as long as such inability continues. During such suspension and in respect of work suspended, the Contractor shall be reimbursed by the UNDP substantiated costs of maintenance of the Contractor's equipment and of per diem of the Contractor's permanent personnel rendered idle by such suspension. 在承包人无法履行义务的限度内，只要承包人无法履行义务的状态持续，承包人在本合同项下的义务和责任应中止。在承包人中止履行义务期间，对于暂时停止的施工作业，开发计划署应向承包人偿付有证据证明的维护承包人设备的费用，以及有证据证明的由于中止施工而向闲置的承包人的固定工作人员按日计付的费用。

例 22. All taxes and duties levied by Chinese government on the Seller, in connection with and in the performance of the Contract, according to Chinese tax laws and the agreement between the government of the People's Republic of China and the government of the Seller's country for the reciprocal avoidance of double taxation and the prevention of fiscal evasion with respect to taxes on income, in effect shall be borne by the Seller. The Seller has the responsibility to pay the above-mentioned taxes directly to the Chinese tax authorities. 中国政府依照中国税法以及中华人民共和国政府与卖方所在国家政府相互避免双重征税和防止逃避缴纳所得税的生效协定，向卖方课征的与本合同有关的和履行本合同过程中的所有赋税须由卖方缴纳。卖方有义务直接向中国税务机关缴纳上述赋税。

品味语义，下面例句中第一个 responsibilities 的意思是职责，第二个 responsibilities 前面有 duties 表示义务这个意思，所以将 responsibilities 译成责任。

例 23. If the Employer and Engineer so agree, the Engineer shall provide one or more Engineer's Representative(s) to assist the Engineer in carrying out his responsibilities at the site. The Engineer shall notify in writing to the Contractor and the Employer the duties, responsibilities and limitations of authority of any such Engineer's Representative(s). 如果雇主和工程师协商一致，工程师应提供一名或多名工程师的代表，协助工程师在现场履行其职责。工程师应将上述代表的义务、责任和权限书面通知承包人和雇主。

最后我们体会一个例句，除了 accountability, 例句包含了我们学习的其他几个词汇：

例 24. If, in relation to the Security in any jurisdiction in which the same may be situated, the constitution of the trusts pursuant to this Agreement and the rights and obligations conferred on any person thereby (whether or not a party to this Agreement) would not be recognized as creating enforceable rights and obligations by applicable law, then this Agreement shall, to such extent, be construed as constituting the equivalent rights and obligations as a matter of contract; provided always that, in the event that the foregoing provisions of this Clause 17.3.4 take effect so that this Agreement operates as a matter of contract, the Security Agent shall have no additional or incremental duties, obligations, responsibilities or liabilities over and above those which would have existed had the said trusts, rights and obligations been so recognized. 就担保物可能处于任何司法管辖区而言，倘若依照本协议构成信托和根据信托授予

任何人（无论是否为本协议的当事人）的权利和义务，依据相关法律可能不会被认可为创设可以执行的权利和义务，那么本协议应当在上述范围内被解释为构成相同的合同权利和义务；但是需要始终满足这样的前提条件：如果第17.3.4条的前述规定生效，以致本协议发挥合同效力，担保事务代理人承担的职责、义务、责任或债务不应当超过假若上述信托、权利和义务获得认可后原本应当存在的职责、义务、责任或债务。

address & redress

(1)

address [ə'drɛs] *n.[C]* ① 地址；② 演讲；*v.t.* ① 在(信封或包裹)上写明地址；② 对……讲话，
　　给……写信；③ 解决，处理，应付
addressee [ˌædre'siː] *n.[C]* 收信人；收件人；收讯者

例 1. All communications shall be sent to the parties hereto at their respective addresses as set forth in writing at the time of this Agreement or at such other address as the Parties may designate by ten (10) days advance written notice to the other Parties. 所有通信应当按照签订本协议时以书面方式列明的各方当事人的地址或者按照双方当事人提前十（10）天书面通知对方的其他地址送交各方当事人。

例 2. *The Draft Measures* should address the protection of intellectual property in technical committees which are developing standards. 《征求意见稿》应当解决制定标准的技术委员会保护知识产权问题。

例 3. Mr. XXX produced an expert report addressing that issue and he valued the Company as at 11 September 2018 at between US$11.4 million and US$15.2 million. 某先生出具了一份处理该争点的专家报告，他估计截至 2018 年 9 月 11 日，这家公司的价值在 1140 万美元至 1520 万美元之间。

例 4. It is not strictly necessary to address these arguments, as I have come to the view that the award of damages in the *Order* should be set aside. 我认为《法官命令》中的损害赔偿裁决应当撤销，因此完全没有必要探讨这些论点。

例 5. To address this concern, we suggest that a similar approach in China would help China reach its goals for NEV adoption without significant market disruption. 为解决这个问题，我们建议中国实行类似的做法，这将有助于中国实现采用新能源汽车的目标，又不会给市场造成重大干扰。

例 6. We commit with a sense of urgency to a single, renewed education agenda that is holistic, ambitious and aspirational, leaving no one behind. This new vision is fully captured by the proposed SDG 4 *Ensure inclusive and equitable quality education and promote lifelong learning opportunities for all*" and its corresponding targets. It is transformative and universal, attends to the "unfinished business" of the EFA agenda and the education-related MDGs, and addresses global and national education challenges. 我们怀着紧迫意识，承诺要制定一个全面的、有雄心、有追求、不放弃任何人的单一和更新的教育议程。这一新愿景完全体现在了拟议的可持续发展目标4（"为所有人确保包容、公平的优质教育并促进终身学习机会"）及其相关具体目标之中。新愿景既具有变革性也具有普遍性，致力于全民教育议程和与教育有关的千年发展目标的"未竟事业"，应对全球和国家的教育挑战。

例 7. A notice may be served by the Foundation upon any Member by personal delivery at or by sending it through the post to the address of the Members appearing in the *Register* (which shall be an address in Hong Kong) and, in the case of the service of notice by post, it shall be deemed to have been served on the third day following that on which the letter containing the same is put in the post. In proving such service, it shall be sufficient to prove that the envelope containing the notice was properly addressed in accordance with this Article and put in the post office as a prepaid letter. 基金会可以采取专人递送方式将通知送达任何会员或者通过邮寄方式将通知寄到《登记簿》上列明的会员地址（该地址应当是香港境内的地址）。如果采用邮寄方式送达通知，在将装有通知的函件在邮局投递之后第三天，应当视为通知已经送达。在证明邮寄送达时，只要证明已经依照本条的规定，在装有通知的信封上正确书写收件人姓名、地址并将其作为预付邮费的信件在邮局投递，即为充分证明。

(2)

redress [ri'dres] *v.t.* 补救，纠正；赔偿；*n.[U]* ['ri:dres] 补救，纠正；赔偿

例 8. The *Vienna Declaration and Platform for Action* clearly and concisely stated that every State should provide an effective framework of remedies to redress human rights grievances or violations. 《维也纳宣言和行动纲领》言简意赅地指出：每个国家均应提供一个有效的补救框架，解决人权方面的冤屈或人权遭受侵犯的问题。

例 9. In case of any found defects, failures or other problem of Deliverable, LICENSOR shall notify AAA timely and AAA shall promptly take any and all necessary action to redress and correct those defects and the likes in order to provide LICENSOR with acceptable Deliverable. 如果发现可交付产品存在瑕疵、缺陷或者其他问题，许可人须及时通知 AAA，AAA 须立即采取一切必要行动重新处理和纠正上述瑕疵和类似问题，以便向许可人提供可以接受的可交付产品。

例 10. Where any director or directors so fail to take reasonable care to protect a company as to expose it to a risk of insolvency, and the company becomes insolvent as a result and therefore goes into liquidation, then, if any creditor of the company suffers loss and is driven to proving in the liquidation for redress, the company's claim against the negligent director or directors cannot be defeated, to the ultimate detriment of any creditor, by any ratification which such director or directors may be able to procure of their own negligent acts or omissions. 倘若任何一名或多名董事未采取合理的谨慎措施保护一家公司，使其蒙受无力偿还债务的危险，而该公司因此破产并因而进行清盘，那么，如果该公司的任何债权人遭受损失，并被迫在清盘过程中为讨回公道而作出证明，而这位或这些有疏失的董事有可能使自己的疏忽行为或不作为得到追认，但这种追认不能否定公司针对该董事的赔偿请求权，否则会令债权人最终遭受损害。

例 11. Also, a less formal process may be to lodge a complaint with the Perma-

13

nent Secretary (most senior civil servant) in the procuring department or to the Chief Executive of the public body or to the Office of Government Commerce seeking redress for breach of the proper procedures. In fact, this is a requirement under the *Public Contract Regulations* before any legal proceedings can be issued. 还有一种非正式的程序，就是可以向进行采购部的事务次官（最高级别的公务员）或公共机构的行政长官或政府商务司投诉，寻求纠正违反正当程序的办法。其实这也是《政府合同条例》规定的一个步骤，然后才可以提起任何法律程序。

allocate, dislocate, locate & relocate

(1)

allocate ['æləkeit] *v.t.* 分配，分派

注意 allocate 构成的词组：allocate sth. to sb./sth., allocate sb. sth. 和 allocate sth. for sth.。

allocation [ˌælə'keiʃən] *n.[C,U]*

例 1. All items of income, gain, loss and deduction will be allocated pro rata to the Limited Partners in accordance with the terms of the *Limited Partnership Agreement.* 所有收入、盈余、损失和扣除的项目将依照《有限合伙协议》载明的条件由有限合伙人按比例分担。

例 2. We therefore are determined to increase public spending on education in accordance with country context, and urge adherence to the international and regional benchmarks of allocating efficiently at least 4% ~ 6% of Gross Domestic Product and/or at least 15% ~ 20% of total public expenditure to education. 所以我们决心根据各国的具体情况，增加对教育的公共支出，敦促遵守国际和地区基准，即将国内生产总值的至少 4%~6% 和 / 或公共总支出的至少 15%~20% 用于教育。

例 3. In 2010–2011, an average of US$3.2 billion in aid was allocated annually to scholarships and imputed student costs, equivalent to a quarter of total aid to education. 2010 年至 2011 年，每年平均拨出 32 亿美元援助金偿付奖学金和估算学生费用，相当于教育援助总额的四分之一。

例 4. The allocation of official aid flows should not be guided by per capita income only. In this context, particular attention needs to be paid to the needs of vulnerable countries such as small island developing states. 官方援助的分配不应当仅以人均收入作为指导。在这样的背景下，需要格外关注像小岛屿发展中国家等脆弱国家的需求。

例 5. If a Force Majeure compels Seller to allocate deliveries of products or services, Seller will make such allocation in a manner that ensures Buyer at least the same proportion of the Seller's total output as was purchased by Buyer prior to the Force Majeure. 如果不可抗力迫使卖方分配产品或服务的交付，卖方分配产品或服务交付的方式，应确保买方得到的产品或服务的数量，与买方在不可抗力之前购买的数量，在卖方总产量中至少占据相同的比例。

(2)

dislocate ['dɪsləʊkeɪt] *v.t.* ① 使脱臼；② = disrupt 扰乱
dislocated ['dɪsləʊkeɪtɪd] *adj.* 脱臼的，错位的
dislocation [ˌdɪsləʊ'keɪʃən] *n.[C,U]*

例 6. The gymnast fell down and dislocated her ankle while she was performing on a balance beam. 这名体操运动员在表演平衡木项目的时候摔了下来，一只脚踝脱了臼。

例 7. Although Mr. Nixon voiced the deepest concern about the US's "significant structural problems" as well as about the "rigidity" of the European Union, he said it would be "very hard to dislocate New York or London as the global financial centers", despite the impact of economic problems and of tougher regulatory demands. 尽管尼克松先生对美国的"重大结构性问题"以及欧盟的"呆板僵化"表示了最深切的忧虑，不过他说，就算有各种经济问题和更严格的监管要求造成的影响，"还是很难撼动纽约或伦敦作为全球金融中心的地位"。

(3)

locate [ləʊ'keɪt] ① *v.t.* to find the exact position of something 确定……的方位

② be located + in (near, on, etc.) 等介词短语构成的定语，表示位于 / 坐落在……地方

③ *v.t.* to put or build something in a particular position or place 在……地方设立

④ *v.i.* to come to a place and start a business, company, etc. 搬到……地方开始营业

注意：第四个义项是美式英语的用法，locate 是不及物动词，后面加上副词或介词。要结合具体语境传达 locate 的意思。

location [ləʊˈkeiʃən] ① *n.[C]* 位置，地点；② *n.[C,U]* 外景地，拍摄地；③ *n.[U]* the act of finding the position of something 确定……的方位

例 8. Since the suspect remained silent throughout the investigation, the police failed to locate the victim's remains. 由于嫌疑人在调查期间始终保持沉默，警方没能找到受害人的遗骸。

例 9. The apartment building is in a lovely location overlooking the Tokyo bay. 这座公寓大楼位置极佳，可以俯瞰东京湾。

例 10. Thanks to its isolated geographical location, the island does not fall victim to tourist boom. 多亏坐落在偏僻的地方，这座岛屿才没有被旅游热潮糟蹋。

例 11. Mangroves are a unique, special and fragile ecosystem located where land meets sea. 红树林是陆地与海洋交界处的一种独一无二、特殊而且脆弱的生态系统。

例 12. Among these obstacles are insufficient resources to hire lawyers, absence of interpretation in their languages during court hearings, and the inaccessibility of courts as these are usually located in urban centers. 其中主要的障碍是没有足够的资源聘请律师，法庭审理过程中没有使用他们的语言进行翻译，而且法院一般设在市中心，不方便寻求救济。

例 13. Location is often the most important criteria for any real estate investment. The Project is located within Stratford-upon-Avon, one of the most prestigious ski and recreational resorts in the world, making it a unique investment opportunity. 位置通常是房地产投资的最重要标准。项目位于埃文河畔斯特拉特福内部，该地是世界上最有声望的滑雪和休闲度假地之一，这使得项目成为一个无与伦比的投资机遇。

例 14. RDA Architecture specializes in the design of custom residences and boutique resort projects in locations around the world. RDA 建筑师事务所擅长世界各地的定制寓所和精品度假地项目的设计。

例 15. Notify QQQ in writing of the location for all records and any address changes where such records are located. 以书面形式将存放所有记录的地点和上述记录存放地点的变更情况告知 QQQ。

例 16. Strictly speaking the address and occupation of a particular witness at the time of the trial is irrelevant to any issue, though either an address or an occupation at the time of the events in issue can be. The evidence is received simply in order to locate the witness in society. 严格地讲，特定证人的地址和职业在庭审时与任何争点没有关系，不过在争议事件发生时地址或是职业可能具有关联性。接收此类证据只是为了弄清证人的社会地位。

例 17. These colleagues, in fact, tend to agree with those who are sceptical about the value of thematic plenary debates and believe that it is more important to locate thematic discussions not in plenaries but in subsidiary bodies, and that such discussions could be reported on factually either by the chairs of the said subsidiary bodies or by the Conference president. 这些同事实际上倾向于赞同那些对主题全体辩论的价值持怀疑态度的人，他们认为在附属机构而不是全体会议上进行主题讨论更为重要，而且可以由这些附属机构的主席或裁军谈判会议主席如实汇报这些讨论。

例 18. The training courses, held in November 2017 and June 2018, also contained practical exercises on detecting firearms during which the participants used training vehicles to gain hands-on experience in locating possible concealments of illicit firearms. 于 2017 年 11 月和 2018 年 6 月举行的培训课程还包括多次侦查枪支的实际演习，学员利用培训车辆获得找到可能隐藏非法枪支地点的第一手经验。

(4)

relocate [ˌriːləʊˈkeit] *v.t. & v.i.* 搬迁；调派

relocation [ˌriːləʊˈkeiʃən] *n.[U]*

例 19. The tenants were relocated to temporary accommodation while the retrofitting was being carried out. 翻修施工期间，租户被重新安置到临时住所。

例 20. A lot of firms have been priced out of London by increasing rents and are relocating to the North of England. 不断上涨的租金使许多商行在伦敦待不下去了，它们正迁到英格兰北部。

例 21. With 22 offices in the Greater San Francisco Bay Area and Lake Tahoe area—more than any other independent real estate firm, they offer a full range of personal and commercial real estate services, including buying, selling, property management, insurance, and relocation services. 它在大旧金山湾地区和塔霍湖地区设有二十二个办事处，数量上胜过任何其他独立房地产商行，提供种类齐全的个人和商业房地产服务，包括买卖、物业管理、保险和安居服务。

例 22. In September 2014, Cambodia signed a refugee relocation agreement with Australia whereby Cambodia would receive and settle refugees from Nauru. 2014 年 9 月，柬埔寨与澳大利亚签署了一项难民重新安置协议，柬埔寨借此接收和安置来自瑙鲁的难民。

例 23. AAA reserves the right, at its expense, to relocate the Premises (or any part thereof), provided that: (a) the alternative Premises must be substantially similar to, and must not be materially less convenient for, BBB; and (b) must provide BBB with at least eighteen (18) months' notice of such relocation. AAA 保留自行负担费用调迁运营场所（或者运营场所的任何部分）的权利，前提条件是：（1）替代的运营场所必须大致相似，而且不得给 BBB 造成严重不便；（2）必须提前至少十八个（18）月向 BBB 发送调迁通知。

amiable & amicable

(1)

amiable ['eimiəbl] *adj.* 友好的，亲切愉快的

amiably ['eimiəbli] *adv.*

amiability [ˌeimiəˈbiləti] *n.[U]*

例 1. In the context of international law, amiable compositor refers to an unbiased third party, often a head of state or high government official, who suggests a solution that disputing countries might accept of their own volition. Also termed amiable compositeur. 在国际法背景下，调解人（amiable compositor）指公允的第三方，通常为国家元首或政府高官，向发生争端的各国提出解决方案的建议，后者可依其自愿决定是否接受。调解人（amiable compositor）亦称 amiable compositeur。

(2)

amicable ['æmikəbəl] *adj.* 友好的，心平气和的

amicably ['æmikəbli] *adv.*

amicability [ˌæmikəˈbiləti] *n.[U]*

例 2. Both Parties shall attempt to settle any dispute amicably before the commencement of arbitration. However, unless both Parties agree otherwise, arbitration may be commenced on or after the fifty-sixth (56) day after the day on which the dispute has arisen for the first time between the Parties, even if no attempt at amicable settlement has been made. 双方应在仲裁开始之前尝试友好解决任何争议。但是，除非双方另外达成协议，否则即使双方未尝试和解，也可在双方首次发生争议之日过后的第五十六（56）天或在这一天之后开始仲裁。

例 3. Unless settled amicably, any dispute shall be submitted to the China International Economic and Trade Arbitration Commission (CIETAC), Shanghai Sub-Commission, for arbitration which shall be conducted in accordance with the commission's arbitration rules. 除非双方以友好方式解决争议，否则应将争议提交中国国际经济贸易仲裁委员会（"贸仲委"）上海分会，按照贸仲委的仲裁规则进行仲裁。

例 4. The Parties shall endeavor to promptly settle any dispute arising out of or in connection with these Articles of Association amicably through friendly consultations. 双方当事人应当尽力通过友好协商，及时友好解决由本章程细则引起的或者与本章程细则有关的任何争议。

例 5. Each Party agrees to use its best good faith efforts to resolve amicably and promptly any dispute that arises from or in connection with this Agreement. 各方当事人同意尽其最真诚的努力友好和从速解决本协议引起的或者与本协议有关的任何纠纷。

例 6. The Parties irrevocably agree that any dispute which might arise from or in connection with this Agreement, which cannot be resolved amicably within 60 days after the dispute arises, shall be finally settled by China International Economic and Trade Arbitration Commission (CIETAC) conducted by three neutral arbiters, in accordance with the rules of conciliation and arbitration of the International Chamber of Commerce, by which each Party hereto is bound. 双方当事人不可撤销地约定：对于本协议可能引起的或可能与本协议有关的任何纠纷，凡双方在该纠纷发生之后六十天内无法友好解决该纠纷，须将该纠纷提交中国国际经济贸易仲裁委员会（"贸仲委"），由三位中立的仲裁员按照对各方当事人具有约束力的国际商会调解和仲裁规则予以终局裁决。

approach & reproach

(1)

approach [əˈprəʊtʃ] ① *v.t. & v.i.* to move towards or nearer to someone or something 接近；

② *v.t..* approach sb. for sth. / approach sb. / sth. about (doing) sth. 联系，接洽，交涉；

③ *v.t. & v.i.* if an event or a particular time approaches, or you approach it, it is coming nearer and will happen soon 临近； ④ *v.t.* 处理，应付； ⑤ *v.t. & v.i.* to be almost equal to something 将近

approach ① *n.[C]* a method of doing something or dealing with a problem 方法，方式； ② *n.[C]* a request from someone, asking you to do something for them 商量，联系，接洽； ③ the approach of sth. ……将要到来 / 发生 ④ *[U]* movement towards or near to something 接近；

注意：名词 approach 的第一个义项后面搭配的介词是 "to"，采取某种方法通常用动词 adopt 或 take。

例 1. The guard dog began to growl when the burglar was approaching the house. 盗贼接近房子的时候，看家狗咆哮起来。

例 2. The manufacturer's solicitor is approaching injured customers about finding an amicable solution. 制造商的代理律师正在与受伤的顾客交涉，争取找到友好解决办法。

例 3. With temperature approaching 45℃ and humidity 80%, every pedestrian is drenched in sweat. 温度将近四十五摄氏度，湿度将近百分之八十，行人全都大汗淋漓。

例 4. The associate has been racking his brains all day to adopt a different approach to the case. 这位律师绞尽脑汁想了一整天，企图换一种办法办这个案子。

例 5. A continuous hazard analysis approach is necessary during the life and operation of the asset. 在资产的寿命期内和运营期间必须采用一种连续危险分析法。

例 6. We will focus our efforts on access, equity and inclusion, quality and learning outcomes, within a lifelong learning approach. 我们将从终身学习的角度，将工作重心放在增加机会、提升公平和包容、质量和学习成果上。

例 7. Yet another eloquent example of the intolerant approach of the occupying authorities to the issues of education is the school history course. 学校历史课程是占领当局采取褊狭的方法处理教育事务的另一个有说服力的事例。

例 8. Where any person is approached in connection with his possible appointment as an arbitrator, he shall disclose any circumstance likely to give rise to justifiable doubts as to his impartiality or independence. 凡与可能被委任为仲裁员的人联系，该人须公开任何有可能导致对其是否具备公正或独立品性产生正当疑虑的情况。

例 9. A problem-based approach will be introduced using cases to reinforce Occasional Infection (OI) diagnosis and treatment skills. 采取以问题为基础的方法，利用案例强化偶然性感染的诊断和治疗技能。

例 10. The completed townhome units will be released in a phased multi-year sell-through approach in conjunction with a tiered pricing system. 已经建成的连排别墅将采取分阶段多年销售方法，配以分层次定价体系投放市场。

例 11. His Honor then turned his attention to an alternative approach to the question of admissibility of evidence with which his Honor was then dealing. 法官大人接下来将注意力转移到他正在处理的证据可采信性问题的替代解决办法上。

例 12. We see no error, either of law or of fact, in the approach taken by his Honor to that matter. 我们没有发现法官大人处理此事的方法存在任何法律或事实上的错误。

例 13. We point out, yet again, that the correct approach for present purposes is one that reads fairly the entirety of the summing-up. Approached in that way, we are wholly unpersuaded that his Honor's relevant directions were unbalanced. We reject the present ground of appeal. 我们再次指出，处理上诉人的上诉理由的正确办法是公正地解读证据总结的全文。由于采用这种办法，完全不能让我们相信法官大人的相关指示有失偏颇。我们拒绝接受这条上诉理由。

approachable [əˈprəʊtʃəbl] *adj.* 和善
反义词 unapproachable [ˌʌnəˈprəʊtʃəbl] *adj.*

(2)

reproach [rɪˈprəʊtʃ] *v.t. (formal)* 责备，批评
注意 reproach 构成的常用词组：reproach sb. for / with sth.。

例 14. You've got nothing to reproach yourself for—a seasoned lawyer would have settled the case in this way. 你没什么可自责的——换个老练的律师也会这么和解。

reproach 也有名词词性：reproach *n.[U]* 责备；*n.[C]* 责备的话语
注意名词 reproach 构成的两个比较重要的词组：
above/beyond reproach = perfect 无可指摘
be a reproach to sb./sth. 是……的耻辱

例 15. Rubbish-strewn beaches are a reproach to this tourist destination which has been bragging about its paradise-like environment. 遍布垃圾的海滩让这个一直吹嘘

自己的环境仿佛天堂的旅游胜地脸上无光。

reproachful [rɪˈprəʊtʃfl] *adj.* 表示责备的

reproachfully *adv.*

arguable & argumentative

(1)

arguable [ˈɑːgjuəbəl] *adj.* = debatable 可争辩的

例 1. It is arguable whether this rule should or could go far. 这项规定应不应当起到作用，能不能起到作用，还没有定论。

阅读法律文件时，经常遇到这样的句型：It is arguable that + 主语从句.。

例 2. It is arguable that the legislation has had significant effect on first-time homebuyers. 有理由说这项立法对首次购房人产生了重大影响。

arguably [ˈɑːgjuəbli] *adv.* 大概，或许，可能（表示有充分理由）

例 3. Our firm is arguably one of the best recommended legal service providers. 我们事务所可以说是口碑最好的法律服务提供者之一。

(2)

argumentative [ˌɑːgjuˈmentətiv] *adj.* ① of or relating to argument or persuasion 争论的；② stating not only facts, but also inferences and conclusions drawn from facts 可争议的；③（指人）好争辩的（含有强词夺理的意思）

例 4. The judge sustained the prosecutor's objection to the argumentative question. 法官支持检察官对于可争议询问提出的异议。

例 5. Argumentative question is a question in which the examiner interposes a viewpoint under the guise of asking a question. This is considered an abuse of interrogation. 可争议的询问是指询问者假借提问，在问题中暗含某种观点。这种做法被认为是滥用询问的表现。

ascribe, circumscribe, describe, inscribe, scribe, subscribe & transcribe

(1)

ascribe [əˈskraib] *v.t.*

注意 ascribe 构成的短语：ascribe sth. to sb./sth.。

这个短语的意思是：① 把……归因于……；② 认为……是……所说（所做）；③ 认为……具有某种品质 / 特点。

例 1. The paramount purpose of such investigation is to determine the circumstances and causes of the emergency incident with a view to avoiding similar incidents in the future, rather than to ascribe blame therefor to any person. 此项调查的首要目的是确定紧急事故的情况及起因，以避免日后发生相似的事故，而非将责任归咎于任何人。

例 2. After intensive handwriting analysis, the forensic expert finally ascribed this anonymous blackmail letter to one of his competitors. 经过深入的笔迹分析，司法鉴定专家终于认定这封匿名敲诈信出自他的一位竞争对手。

例 3. "Beneficiary", "conflict of interest","secret profit" and "duty of disclosure" shall have the respective meanings ascribed to them by the *Companies Act 1985* or the *Companies Ordinance,* as the case may require. "受益人""利害冲突""秘密收益"及"披露义务"具有《1985 年公司法》或《公司法例》（视情况需要而定）分别给予各词的涵义。

例 4. While consensus has been sought as far as possible, it was considered most in accord with a practical manual to include some elements where consensus could not be reached, and it follows that specific views expressed in this Manual should not be ascribed to any particular persons involved in its drafting. 虽然已尽可能寻求达成共识，不过，把一些无法达成共识的内容收录在内，这种做法被认为最符合实用手册的特点，因此，不应认为本手册中表达的特定观点是参与起草工作的个别人员的观点。

(2)

circumscribe ['sɜːkəmskraib] *v.t.* ① 限制，约束，制约；② 画……的外接圆

例 5. The Delegation of Indonesia thanked the Delegation of the EU, on behalf of the EU and its Member States, for the statement made clarifying its position on disclosure requirements. It asked the Delegation of the EU how it saw the relationship between geographical indications and disclosure requirements and whether it considered geographical indications as another form of disclosure requirements. It believed that the legal framework of geographical indications could be used to circumscribe the debate and provide for legal clarity to the discussions on origin and source. 印度尼西亚代表团感谢欧盟代表团代表欧盟及其成员国发表的声明，此项声明阐明了其关于披露要求的立场。它询问欧盟代表团如何看待地理标志与披露要求之间的关系以及欧盟是否将地理标志看作是另一种形式的披露要求。它认为，可以利用地理标志的法律框架约束辩论，并为关于原产地和来源的讨论提供法律上的明晰。

(3)

describe [di'skraib] *v.t.* 描述，描写，描绘

例 6. On an agreed date and in an agreed format, Contractor will provide AAA with the written reports described in Exhibit B attached to this Agreement. 承包商将在商定的日期并采用商定的格式向 AAA 提供本协议附件 B 所述的书面报告。

例 7. The captions used in this Agreement are for the Parties' convenience and do not define, limit or describe the scope or intent of this Agreement. 本协议中使用的标题是为双方当事人的方便，并不界定、限制或描述本协议的范围或意图。

例 8. At the Client's request and the Consultant's expense, the Consultant will provide the Client with audited financial statements and/or the type of Dunn & Bradstreet report described in the request. 顾问将根据客户的要求，并由顾问承担费用，向客户提供经过审计的财务报表和／或该要求中所描述的那一类邓白氏报告。

例 9. Section IV describes the steps taken by the Executive Secretary to further develop the Coordination Mechanism and to enhance synergies with relevant initiatives; the final section presents the conclusion and recommendations, including elements of a possible decision on capacity-building. 第四节叙述执行秘书为进一步发展协调机制和促进与有关举措的协同作用而采取的步骤；最后一节提出结论和建议，包括关于能力建设的可能决定的要素。

例 10. The Company shall perform the services (the "Services") described in Schedule 2 hereto. The scope of the services may be varied from time to time by the mutual agreement of Parties in writing. 公司应履行本协议附表 2 所描述的服务（"服务"）。经双方书面同意，可以随时变更服务范围。

例 11. The terms and conditions set out in this letter shall apply to any services performed by us upon your request, or upon the request of any subsidiary in your group of companies, in addition to the services described above, whether as part of the same matter or separately, unless agreed otherwise. 除非另有约定，本函载明的各项条件适用于按照贵司的要求，或者按照贵司集团内部任何子公司的要求，由本所履行的除上文描述的服务以外的任何服务，这些服务作为上述服务的组成部分还是作为单独的服务则在所不论。

(4)

inscribe [inˈskraib] *v.t.* 题写，镌刻

例 12. Each donor will have his or her name inscribed on a special stone tablet erected in the Temple. 每位捐赠人的姓名将镌刻在本寺专门树立的一块石碑上。

例 13. A number of specific conservation issues had already been identified and assessed when the property was evaluated and inscribed on the World Heritage List in 2013. 在 2013 年对该处世界遗产进行评价并将它列入世界遗产名录时，已经认定并且评估了若干特别保护问题。

例 14. The *1972 Convention Concerning the Protection of World Cultural and Natural Heritage* is an effective instrument for the protection of mangrove ecosystem. Properties inscribed on the *World Heritage List* with significant mangroves include the Great Barrier Reef in Australia, the Belize Barrier Reef Reserve System, the Malpelo Fauna and Flora Sanctuary in Colombia, the Cocos Island National Park in Costa Rica, the Lagoons of New Caledonia in France, the Komodo National Park in Indonesia, the Phoenix Islands Protected Area in Kiribati, the Aldabra Atoll in the Seychelles, East Rennell in the Solomon Islands and the Everglades National Park in the United States. 《一九七二年保护世界文化和自然遗产公约》是一项旨在保护红树生态系统的有效文书。被记入《世界遗产名录》的生长着重要红树林的自然遗产包括澳大利亚的大堡礁、伯利兹堡礁保护区系统、哥伦比亚的马尔佩罗动植物保护区、哥斯达黎加的考克斯岛国家公园、法国的新喀里多尼亚环礁湖、印度尼西亚的科摩多国家公园、基里巴斯的凤凰群岛保护区、塞舌尔的阿尔达布拉环礁、所罗门群岛的东雷奈勒以及美国的大沼泽地国家公园。

(5)

scribe [skraib] *n.[C]* （印刷术发明之前的）抄写员，抄书吏

例 15. The Seated Scribe in the Louvre is thought by some archaeologists to portray someone connected with a certain Pharaoh of the fifth dynasty in Ancient Egypt. 有些考古学家认为卢浮宫收藏的抄书吏坐像刻画的人物是古埃及第五王朝某一位法老的亲戚。

(6)

subscribe [səbˈskraib] *v.t.* & *v.i.* 认购；订阅，订购，认捐

注意：subscribe to sth. 除表示订阅、认购外，还有赞同、支持的意思。

例 16. Investors will have the first right to subscribe for any future issue of shares by the Company (in a pro-rata fully-diluted basis) and the first right to purchase any shares transferred by the Common Shareholders in the Company, other than for tax and estate planning purposes, pro-rata in proportion to their respective shareholding (on a deemed converted basis) in the Company. 投资人有权为非税务和产业规划用途，按照他们在公司中各自的持股比例（在被视为转换的基础上），（在充分稀释的基础上按比例）优先认购公司今后发行的股份，而且有权优先购买公司的普通股股东转让的股份。

例 17. At a board meeting, the directors decided that, owing to lack of funds, the parent company should subscribe for 2,000 shares in AAA, and that the company's five directors and the company's solicitors should subscribe for 500 shares each. However, the chairman, GGG, did not subscribe for shares personally, but instead persuaded a friend of his and two companies in which he was interested to subscribe. 在董事会的一次会议上，董事们决定，由于资金不足，母公司认购 AAA 的股份 2000 股，公司的五名董事及公司的律师各认购 500 股。然而，董事长 GGG 本人并未认购股份，而是说服了他的一位朋友和与他有利害关系的两家公司认购股份。

例 18. If you would like to receive a notification when a new allegation has been added, you can subscribe to receive updates on data. 如果您想要在录入新指控的时候得到通知，您可以办理订阅，接收最新资料消息。

例 19. Rules of procedure are adopted by the Committee unilaterally, they are not subscribed to by States parties. 程序规则是委员会单方面通过的，没有得到各缔约方赞同。

例 20. South Africa does not Subscribe to the view that a fissile material treaty is the only item ripe for negotiation or that this should become a condition for further progress towards nuclear disarmament. 南非不同意这样一种观点，即裂变材料条约是唯一时机成熟的谈判项目，或者这应当成为谋求核裁军取得进展的条件。

(7)

transcribe [træn'skraib] *v.t.* 誊写，抄录

例 21. Evidence given under this Section shall be recorded, transcribed, read over to and signed by the witness and also by the judge. 证人根据本条所作证供，必须予以记录、誊写及向证人宣读，并由证人及法官签署。

例 22. Any documentary evidence submitted to the Court which is illegible shall be transcribed into legible form and the transcribed version placed immediately before the illegible copy. 呈送本庭的任何书面证据如不能辨读，则必须以可辨读形式誊写，而经誊写的版本须放置于紧接该不能辨读的文本之前。

aware, beware & unaware

(1)

aware [əˈwɛə] 是表语形容词，仅跟在 be 动词或其他系动词后面。

aware 常用的句式是 be aware of sth./that + 宾语从句。意思是"意识到，知道，察觉"。

例 1. I am painfully aware that there is only one week away from the deadline. 我痛苦地意识到离最后期限只有一周了。

例 2. Tourists are well aware that the city is no longer what it used to be. 观光客们很清楚：这座城市不是从前的样子了。

例 3. The Vendor and the Purchaser must promptly notify the other in writing as soon as they become aware that any Condition Precedent is satisfied or becomes (or is likely to become) incapable of being satisfied. 卖方和买方一旦意识到任何先决条件已经满足或者无法（或者有可能无法）满足，必须即刻以书面形式通知对方。

例 4. Within their respective functions, lawyers, prosecutors and especially judges have an obligation and responsibility to uphold international human rights law. For that reason, they must be aware of and trained to use human rights law, principles and jurisprudence, as well as receive education regarding the obligations thereof. 律师、检察官，特别是法官，在各自职责范围内有维护国际人权法的义务和责任。为此，他们必须知晓并被训练利用人权法律、原则和判例，他们还必须接受关于其义务的训导。

例 5. The Purchaser must notify the vendor representative (listed in Clause 10)

("Vendor Representative") in writing of any potential claim for breach of Vendors' Warranty arising as a result of any claim by a third party against the Purchaser or the Company ("Third Party Claim") as soon as reasonably practicable after becoming aware of such Third Party Claim. 倘若由于第三方向买方或者对象公司提出权利请求，可能引起声称违反卖方担保的潜在权利请求（"第三方权利请求"），买方必须在知晓该第三方权利请求之后尽快采取书面方式通知（第 10 条所列的）卖方代表（"卖方代表"）。

aware 前面还可以加上副词，表示具有某种意识或觉悟。

例 6. After a one-month campout in the mountain, both adults and their children have become environmentally aware. 在山里露营一个月之后，大人和孩子都有了环境意识。

例 7. It is said that a lawyer who pursues a career in tax law should be both legally aware and politically aware. 据说，要在税法领域有造诣的律师既要通晓法律还得政治过硬。

awareness [əˈwɛənəs] n.[U] 觉悟，意识

例 8. The Office of the high Commissioner of Human Rights (OHCHR) organized or participated in commemoration events, distributed promotional and informational material and contributed opinion pieces to increase awareness. 为了提高人们的觉悟，人权高专办组织或参加了各类纪念活动、散发了宣传和信息资料，并且撰写了观点文章。

例 9. This legal training institute conducts many seminars, courses and vocational training days in order to raise their awareness to human rights issues. 这个法律培训学院举办许多研讨会、课程和职业培训日活动，以便提高学员们对人权问题的认识。

(2)

beware [ˌbiˈwɛə] *v.t. & v.i.*

注意：beware 是动词，只能用不定式形式或表示命令。

beware 最初作为及物动词，后面直接搭配宾语，例如：Beware the ides of March. 当心三月十五日。

现在 beware 后面要加上介词 of：beware of (doing) sth.

例 10. Beware of the dog. 小心有狗。

例 11. But beware of men: for they will deliver you up to the councils, and they will scourge you in their synagogues; 你们要防备人，因为他们要把你们交给公会，也要在会堂里鞭打你们；（原文选自英文圣经钦定本马太福音第 10 章，译文选自《圣经和合本》。）

注意区别 beware of sth. 和 be wary of sth.：wary [ˈwɛəri] 是形容词，既可以做表语，也可以做定语。意思是小心谨慎，构成的词组是 be wary of sth./doing sth.。

例 12. Nowadays not only children but adults are taught to be wary of strangers. 如今不仅孩子连大人都被教导要当心陌生人。

例 13. Keep a wary eye on the weather before you go camping in the mountain. 去山里露营之前要留心天气状况。

(3)

unaware [ˌʌnəˈwɛə] *adj.*

unaware 是形容词，只能做表语。搭配的词组是 be unaware of sth./that 宾语从句。意思是不知道，没有意识到，没有察觉。

例 14. On the worst complexion the actions of the customs officers were committed in an act of hot pursuit. The more favorable view is that they were simply unaware in those heavy seas where they were in relation to territorial limits. 最糟糕的局面是海关公务人员实施的紧追行为。更有利的看法是在波涛汹涌的大海上他们不知道领海线在何处。

unawares [ˌʌnəˈwɛəz] *adv.*
take/catch sb. unawares 令某人始料不及 / 猝不及防

例 15. The suspect was taken unawares, without the chance to dispose of the evidence. 嫌疑人被逮个正着，没机会销毁证据。

beneficial & beneficiary

beneficial [ˌbɛnəˈfiʃəl] *adj.* 有益的；令……受益的

beneficiary [ˌbɛniˈfiʃəri] *n.[C]* 受益人

注意区分 beneficial 和 beneficent，以及 beneficiary 和 benefactor 这两组形近词。

beneficent [biˈnɛfisənt] *adj.* 慈善的，行善的

benefactor [ˈbɛniˌfæktə] *n.[C]* 赞助人

例 1. BANK A shall provide any information and proof to identify tax status of BANK A or Korean Unit Trust or its beneficial unit holder as BANK B requests reasonably according to the Applicable Laws. 在乙银行按照可适用法律提出合理要求的情况下，甲银行应当提供信息和证据以确认验明甲银行或者韩国单位信托公司或者它的受益单位持有人的纳税状况。

例 2. The Fund will obtain appropriate representations and undertakings from purchasers of the Limited Partnership Units to assure that the conditions of "beneficial ownership" will be met on an ongoing basis. 本基金将向有限合伙份额的购买人取得适当的声明和承诺，以确保始终满足"受益所有权"的条件。

例 3. Beneficial ownership for purposes of this Section shall be deemed to include all shares which would be determined to be beneficially owned (whether directly by such person or entity or indirectly through any affiliate or otherwise) under Rule 13d-3 of the Securities and Exchange Commission as in effect on the date of filing of these Restated Articles of Incorporation with the Oregon Corporation Commissioner as well as all shares of the Corporation which the other entity has the right to acquire, pursuant to any agreement or otherwise. 本节所称实益拥有权应视为包括根据在向俄勒冈州

公司事务专员提交本重述公司章程之日施行的证券交易委员会规章 13d-3，将被认定为实益拥有的所有股份（无论是由该人或实体直接实益拥有还是通过任何关联方或其他方式间接实益拥有），以及另一实体依据任何协议或以其他方式有权取得的本公司的所有股份。

例 4. The pension plan is a union-negotiated, collectively-bargained defined benefit pension plan established on November 1, 1973 and currently has approximately $1.5 billion in assets, over 9000 members and pensioners and beneficiaries. The fund is governed by a board of trustees representing members of the plan. 该退休金计划于 1973 年 11 月 1 日设立，是一项由工会协商、集体谈判的定额给付退休金计划。它目前拥有大约 15 亿加元资产，9000 多位会员、退休金领取人和受益人。该基金由一个代表该基金计划成员的受托人理事会管理。

例 5. That the trusts set forth in said petition constitute a public benefaction with no specially designated beneficiaries and with no persons legally or directly interested in its management other than the People of the State of California. 上述申请书中阐述的信托安排构成一笔没有特别指定受益人的公共慈善资金，除加利福尼亚州人民以外，任何人对这笔资金的管理不得享有任何法律上的利益或直接的利益。

例 6. The moving spirit of the Founders in the foundation and endowment of the Leland Stanford Junior University was love of humanity and a desire to render the greatest possible service to mankind. The University was accordingly designed for the betterment of mankind morally, spiritually, intellectually, physically, and materially. The public at large, and not alone the comparatively few students who can attend the University, are the chief and ultimate beneficiaries of the foundation. 推动创办人创建和资助小利兰斯坦福大学的是对于人类的热爱和为人类提供最杰出服务的愿望。因此创办斯坦福大学是为了从道德、心灵、智识、体魄和物质诸方面改善人类的境况。普罗大众——而不仅仅是相对寥寥的能够在斯坦福大学求学的学生——是基金的主要的也是最终的受益人。

例 7. The Shanghai Timber Market is also very beneficial to the development of the forest products industry in China because it is the first forest products national sub-market in the eastern region of the country. 上海木材市场还非常有利于中国森林产品行业的发展，因为它是中国东部第一个森林产品国内次级市场。

例 8. Party B will not sell, transfer, mortgage, pledge, grant any option rights or otherwise dispose of any asset, business or legal or beneficial interest, or permit the creation of any other security interest over the same without the prior written consent of Party A. 事先未经甲方书面同意，乙方不会对任何资产、业务或者法定权益或受益权益进行出售、转让、抵押、质押、设定任何期权或以其他方式进行处分，也不会允许在上述资产、业务或者法定权益或受益权益之上创设任何其他担保物权。

例 9. Furthermore, to the extent of the provisions under PRC law, a trust under which BANK A is the beneficiary shall be deemed to be established one (1) day before the Bankruptcy Incident, pursuant to which BANK B, as sub-custodian of BANK A, holds all the Securities, cash and other asset in the Securities Account and RMB Special Account and any other account under BANK A's name, and any other securities, cash or assets held by BANK B on behalf of BANK A in any form, until such securities, cash or assets are returned to BANK A or paid according to its instruction. 此外，在中华人民共和国法律规定的范围内，甲银行作为受益人的信托应被视为在破产事件之前一日设立，乙银行依据该信托担任甲银行的次级托管人，持有证券账户、人民币专用账户和以甲银行名义开立的任何其他账户中的所有证券、现金和其他资产，以及乙银行代表甲银行以任何形式持有的其他证券、现金或者资产，直至将上述证券、现金或者资产返还甲银行或者依照甲银行的指示支付上述证券、现金或者资产。

best endeavor & reasonable endeavor

翻译法律文件的时候，经常遇到 best endeavor 和 reasonable endeavor。前者常翻译成"最大努力"或"尽力"，后者常译成"合理努力"。

例 1. ABC agrees to provide, or use its best endeavors to cause the manufacturer or ABC Software licensor to provide, such warranty services as are required under the warranties set forth in Section 5 (a) hereof. ABC 同意提供，或者尽其最大努力促使生产商或 ABC 软件特许权人提供，根据本项目协议第 5（a）条列明的保证所要求的保证服务。

例 2. When a Party breaches the Applicable Laws or fails to prove its ability to carry out its duties of the Agreement, the other Party may terminate this Agreement with immediate written notice. In this case of termination, a Party shall make best endeavor to transfer the assets, records and books to the designated by the other Party, and shall not be entitled to reimburse any cost or expense, except out of pocket expense. 一方当事人违反可适用法律的规定或不能证明自己有能力履行本协议规定的义务，对方当事人可以立即凭书面通知终止本协议。在此种情况下，当事人须尽最大努力将资产、记录和账簿转交对方当事人指定的人，并且无权报销除自付费用外的任何费用或开销。

例 3. 1.1 Before the Recipient may disclose the Disclosing Party's Confidential Information under Clause 5.1 above, it will (to the extent permitted by law and where practicable) use its best endeavors to:

1.1.1 inform the Disclosing Party of the full circumstances and the Disclosing Party's Confidential Information to be disclosed;

1.1.2 take all such steps as the Disclosing Party may reasonably require to limit such disclosure to only that portion legally required to be disclosed; and

1.1.3 to obtain assurances as to confidentiality from the body to whom the Disclosing Party's Confidential Information is to be disclosed.

1.1 在收受方根据上述第 5.1 条披露开示方的机密信息之前，它要（在法律允许的范围内，并在可行的情况下）尽其最大努力：

1.1.1 将全部情况和需要披露的开示方的机密信息告知开示方；

1.1.2 采取开示方可能合理要求的一切措施，将所作披露限制在依法需要披露的部分；而且

1.1.3 凡向任何机构披露开示方的机密信息，收受方要获得该机构对于机密信息作出的保密保证。

例 4. AAA agrees to use all reasonable endeavors to implement any reasonable cost-cutting measures for the AAA Group, including measures to reduce salary costs. AAA 同意采取所有合理努力，为 AAA 集团实施一切合理的成本缩减措施，包括工资成本缩减措施。

例 5. The Shareholders shall not, and shall use all reasonable endeavors to procure that every person connected with or associated with each such Shareholder shall not, disclose to any person, firm or corporation or use to the detriment of the MANAGEMENT COMPANY or any of the Shareholders any Confidential Information which may have come to its knowledge in its capacity as a Shareholder concerning the affairs of the MANAGEMENT COMPANY or of any company in which the MANAGEMENT COMPANY has an investment or of any group company of that company, unless required to do so pursuant to a court or administrative order, law or regulation, including regulations of stock exchanges or similar regulatory authorities. 全体股东不得向任何人、企业或公司披露，亦不得在损害管理公司或任何股东的利益的情况下，使用由于它具有股份身份而可以知悉的涉及管理公司的事务，或者涉及管理公司投资的任何公司的事务，或者涉及前述公司的任何集团公司的事务的任何机密信息，而且全体股东应当作出所有合理的努力，保证与各该股东有关

的每一个人不得实施上述行为，除非依照法院或者行政命令、法律或者规章——包括股票交易所或者类似的管理机关的规章条例——必须予以披露。

例 6. Each of the Vendors and the Purchaser (as the case requires) must use its respective reasonable endeavors to ensure that the Conditions Precedent are fulfilled as soon as possible. To this end each Party must do all acts and things and sign, execute and deliver all assurances, references and provide all information as may be lawful, reasonable or reasonably required by the Purchaser and the Vendors. 各个卖方与买方（按具体情形需要）必须尽到各自的合理努力，以期确保尽快实现先决条件。为此目的，各方当事人必须完成所有合法、合理或者买方和卖方合理要求的行为和事情，签署和交付所有合法、合理或者买方和卖方合理要求的不动产转让证书，并且提供所有合法、合理或者买方和卖方合理要求的信息。

例 7. Each Party agrees, at its own expense, on the request of any other Party, to do everything reasonably necessary for the purposes of or to give effect to this Agreement and the transactions contemplated by it (including the execution of documents) and to use all reasonable endeavors to cause relevant third Parties to do likewise. 各方当事人同意，根据对方当事人提出的要求，由本方承担费用，采取一切合理必要的措施，以实现本协议的目的或者完成本协议和本协议筹划的交易（包括签署文件），并尽一切合理努力促使相关第三方亦复如此。

bonus & onus

(1)

bonus ['bəunəs] *n.[C]* ① 奖金，红利，花红，津贴；② 额外的好处 it is a real bonus that...,
 with the added bonus of sth.

bonus 的第一个义项在金融类法律文件中出现频率很高。

例 1. "Dividends" means, in relation to the Equity Interests, all present and future: "股息" 是指有关股权的所有当前和今后的：

(a) rights, Equity Interests, money or other assets accruing or offered by way of redemption, bonus, option or otherwise in respect of the Equity Interests; （a）以回赎、红利、期权或者其他方式产生或者提供的有关股权的权利、股份利益、金钱或者其他资产；

例 2. In this Agreement, unless the context otherwise requires, Distribution includes a share issued by a company to a shareholder in the company where the share is issued as a bonus share. 在本协议中，除文意另有所指外，派发包括任何公司以红股形式发行给其股东的股票在内。

例 3. In consideration of the premises and in consideration of the Purchase Price to be satisfied in the manner and at the times stipulated herein, the Vendor hereby agrees to sell to the Purchaser and the Purchaser hereby agrees to purchase from the Vendor the Sale Shares on the basis of the representations, warranties, covenants and terms of agreement as set out herein, free from all charges or liens or any other encumbrances thereto and with all rights attaching thereto as at the date hereof including, but without limitation, all bonuses, rights, dividends and distributions declared, paid or made in respect thereof from the date hereof subject to the terms and upon the conditions hereinafter contained. 鉴于上述各点以及按照本协议所规定的方式和时间进行支付的购买价款，卖方特此同意根据本协议列明的表述、担保、契诺和条款向买方出售待售股份，买方特此同意根据上述表述、担保、契诺和条款从卖方处购买待售股份，在本协议订立之日，该股份未设定担保、留置或者其他债务负担，而且该股份附带各项权利，包括但不限于从本协议订立之日起按照本协议所含条款和下文载明的条件宣告、支付或进行的待售股份的各类红利、权利、股息以及派发。

bonus 的第二个义项在托福、雅思词汇书中也经常提到。

例 4. It is a real bonus that this apartment for rent on Airbnb is conveniently situated near the Metropolitan Museum of Art. 这间在爱彼迎上招租的公寓有一个实实在在的好处——就是位置便利，离大都会艺术博物馆不远。

(2)
onus ['əunəs] *n.[C]* = the responsibility for something 责任，义务
onus 常构成这样的句式： the onus is on sb. to do sth.。

例 5. The onus is on the landlord to ensure that the property is habitable. 房东有责任保证这个房产适宜居住。

例 6. The onus is on the prosecution to disprove this alibi. 检方有义务证明这项不在场证明不实。

onus probandi ['əunəs prə'bændai]
onus probandi 是拉丁文，常简写作 onus，等于 burden of proof，也就是我们翻译法律文件时经常用到的"证明责任"。

例 7. When this ground of appeal is considered is conjunction with Ground 4(e), the appellant contends that there has been a failure to fully explain the burden of proof such that the jury would have been laboring under the misconception that the Crown stood on an equal footing with the appellant and the issue was which of the competing cases (that of the Crown or of the appellant) was to be preferred. 当结合第四条理由的（e）段来考虑本条上诉理由时，本上诉人辩称，承审法官没有充分解释举证责任，于是陪审团就会受到这样的误解的影响，那就是公诉方与本上诉人处于平等的地位，而争点是陪审团愿意选择相互对立的案情（公诉方呈述的案情或本上诉人呈述的案情）中的哪一个案情。

例 8. It is a counsel of prudence to give a Liberato direction in most, if not all, cases. It is a sensible direction which further emphasises the standard and the burden of proof. 在大多数案件中（即便不是全部案件），作出莱伯拉托案指示乃是一项审慎原则。莱伯拉托案指示是一项进一步强调证明标准和证明责任的明智指示。

例 9. The Court admits that the burden of proof is on UT, ante, at 7, and that "a university bears a heavy burden in showing that it had not obtained the educational benefits of diversity before it turned to a race-conscious plan," ante, at 13−14. 本庭承认，德州大学承担证明责任（见上文第七页），而且"一所大学承担艰巨的证明责任，需要证明多元化并没有让它在教育上获益，之后它采取了有种族意识的方案。"（见上文第十三至十四页）。

例 10. Rule 301 — Presumptions in Civil Cases Generally

In a civil case, unless a federal statute or these rules provide otherwise, the Party against whom a presumption is directed has the burden of producing evidence to rebut the presumption. But this rule does not shift the burden of persuasion, which remains on the Party who had it originally.

规则 301 关于民事案件中推定的一般规定

在民事案件中，除非联邦制定法或本证据规则另有规定，一项推定所针对的当事人承担反驳该推定的举证责任。但本条规则并不转移说服责任，说服责任仍然由原来承担该责任的当事人承担。

breach & default

breach 和 default 在英文法律文件中使用频率极高，在不同的语境中有不同的含义，可以指违反法律、侵害他人权利、不履行自己的义务或职责等；其行为方式可以是作为，也可以是不作为。在涉及合同的背景下，它们都可以指合同一方当事人未履行合同的条款、允诺或条件。不过，它们还是有细微的区别，下面我们先结合工具书对它们的含义做一下梳理。

(1)

breach [briːtʃ] *v.t.* & *n.[C]* a violation or infraction of a law or obligation. 违反

(2)

default [diˈfɔːlt] *n.[U]* & *v.i.* the omission or failure to perform a legal or contractual duty; esp., the failure to pay a debt when due

动词 default 的意思是：① to be neglectful; esp., to fail to perform a contractual obligation ② to fail to appear or answer ③ to enter a default judgment against a litigant

根据以上定义，我们可以看出：breach 和 default 都有违反法律义务和合同义务的意思，不过 default 有疏于履行的意思，侧重于不履行合同义务，特别是不偿还到期债务，也就是常说的"欠钱不还"。另外，default 还有诉讼当事人庭审缺席和法庭作出缺席判决的意思。

下面结合例句体会这两个词在实践中的用法：

例 1. Without prejudice to the provisions of Article 7, if Force Majeure occurs and prevents either Party from performing any of its obligations under this Agreement, the performance of such obligations shall be suspended during such period of delay, which shall not constitute a breach of this Agreement. 在不损害第七条的规定的情况下，如果发生不可抗力，致使一方当事人无法履行其在本协议项下的义务，在

不可抗力导致的延迟期间应当中止履行，中止履行不构成违反本协议。

例 2. Waiver by either Party of any breach of any provision of this Agreement shall not be considered as or constitute a continuing waiver or a waiver of any other breach of the same or any other provision of this Agreement. 任何一方对违反本协议任何条款的情形放弃权利不应被视为而且亦不构成持续放弃权利或对违反本协议该条款或本协议任何其他条款的情形放弃权利。·

例 3. Notwithstanding any other provision set forth in this Agreement, including amendments, attachments, or any other document incorporated herein, this Section sets forth AAA's entire responsibility and liability and the Company's entire remedy with respect to any breach of this Agreement, and any third Party claims, related to Materials Declaration Requirements, and that absent this provision, AAA would not enter this Agreement. 即使本协议，包括修正案、附件或被纳入本协议的任何其他文件，作出任何其他规定，本节列明对于任何违反本协议的情形，AAA 承担的全部责任和公司获得的全部补救，以及与材料申报要求有关的任何第三方申索，如果没有这一规定，AAA 就不会签订本协议。

例 4. Either Party may terminate this Agreement based on the material breach by the other Party of the terms of this Agreement, provided that the Party alleged to be in material breach receives written notice setting forth the nature of the breach at least 30 days prior to the intended termination date. During such time the Party in material breach may cure the alleged breach and if such breach is cured within such 30 day period, no termination will occur and this Agreement will continue in accordance with its terms. If such breach shall not have been cured, termination shall occur upon the termination date set forth in such notice. 任何一方均可以另一方严重违反本协议条款为根据终止本协议，但被指称严重违约的一方须至少在意图终止本协议的日期之前三十天收到说明其违约性质的书面通知。在此期间，严重违约方可以纠正被指称的违约行为，如果在这三十天内纠正了该违约行为，则不会发生终止本协议的情形，本协议将按照其条款继续有效。倘若该违约行为未得到纠正，

则在上述通知中规定的终止日期终止本协议。

例 5. Each Party acknowledges that a breach of any of the terms of this Section may cause the non-breaching Party irreparable damage, for which the award of damages would not be adequate compensation. Consequently, the non-breaching Party may institute an action to enjoin the breaching Party from any and all acts in violation of those provisions, which remedy shall be cumulative and not exclusive, and shall be in addition to any other relief to which the non-breaching Party may be entitled at law or in equity. 每一方承认违反本节的任何条款可能给守约方造成无法用金钱弥补的损害，对此，判给守约方损害赔偿金不构成充分补偿。因此，守约方可以提起诉讼，以便禁止违约方作出任何违反上述规定的行为，这种补救属于累积补救，而非排他性补救，并且对守约方在法律上或在衡平法上有权获得的任何其他救济构成补充。

例 6. An award may be set aside by the Court if the Party who applies to the Court to set aside the award proves to the satisfaction of the Court that a breach of the rules of natural justice occurred in connection with the making of the award by which the rights of any Party have been prejudiced. 如果向高等法院申请撤销仲裁裁决的当事人证明并令高等法院确信发生了与作出仲裁裁决有关的违反自然公正原则的情形，导致任何一方当事人的权利受到损害，高等法院可以撤销仲裁裁决。

例 7. Where the law in the Special Part of this Code or in any other law defines in a restrictive manner offences that may be prosecuted only upon the preferring of charges by the injured or aggrieved person or those claiming under him, the Court has no power to try the offence and a penalty cannot be pronounced in default of this condition precedent. 凡在本法典分则或任何其他法律中以限制性方式规定只有经受伤害者或受屈者或有权以其名义申索的人提出控告，才能对某些罪行进行检控，如未满足这项先决条件，法院就无权审判该罪行并宣告处罚。

例 8. The Parties may agree on the method of reckoning periods of time for the purposes of —

(a) any provision agreed by them; or

(b) any provision of this Act having effect in default of such agreement.

双方当事人可以约定计算下列条文所指期限的方法：

（a）由双方当事人约定的任何条文；或者

（b）在双方当事人没有作出约定的情况下予以适用的本法的任何条文。

例 9. Finally, it should be noted that the European Commission may take action against any member state that fails to appropriately implement the EU Directives on public procurement. Complaint to them may be made by aggrieved Parties. Action may be taken in the European Court of justice against the defaulting state. 最后，应当注意的是，欧盟委员会可以对任何未妥善执行欧盟公共采购指令的成员国提起诉讼。受害方可以向欧盟委员会提出申诉。可在欧洲联盟法院对失职的成员国提起诉讼。

例 10. Default interest (if unpaid) arising on an Unpaid Sum will be compounded with the Unpaid Sum at the end of each Interest Period applicable to that Unpaid Sum but will remain immediately due and payable. 未付款额所产生的违约利息（如未付）在该笔未付款额适用的每一利息期结束时与未付款额合并累计复利，但仍继续即时到期应付。

例 11. "Default" means an Event of Default or any event or circumstance specified in Clause 20 (*Events of Default*) which would (with the expiry of a grace period, the giving of notice, the making of any determination under this Agreement or any combination of any of the foregoing) be an Event of Default. "违约"指违约事件或第 22 条（违约事件）所述（在宽限期届满、发出有关通知并按任何融资文件作出决定后或前述各项任何组合的情况发生后）构成违约事件的事件或情况。

例 12. The *Companies Act 1985*, s310 renders void any provision (whether contained in the company's articles or otherwise) exempting or indemnifying any officer of the company from liability for negligence, default, breach of duty or breach of trust.《1985 年公司法》第 310 条规定，对于公司任何高级职员的疏忽、失责、违反职责或违背信托义务行为，凡豁免其责任或对其予以弥偿的条款（无论是否载于公司章程）均属无效。

carry on & carry out

(1)

carry on = to continue or proceed 继续

carry on 可以作为及物动词，也可以作为不及物动词。作为及物动词，后面搭配名词、动名词。

例 1. The plaintiff is an engineering and construction company based in England whilst the defendant carries on business as a bank in Hong Kong. 本案原告是一家设在英格兰的工程建设公司；本案被告是一家在香港开展业务的银行。

例 2. If a notice or other document is addressed, prepaid and delivered by post—

(a) to the addressee's usual or last known place of residence or, if he is or has been carrying on a trade, profession or business, his usual or last known place of business; or

(b) if the addressee is a body corporate, to the body corporate's registered office, it shall be treated as effectively served.

如果通知或其他文书按照下列方式注明通信地址、预付邮费和投递，则通知或其他文书应被视为有效送达：

（a）送达收件人的惯常居住地或最后为人所知的居住地，或者如果收件人正在或一直从事某种行业、职业或营业，则送达其惯常的营业地或最后为人所知的营业地；或者

（b）如果收件人是法人，送达该法人的登记住所。

(2)

carry sth. out 执行，贯彻，落实，完成

例 3. "Technical Documentation" shall mean the in-depth-description of the functionalities of the Products reasonably enabling any skilled person in the field of technology to understand, analyze and operate the functions of the Products and to carry out customizing. "技术文献"应指对产品的功能进行的深入说明，从而使任何熟练的技术人员能够理解、分析和操作产品的功能，并且能够完成定制。

例 4. Agreed Orders of AAA shall only be governed by and carried out according to the terms and the conditions of this Agreement. Agreed Orders of other Ordering Entities shall only be governed by and carried out according to the terms and the conditions of this Agreement if reference is made to this Agreement the respective Order or in the respective Adoption Agreement. AAA 签发的约定订单仅受本协议载明的各项条件约束并且仅依照上述条件履行。只有引述本协议、各份订单或者各项认可协议，其他订货实体签发的约定订单才受本协议载明的各项条件约束并且按照上述条件履行。

例 5. Service Provider shall perform the Services in accordance with the provisions of this Agreement and its schedules and shall in performance hereof comply with all reasonable instructions from Customer and exercise all reasonable skill, care and diligence to be expected of a service provider carrying out services similar to the Services. 服务商应当依照本协议及本协议各附件载明的各项条件履行约定服务，服务商在履行该服务时应当遵守客户作出的各项合理指示，并且具备履行类似约定服务的其他服务商所应具备的所有合理的技能、谨慎及勤勉。

例 6. In British Columbia, the *Oil and Gas Activities Act* (British Columbia), which came into force on October 4, 2010 and, among other things, repealed the *Pipeline Act* (British Columbia), provides that no person may carry out any oil or gas activity, which includes the construction and operation of a pipeline, without a permit. 在不列颠哥伦比亚省，于 2010 年 10 月 4 日生效的《油气活动法》（不列颠哥伦比亚省），除了其他事情外，废止了《管道法》（不列颠哥伦比亚省），规定如未获得执照，任何人不得开展任何油气活动，包括修建和运营管道。

例 7. The Seller shall carry out design, Contract Equipment manufacturing, selection of materials, inspection and test of the Contract Equipment according to the international standards in force and/or to the Seller's and/or manufacturer's standards and codes, details as per Section 1, Section 2 and Section 4. 卖方应当按照有效的国际标准及 / 或按照卖方的及 / 或制造商的标准和规范，完成设计、合同设备制造、材料甄选、检验及合同设备测试。有关详情由《技术规格》第 1 条、第 2 条和第 4 条加以规定。

cartilage & curtilage

(1)

cartilage [ˈkɑːtəlidʒ] *n.[C,U]* 软骨

gristle [ˈgrisəl] *n.[U]* 脆骨，软骨

注意：gristle 是指供食用的动物的肉里面的脆骨，cartilage 是指人体的软骨。

要注意区分 cartilage 和 curtilage。

(2)

curtilage [ˈkɜːtəlidʒ] *n.[C]* 庭院，宅地，园地

参看《布莱克法律词典》的解释：

The land or yard adjoining a house, usu. within an enclosure. Under the Fourth Amendment, the curtilage is an area usu. protected from warrantless searches. Also termed (in Latin) curtillium.

参看《元照英美法词典》的解释：

指与住所直接相连的土地或院子，通常由栅栏或灌木等加以围绕。在普通法中，以契约转让住宅和宅基时，庭院则一并转让而不用明确表述。在判定自卫权的存在时，家的庭院一般阐释为至少包括环绕住宅的院子和车库、畜栏以及其他外屋所占据的地方。在美国宪法第四条修正案中，对住所禁止非法搜查亦及于庭院。

例 1. The law provides that buildings and other structures that pre-date July 1948 and are within the curtilage of a listed building are to be treated as part of the listed building. 该法规定，凡建成于 1948 年 7 月以前且坐落在某一文保建筑的庭院内的建筑物及其他结构物应被视为该文保建筑的组成部分。

categorical, categorize & category

(1)

categorical [ˌkætiˈɡɒrikl] *adj.* 直接的，无条件的；分类的

categorically [ˌkætiˈɡɒrikli] *adv.* in such a sure and certain way that there is no doubt

例 1. The defense attorney employed persistent dilatory tactics to evade any categorical statement as to the defendant's legal capacity. 辩护律师没完没了地用拖延战术避免就被告人的法律行为能力作出任何明确的陈述。

例 2. The defendant has categorically denied his guilt all along, despite the fact that the prosecutor has produced irrefutable evidence against him. 尽管检察官出示了不容辩驳的有罪证据，被告人却始终断然否认有罪。

例 3. Either of the two forms may be used for obtaining partner approval; however, it is most common to distribute the Detail Estimate since it provides an itemized, categorical description of anticipated costs. 这两种表格中的任何一种都可以用来获得合作伙伴的批准；但是，详情估算表可以对预期成本作逐项分类说明，所以派发这种表的做法最常见。

例 4. In his report to the General Assembly, the Special Rapporteur on torture and other cruel, inhuman or degrading treatment or punishment noted that there is no categorical evidence that any method of execution in use today complies with the prohibition of torture and cruel, inhuman or degrading treatment. 调查酷刑和其他残忍、不人道或有辱人格的待遇或处罚问题的特别报告员在他提交联合国大会的报告中提到，没有任何确定无疑的证据能够证明目前使用的任何处决方法符合禁止酷

刑和残忍、不人道或有辱人格的待遇的规定。

(2)

categorize [ˈkætigəraiz] *v.t.* = classify 归类

例 5. Directors' duties may be categorised into three broad types. The first two types are fiduciary in nature. 可以将董事的职责分为三大类。前两种类型本质上属于信托。

例 6. The present summary report provides an overview of the findings of the Working Group under its multi-year workplan, categorizes the range of mechanisms for international cooperation and explains legal provisions in various types of international mechanisms, in particular bilateral cooperation agreements that serve as examples for consideration, as appropriate. 本摘要报告概述工作组在其多年期工作计划之下得出的调查结果，对各类国际合作机制进行分类，并酌情解释各类国际机制——特别是作为审查事例的双边合作协定——的法律条款。

例 7. Technical cooperation projects are categorized as contributing to one of the Organization's thematic priorities: (a) creating shared prosperity, (b) advancing economic competitiveness and (c) safeguarding the environment. 技术合作项目被归类为有助于工发组织的某一专题优先事项：（a）创造共同繁荣，（b）提高经济竞争力以及（c）保护环境。

例 8. One attempt to make progress in this regard were the presentations made by the Office's Director to the Executive Board in 2015 and in 2016, which flagged important pending recommendations, categorized by main areas of the Organization's activities, where action was needed. 推动这方面取得进展的一个尝试是，人权高专办主任在 2015 年和 2016 年向执行局作了介绍，其中按本组织需要采取行动的主要活动领域分类，列出了重要的待决建议。

(3)

category [ˈkætigəri] *n.[C]* 类别，范畴

例 9. In addition, different categories of formal arrangements or programme-related instruments, either legally binding on the Parties or affecting their interests in some way, have been concluded. 此外，还缔结了不同类型的正式安排或与计划有关的文书，它们或者对各方具有法律约束力，或者在某种程度上影响到各方的利益。

例 10. Another category of antitrust offenses involves discrimination which harms customers or competitors. Violations can occur both in selling to customers or in purchasing from suppliers. 另一类反垄断犯罪涉及损害客户或竞争对手的歧视。在向客户销售或向供应商采购时都会发生这种违法行为。

例 11. The EU rules do not apply to all procurements. Only those above the thresholds and within certain categories of products are affected. These rules affect relevant procurements by all central and local government bodies in the UK as well as other publicly funded bodies and certain utility providers even if they are private companies. 并非所有采购均须遵守欧盟规章。那些超过最低额度的采购和在某些类别的产品范围内进行的采购才受到影响。这些规章会影响英国所有中央和地方政府机构的相关采购，另外，其他受政府资助的机构和某些公用事业供应商，即使他们是私营公司，相关采购也会受影响。

例 12. When considering the question of the range of procurement methods that a procurement system makes available to procuring entities, it is important to note at the outset that there are basically two main categories of provisions on procurement methods. 在考虑采购体系为采购实体提供的采购方法的范围问题时，必须首先注意关于采购方法基本上有两大类。

例 13. User charges that may be imposed by the competent charging authorities or bodies of each Party on the airlines of the other Party shall be just, reasonable, not unjustly discriminatory, and equitably apportioned among categories of users. 各方的主管收费机关或团体对另一方的航空公司征收的用户收费应当公正、合理，不得有不当歧视，并且应当按用户类别公平分摊。

例 14. The right to strike is weakened by excluding certain categories of workers from the right, excessive prerequisites to hold a legal strike, inappropriate legal changes that allow public authorities to suspend or declare a strike illegal and government and public arguments favoring restrictions on the right to strike. 不让一些类别的工人拥有罢工权，对举行合法罢工设定过高要求，对法律作出不当改变，政府部门有权取消罢工或宣布罢工非法，加上政府和公众支持对罢工权设限，这些因素都削弱了罢工权。

例 15. What then is a person who is criminally concerned, or an accomplice? He is in fact an accessory before the fact or a principal or an accessory after the fact. That is, he is a person who helps in the preparation of the crime or commits a crime or assists a criminal to escape liability. There seems to be absolutely no doubt that Mr. ABC falls firmly into that category. 那么，一个牵涉入犯罪，或者与他人共同实施犯罪的人是什么人呢？其实，他是事前从犯，主犯或事后从犯。也就是说，他帮助预备犯罪或实施犯罪或协助犯罪分子逃避刑责。ABC 先生肯定属于这类人，这一点毫无疑问。

例 16. AAA shall, subject to applicable laws and regulations and the terms and conditions of this Agreement, use its affiliates, entities or third Party designees in the Territory, to act as the distributor for only goods which fall within categories of goods set out in Schedule 1 hereto. AAA 根据可适用的法律法规和本协议的条款和条件，在约定地域内利用其关联企业、实体或第三方指定人员，仅对属于本协议附件 1 所列类别的货物担任经销商。

cease, decease & predecease

(1)

cease [si:s] *v.t. & v.i.* 停止

例 1. The authority of an arbitrator shall cease upon his death. 仲裁员亡故时其职权即告终止。

例 2. The reconstitution of the arbitral tribunal shall not affect any right of a Party to challenge the previous proceedings on any ground which had arisen before the arbitrator ceased to hold office. 重新组成仲裁庭不影响当事人享有根据仲裁员离任之前产生的理由针对先前的程序提出异议的权利。

例 3. The Company agrees that the process by which any Proceedings are begun in England may be served on it by being delivered to AAA at ..., United Kingdom (Attention: Mr. BBB). If such appointment ceases to be effective the Company shall immediately appoint a further person in England to accept service of process on its behalf in England and, failing such appointment within 15 days, any Facility Agent shall be entitled to appoint such a person by notice to the Company. 公司同意，据以在英格兰提起诉讼的诉讼书状可以通过送交联合王国……的 AAA（收件人：BBB 先生）送达公司。如果上文指定的收件人不再有效，公司应当立即在英格兰指定其他人员代表公司在英格兰接收送达的诉讼书状，如果公司没有在十五日内指定有关人员，贷款事务代理人应当有权通过给予公司的通知，指定接收送达诉讼书状的人员。

例 4. Every member of the Foundation undertakes to contribute to the assets of the Foundation, in the event of its being wound up while such person is a member or within one year thereafter, for payment of the debts and liabilities of the Foundation contracted before such person ceases to be a member and the costs, charges and expenses of winding up and for the adjustment of the rights of the contributories among themselves, such amount as may be required but not exceeding HK$ 100. 基金会的每一位成员承诺，如果基金会停业清理，此时他仍然是基金会的成员或者在终止成员身份后一年之内，他将向基金会的资产出资，用以偿还在他终止基金会成员身份之前，基金会所缔结的债务以及偿付停业清理的费用，并且用以在出资人之间调整他们的权利。可能要求的出资不得超过一百港元。

(2)

decease [di'si:s] *n.[U]* 去世
deceased [di'si:st] *adj. & n.[C]* 去世的（人）

例 5. An arbitration agreement shall not be discharged by the death of any Party to the agreement but shall continue to be enforceable by or against the personal representative of the deceased Party. 仲裁协议不因协议任何当事人亡故而被解除，而是由亡故者的遗产代理人继续执行或者继续针对该遗产代理人执行。

例 6. Where the deceased has not expressed his will in the form mentioned in Article 24, the conditions of his funeral shall be fixed by his surviving spouse or by his nearest relatives. 若死者没有按照第二十四条提及的形式明示自己的遗嘱，应当由他在世的配偶或最近的亲属确定他的丧葬条件。

(3)

predecease [ˌpri:di'si:s] *v.t.* 先于……死亡

例 7. One or more predeceased children of the person represented shall themselves be represented according to the same principles. Succession shall not take place beyond relatives of the sixth degree. 被代位继承人的一个或多个先去世的子女应当按照相同的原则被代位继承。第六亲等以外的亲属不得参加继承。

censor, censure & census

(1)

censor ['sɛnsə] *n.[C]* （新闻、电影、书刊、戏剧等的）审查员；*v.t.* 审查（新闻、电影、书刊、戏剧等）

censorship ['sɛnsəʃip] *n.[U]* 审查（制度）；检查（制度）

(2)

censure ['sɛnʃə] *n.[U]* an official reprimand or condemnation; harsh criticism

v.t. to reprimand; to criticize harshly 谴责，训斥

例 1. The judge's careless statements subjected her to the judicial council's censure. 这位法官发表了随意的言论，招致司法委员会训诫。

例 2. The Senate censured the senator for his inflammatory remarks. 这名参议员因为说了煽动性的话而受到参议院谴责。

(3)

census ['sɛnsəs] *n.[C]* the official counting of people to compile social and economic data for the political subdivision to which the people belong 人口普查

charter, hire, lease, let, rent & tenancy

辨析几个表示租赁的词：

(1)

charter ['tʃɑːtə] *v.t.* & *n.[U]* to hire or rent an airplane, ship, or other vessel 包租（交通工具）

chartered ['tʃɑːtəd] *adj.* 包租的

注意：与其他表示租赁的词语相比，charter 相对特殊，它的对象是飞机、船舶等交通工具，名词 charter 可以作为 charter agreement 的同义语，表示租约。

例 1. The Aircraft shall be properly equipped for the purposes for which it is being chartered. 飞机应按照包机目的妥善配齐人员设备。

例 2. The Carrier shall not advertise or otherwise make public that the Carrier is chartering aircraft or providing services to the UN, nor shall the Carrier, in any other manner whatsoever, use the name, emblem or official seal of the UN, or any abbreviation of the name of the UN in connection with its business or otherwise. 承运人不得刊登广告或以其他方式公开宣传承运人正在向联合国出租飞机或向联合国提供服务，也不得在与承运人业务有关联的情况下或在其他情况下，以无论其他何种方式使用联合国的名称、标志或公章或者使用联合国名称的缩写。

例 3. Nothing in or relating to this Charter Agreement shall be deemed a waiver, express or implied, of any of the privileges and immunities of the UN, including its subsidiary organs. 本租机协议中记载的或与本租机协议有关的任何内容，均不得视为明示或默示放弃联合国（包括其附属机构）的任何特权和豁免。

例 4. Any airline designated by either Party performing international charter air transportation originating in the territory of either Party, whether on a one-way or round-trip basis, shall have the option of complying with the charter laws, regulations, and rules either of its homeland or of the other Party. If a Party applies different rules, regulations, terms, conditions, or limitations to one or more of its airlines, or to airlines of different countries, each designated airline shall be subject to the least restrictive of such criteria. 由任何一方指定的航空公司执行从任何一方领土上起航的国际包机运输任务，无论采用单程形式还是往返形式，该航空公司都可以选择遵守本国或对方的包机法律、规章和规则。如果一方对本方的一个或多个航空公司或者对不同国家的航空公司适用不同的规则、规章、条款、条件或限制，每个被指定的航空公司应遵守限制最少的此类标准。

下面几个表示租赁的词语在法律文件中经常同时出现，我们先讲解这几个词汇，然后结合相关例句体会这些词语的用法。

(2)

hire ['haɪə] *v.t.* ① to procure the temporary use of property, usu. at a set price 租用；② to engage the labor or services of another for wages or other payment 雇请；*n.[U]* 租用

hired ['haɪəd] *adj.* 租来的；雇请的

根据 *Cambridge Advanced Learner's Dictionary* 的解释，在英国英语中，hire 通常表示短期租用某物。rent 通常表示长期租用某物。在美国英语中，rent 既可以通常表示长期租用某物，也可以表示短期租用某物。

实践中，hire 表示租赁，既可以表示承租人租用，也可以表示出租人出租，表示出租的时候用短语 hire sth. out。hire 的对象可以是动产，也可以是不动产。参见下面的链接：

租赁对象是动产：If you are going on holiday and hiring a vehicle, or you are a company hiring out vehicles, these changes may affect you. https://www.gov.uk/government/news/hiring-a-vehicle。

租赁对象是不动产：https://www.theabbeydalepicturehouse.com/hire/，https://www.camdenhouse.com/，https://www.lauderdalehouse.org.uk/hire-house，https://www.wycombehouse.com/hall-hire/，https://www.gumtree.com/property-to-rent/london/hire。

hire 似乎相当于中文的短租，但它和 rent 在租赁时间上的区别不甚明显，在爱彼迎（Airbnb）网站上选一个房间租一晚，也经常使用 rent。参见：https://www.airbnb.com/s/all?query=rent+a+room。

(3)

lease [li:s] *v.t.* ① to grant the possession and use of (land, buildings, rooms, movable property, etc.) to another in return for rent or other consideration; ② to a lease of; to hold by a lease

n.[C] ① A contract by which a rightful possessor of real property conveys the right to use and occupy the property in exchange for consideration, usu. rent. The lease term can be for life, for a fixed period, or for a period terminable at will. ② such a conveyance plus all covenants attached to it ③ the written instrument memorializing such a conveyance and its covenants. Also termed lease agreement; lease contract. ④ the piece of real property so conveyed ⑤ a contract by which the rightful possessor of personal property conveys the right to use that property in exchange for consideration

根据《布莱克法律词典》的定义，我们可以看出动词 lease 包含出租和承租。名词 lease 指租赁这种法律关系，体现这种法律关系的文书（也就是租约）以及租赁关系的标的，而标的可以是动产，也可以是不动产。

(4)

let *v.t. & n.[C]* to offer property for lease; to rent out 出租

注意：动词 let 的现在分词、过去式和过去分词分别是 letting、let、let。

let sth. out to sb. 把……租给某人

let 仅表示出租，它的对象是不动产。

(5)

rent [rentl] *n.[C,U]* consideration paid, usu. periodically, for the use or occupancy of property (esp. real property) 租金；*v.t.* 租赁（出租或租用）

for rent 出租，招租

rent sth. out to sb. 把某物出租给某人

动词 rent 的对象可以是动产，也可以是不动产。名词 rent 表示租赁的对价，也就是租金。

rental ['rentl] *n. [C, U]* 租赁；租金

(6)

tenancy ['tenənsi] *n. [C, U]* 租赁；租赁期限

tenancy 表示租赁的法律关系或租赁的期间。标的是不动产。

注意区分 lessee & tenant 以及 lessor & landlord。

lessee 和 tenant 都表示承租人，区别在于 lessee 既可以指租用不动产的人，也可以指租用
    动产的人。tenant 仅指租用不动产的人。

同理，lessor 和 landlord 都表示出租人，区别在于 lessor 既可以指出租不动产的人，也可
    以指出租动产的人。landlord 仅指出租不动产的人。

例 5. to purchase, lease, take in exchange, hire or otherwise acquire any personal
property and any rights or privileges that the company considers necessary or convenient for the purposes of its business; 购买、租赁、换取、租用或以其他方式收购该
公司认为就其业务而言属于必要或适宜的任何动产及任何权利或特权；

例 5 选自一家香港公司的公司章程大纲（memorandum of association），注意例句用了
    lease 和 hire 这两个表示租赁的词，它们的对象是动产及权利和特权。

例 6. to take land in Bermuda by way of lease or letting agreement for a term not
exceeding twenty-one years, being land "bona fide" required for the purposes of the
business of the company and with the consent of the Minister granted in his discretion
to take land in Bermuda by way of lease or letting agreement for a similar period in
order to provide accommodation or recreational facilities for its officers and employees
and when no longer necessary for any of the above purposes to terminate or transfer
the lease or letting agreement; 以租约或租赁协议方式在百慕大获得期限不超过
二十一年之土地，即为进行该公司业务"真正"需要的土地，并经司法部长酌
情同意就以租约或租赁协议方式在百慕大获得类似期限之土地，以为其高级人
员及雇员提供住宿或休闲设施，并于不再需作任何上述目的时终止或转让该租
约或租赁协议；

例 7. Sublet: A sublet occurs when the tenant moves out of the rental unit, lets another person (the "sub-tenant") live there until a specified date, and can return to live in the unit before the tenancy ends. The tenancy agreement and the landlord-tenant relationship do not change.

A tenant who sublets a rental unit cannot:

(1) charge a higher rent than the landlord does for the rental unit;

(2) collect any additional fees for subletting the rental unit; or

(3) charge the sub-tenant for additional goods or services.

Residential Tenancies Act, 2006 (Canada)

转租：当租户搬出出租单元，让另一个人（"转租户"）住进出租单元，直到指定的日期，而且租户可以在租期结束之前返回该单元居住，就会发生转租。租赁协议和房东租户关系不变。

将出租单元进行转租的租户不能有下列行为：

（1）收取的租金高于房东就出租单元收取的租金；

（2）就转租出租单元收取任何额外费用；或者

（3）就其他物品或服务向转租户收取费用。

2006年《住宅租赁法》（加拿大）

例 8. Possible expansion of the business scope of the Developer may include (1) management of the rental of the townhomes completed and sold in the Project, and (2) per the option granted in the Agreements, the development of the 6 remaining Option Lots. 开发商有可能扩大的营业范围包括：（1）管理本项目中已经建成和售出的连排别墅的租赁事宜；（2）按照协议中授予的选择权，开发六块剩余的备选地块。

例 9. The General Partner has hired AAA, the current developer of XYZ Resort with over 25 years of resort development experience across the U.S., to provide certain pre-development services. The General Partner intends to hire BBB Architecture and CCC Planning, Engineering & Surveying, the original architectural and engineering firms for the first 12 townhomes in the Community, to update and finish all the design and engineering drawings. 普通合伙人已经聘请 XYZ 度假村的当前开发商 AAA 来提供某些开发前期服务，AAA 在美国各地开发度假地的经验超过二十五年。普通合伙人打算聘请 BBB 建筑师事务所和 CCC 规划、工程和测绘事务所来更新和完成所有设计和工程图纸，它们就是承建社区最初十二座连排别墅的建筑事务所和工程事务所。

例 8 和例 9 选自美国律师起草的同一份文件，大家可以看出句中使用 rental 表示租赁，使用 hire 的义项是雇请。

例 10. All software used in connection with the Equipment, Parts or Services, either purchased or rented from Seller, is copyrighted and owned by Seller and licensed to Buyer. 买方向卖方购买或租赁的用于设备、零件或服务的所有软件，均受版权保护，归卖方所有并特许买方使用。

例 11. a. Seller shall release, indemnify, defend and hold Buyer Group harmless from and against any and all Claims in respect of personal or bodily injury to, sickness, disease or death of any member of Seller Group or Seller Group's subcontractors or their employees, agents or invitees, and all Claims in respect of damage to or loss or destruction of property owned, leased, rented or hired by any member of Seller Group or Seller Group's subcontractors or their employees, agents or invitees. 对于卖方集团或者卖方集团的分包人或者其雇员、代理人或者受邀请人的任何成员所受到的对人伤害或者人身伤害，所发生的不适、疾病或者死亡，以及对于卖方集团或者卖方集团的分包人或者其雇员、代理人或者受邀请人的任何成员拥有或者租赁的财产所遭受的破坏或者灭失或者毁损，卖方应当使买方集团免于承担与之有关的任何和所有权利请求。

b. Buyer shall release, indemnify, defend and hold Seller Group harmless from and against any and all Claims in respect of personal or bodily injury to, sickness, disease or death of any member of Buyer Group or Buyer Group's other contractors or their employees, agents or invitees, and all Claims in respect of damage to or loss or destruction of property owned, leased, rented or hired by any member of Buyer Group or Buyer Group's other contractors or their employees, agents or invitees. 对于买方集团或者买方集团的其他承包人或者它们的雇员、代理人或者受邀请人的任何成员所受到的对人伤害或者人身伤害，所发生的不适、疾病或者死亡，以及对于买方集团或者买方集团的其他承包人或者它们的雇员、代理人或者受邀请人的任何成员拥有或者租赁的财产所遭受的破坏或者灭失或者毁损，买方应当使卖方集团免于承担与之有关的任何和所有权利请求。

例 12. Should Tenant hold over and remain in possession of the Premises after the expiration of the Term without Landlord's consent, it shall not be deemed or construed to be renewal of this *Lease*, but shall only operate to create a month-to-month tenancy which may be terminated by either Party at the end of any month upon thirty (30) days' written notice to the other Party. During any holding over period, the *Lease* shall otherwise remain in full force and effect, except that Base Rent shall be one hundred percent (100%) of the Base Rent then in effect. 假若承租人在期限结束之后，未经出租人同意，继续占有场所，承租人的行为不应被视为或解释为重订《租约》，而是仅应作为创设了按月租赁，任何一方当事人均可以在提前三十（30）日书面通知对方后，在任何月份结束时终止这种租赁关系。在逾期占有租赁物期间，《租约》仍应保持充分的效力，但逾期占有期间的基本租金应当是当时施行的基本租金的百分之一百（100%）。

我们可以看出，在上面的例句中，lease 表示租赁契约，rent 表示租金，tenancy 表示租赁法律关系或状态。

例 13. lessee consent/notice issues—lessees will generally require quiet enjoyment letters from any person holding a mortgage over the aircraft and leases may contain other limitations on the creation of aircraft mortgages. Aircraft mortgages would, by definition, require involving the lessees in the process and this can be time-consuming and costly; 承租人的同意／通知问题——承租人往往要求对于飞机享有抵押权的人出具安宁用益权利保证函，而且租约可能包含针对创设飞机抵押的其他限

制。根据定义，飞机抵押需要承租人介入飞机抵押过程，这可能耗费时间和资金；

例 14. The original lettable space is 7,100 square meters. At this moment, the lettable area given by your Mr. John Doe is 6,700 square meters as informed by Mr. Richard Roe of XYZ. We have yet to confirm the actual area till our interior designer recomputes the lettable areas. If the new lettable floor area is short of 8% to 10%, then we request the external bridge open areas for some seating arrangement for the café or food & beverage outlets during good weather condition. 原有的可出租面积是 7100 平方米。目前，根据 XYZ 的 Richard Roe 先生告知我方的情况，贵司 John Doe 提供的可出租面积只有 6780 平方米。迫我方内部设计师重新计算出可出租面积，我方才能确认实际面积。如果新得出的可出租楼面面积缺额达到 8%~10%，我方要求在天气状况良好时，在外部天桥露天区域为咖啡店或者餐饮店安排若干座位。

例 15. XYZ leases its aircraft on a "dry" basis, under which lessees are responsible for all operating expenses including fuel, crew, taxes and insurance. In addition, the lessees pay for the maintenance and repair of the airframe and for engine overhauls during the term (and may be eligible for reimbursement from maintenance reserves already paid, where applicable) and are responsible for compliance with stipulated aircraft return conditions at lease maturity. Some leases provide for XYZ to contribute to the cost of implementing airworthiness directives which exceed a certain dollar threshold. XYZ 在 "干租" 的基础上出租它的飞机，据此，承租人负责包括燃料、机组人员、税费和保险在内的所有运营费用。此外，承租人在承租期限内还支付机体的维护和修理费用和发动机的大修费用（在可行的情况下，承租人可以从已经支付的维护准备金中报销上述费用），在租约到期时承租人负责遵守返还飞机的规定条件。某些租赁协议规定 XYZ 缴纳超过一定以美元计算的最低额度的执行适航指令的费用。

例 16. The Pledgor shall not (nor shall the Pledgor agree to) enter into a single transaction or a series of transactions (whether related or not and whether voluntary or involuntary) to sell, lease, transfer, assign or otherwise dispose of any Pledged Asset except, in the case of Dividends, as permitted by Clause 4.3 (*Dividends before enforcement*) or as permitted under the terms of the *Facility Agreement*. 出质人不得（亦不得同意他人）订立出售、租赁、转移、转让或者以其他方式处置质押资产的单项交易或者系列交易（无论是否存在关联，无论是否出于自愿），但第4.3条（执行前的股息）所准许有关股息的处置，或者根据《贷款协议》获准的处置除外。

例 17. During the term of this Agreement, the Mortgagor shall not lease, assign, transfer or otherwise dispose of the Mortgaged Property in whole or in part (save for the Permitted Leases) without the prior written consent of the Lender. Any purported lease, assignment, transfer or other disposal of the Mortgaged Property in whole or in part except as expressly permitted in this Clause shall be invalid. 在本协议的存续期间内，事前未经贷款人书面批准，抵押人不得租赁、让与、转让或以其他方式处置全部或部分抵押不动产（获准的租赁除外）。除了本条明示准许的处置以外，任何意欲对抵押不动产的租赁、让与、转让或者其他处置无效。

例 18. Notwithstanding the provisions of Clause 4 of this Memorandum of Association, nothing herein contained shall prevent the payment, in good faith, of reasonable and proper remuneration to any officer or servant of the Foundation or to any member of the Foundation, in return for any service actually rendered to the Foundation, nor prevent the payment of interest at a rate not exceeding 2 percent above the prime rate established by The Hongkong and Shanghai Banking Corporation Limited for Hong Kong dollar loans on money lent or reasonable and proper rent for premises demised or let, by any member to the Foundation, but so that no member of the Board of Governors of the Foundation shall be appointed to any salaried office of the Foundation or any office of the Foundation paid by fees and that no remuneration or other benefit in money or money's worth shall be given by the Foundation to any such person except repayment of out-of-pocket expenses and interest at the abovementioned rate on money lent or reasonable and proper rent for premises demised or let to the Foundation, provided that such provision shall not apply to any payment to any company of which such person may be a member and in which such person holds not more than one-hundredth part of the capital or controls not more than one-hundredth part of the votes and such person shall not be bound to account for any share of profits received in respect of any such payment. 即便本章程大纲第 4 条有如是规定，本章程大纲中任何内容不妨碍基金会就其高级管理人员或雇员或基金会的任何成员为其实际提供的服务，善意地向该高级管理人员、雇员或成员支付合理且适当的报酬，也不妨碍基金会按照一定利率（不得比香港上海汇丰银行有限公司为港元贷款规定的优惠利率高出百分之二）就任何成员借给基金会的款项支付利息或者就任何成员租给基金会的场所支付合理且适当的租金，但是不得任命基金会理事会的成员担任基金会的任何有固定薪金的职务或者任何领取报酬的职务，基金会亦不得给予上述人员任何金钱或具有金钱价值的报酬或其他好处，除非偿付他们垫付的费用和按照上述利率就借给基金会的款项支付利息或者就租给基金会的场所支付合理且适当的租金；如果上述人员是某一公司的成员，而且上述人员持有该公司不超过百分之一的资本或者控制该公司不超过百分之一的表决权，则上面的规定不适用于对该公司的偿付，上述人员也没有义务说明他们所收到的与对该公司的偿付有关的股份或利润。

collapse, elapse, lapse & relapse

(1)

collapse [kəˈlæps] *v.i. & n.[C,U]* 倒塌，坍塌，崩溃，垮掉，昏倒；*v.t. & v.i.*（esp. 家具）折叠

例 1. Based on a Market Demand Study prepared by AAA and the Price Estimate Analysis performed by BBB, the U.S. real estate market, the regional Greater San Francisco real estate market, and the local Lake Tahoe real estate market all appear to be in a gradual recovery from the collapse that started in 2008. 根据 AAA 编写的一份市场需求研究和 BBB 完成的价格估算分析，美国房地产市场、大旧金山区域房地产市场以及塔霍湖地区房地产市场均呈现从 2008 年开始的崩溃中逐步复苏的局面。

例 2. The local planning authority may refuse to give its approval of any plans of extension where the carrying out of such extension (i) will cause, or will be likely to cause, a total or partial collapse of any adjoining or other building, or (ii) will render, or will be likely to render, any adjoining or other building so dangerous that it will collapse, or be likely to collapse, either totally or partially, and it is not satisfied that the collapse or the likelihood of the collapse, or such danger or the likelihood of such danger to the building, can be avoided. 凡有下列情况，当地规划部门可拒绝批准扩建工程的任何图则：进行扩建施工（一）将会导致或相当有可能会导致任何毗邻的或其他的建筑物整体或局部坍塌，或（二）会使或相当有可能会使任何毗邻的或其他的建筑物变得危险，以致于会或相当可能会整体或局部坍塌，而当地规划部门确信不可避免坍塌或发生坍塌的可能性，或对建筑物构成的上述危险或构成上述危险的可能性。

74

(2)

elapse [i'læps] *v.i.* 时间逝去

例 3. Any interest, commission or fee accruing under this Agreement will accrue from day to day and is calculated on the basis of the actual number of days elapsed and a year of 360 days. 根据本协议产生的任何利息、佣金或费用将逐日累算，并且根据实际经过的天数计算，一年按照 360 日计算。

例 4. "Actual Time for Completion" means the actual period for completion of the Works (as defined below) which shall commence on the date on which the EPC Contract becomes effective and elapse on the day on which the Taking-Over Certificate (as defined below) is issued. "实际竣工时间"是指完成工程（参见下文定义）的实际期间，该期间自总承包合同生效之日起，自签发交接证书（参见下文定义）之日止。

例 5. The Foundation shall, in each year, hold a general meeting as its annual general meeting in addition to any other meetings in that year and shall specify the meeting as such in the notice calling it. Not more than 15 months shall elapse between the date of one annual general meeting and the date of the next annual general meeting, provided that, so long as the Foundation holds its first annual general meeting within 18 months of incorporation, it need not hold an annual general meeting in the year of incorporation or the following year. 基金会每年应当召开一次全体会议作为它的年度全体会议（当年召开的其他会议除外），基金会应当在召集会议的通知中指明本次会议是年度全体会议。两次年度全体会议的日期间隔不得超过 15 个月，但是，只要基金会自它成立之日起 18 个月内召开它的第一次年度全体会议，基金会在它成立的当年或者下一年就无须再次召开年度全体会议。

(3)

lapse [læps]

v.i. ① (of an estate or right) to pass away or revert to someone else because conditions have not been fulfilled or because a person entitled to possession has failed in some duty ② (of a devise, grant, etc.) to become void 权利（或特权）的终止（或失效）

n.[C] ① a period of time passing between two things happening 时间间隔； ② the termination of a right or privilege because of a failure to exercise it within some time limit or because a contingency has occurred or not occurred 权利（或特权）的终止（或失效）； ③ a temporary failure 失误

例 6. Each contract disclosed in any Schedule to this Agreement or required to be disclosed pursuant to this Section is a valid and binding agreement of Either Founder and is in full force and effect, and to the knowledge of Either Founder, no other Party thereto is in default or breach in any material respect under the terms of any such contract, and, to the knowledge of Either Founder, no event or circumstance has occurred that, with notice or lapse of time or both, would constitute any event of default thereunder. 本协议任何附件中披露的或根据本节要求披露的每份合同是创办人之一的有效且有约束力的协议，具有完全效力，据创办人之一所知，该合同的任何一方均未在任何重大事项上违约或违约。根据任何此类合同的条款，并且据创办人所知，没有发生任何事件或情况，在通知或时间推移或两者同时发生时，将构成任何违约事件。

例 7. According to Paragraph 42 of the document, if the period entered was shorter than intended, the registration would remain effective against third parties even after it had lapsed and the notice was no longer searchable—i.e., the information that the registrant had intended to enter could be relied upon—unless a third Party could prove that it had searched the registry and failed to find the notice concerned, and had thus been seriously misled. 根据这份文件第 42 节，如果输入的期限比预定期限短，即使期限已过且通知无法再查询（也就是可以依据的登记人本来打算输入的信息），登记仍然具有对抗第三方的效力，除非第三方能够证明自己已经查询过登记处，却没有找到有关的通知，因此被严重误导。

(4)

relapse [ri'læps] *v.i.* 疾病复发；故态复萌

['ri:læps] *n.[C]* 疾病复发；故态复萌

 例 8. Amina Mohammed, the UN Deputy Secretary-General, also underscored the need to consolidate peace and avoid a relapse into conflict, and in doing so reiterated the importance of implementing the *2030 Agenda for Sustainable Development.* 联合国常务副秘书长阿米娜·穆罕默德还强调必须巩固和平、避免冲突重演，为此重申实施《2030 年可持续发展议程》的重要意义。

comparable & comparative

(1)

comparable [ˈkɔmpərəbl] *adj.* 可比较的，类似的，相当的

例 1. The amenities in this neighborhood is hardly comparable to those in London's Kensington and Chelsea, though their residential properties are comparably priced. 这个小区的生活设施几乎不能与伦敦的肯辛顿和切尔西相提并论，可是它们的住宅价格却不相上下。

例 2. In the event of damage to or loss of the Property through no fault of the Seller, the Seller may, subject to the prior consent by the Buyer, provide residential units of comparable size, location, and orientation to the Buyer. 倘若非因卖方过错发生物业受损或灭失，卖方在事先征得买方同意的情况下，可以为买方提供面积、地点和朝向相仿的住宅。

例 3. "Writing", "written" and comparable terms refer to printing, typing and other means of reproducing words (including electronic media) in a visible form. "以书面（Writing）" "书面（written）" 和类似术语是指采用打印、打字和其他手段复制可见文字（包括电子媒介）。

例 4. The package of benefits provided by the employer for the retirees who are below age 65 is at least comparable to benefits provided under title XVIII of the *Social Security Act* (42 *U.S.C.* 1395 et seq.). 雇主为 65 岁以下的退休人员提供的一揽子福利至少相当于根据《社会保障法》第 18 编（《美国法典》第 42 编第 1395 条及以下各条）提供的福利。

例 5. Prior to making a purchase of an item listed on the FPI Schedule, contracting officers are supposed to determine whether the item available from FPI is comparable in price, quality and delivery time to the supplies available from the private sector that best meet the needs of the procuring entity. 在采购联邦监狱产业公司计划表中所列的物品之前，负责签订合同的人员应当确定可以从联邦监狱产业公司购得的物品在价格、质量和交付时间方面是否与可以从私营部门购得的最能满足采购单位需求的物品相若。

例 6. Nevertheless, AAA may charge a marketing fee for its services where AAA can demonstrate that such fees are reasonable and/or customary for a given market area or class of service. Any such marketing fee shall be comparable to fees charged by or to non-affiliated entities. 然而，若 AAA 能够证明对于特定的市场区域或服务类别，收取营销费用合理且 / 或合乎习惯，AAA 可以对其服务收取该费用。任何此类营销费用应与非关联实体收取的或向它们收取的费用相当。

comparable 的反义词是 incomparable。

incomparable [inˈkɔmprəbl] *adj.* 无与伦比的

incomparably [inˈkɔmpərəbli] *adv.*

例 7. *Finding Nemo* is, in their view, and not without good reason, incomparably better than *Finding Dory*. 在他们看来，《海底总动员》远远胜过《多莉去哪儿》，这么看不无道理。

(2)

comparative [kəmˈpærətiv] *adj.* 比较的，对比的；比较级的； *n.[C]* 比较级

例 8. This Comparative Table is provided for the convenience of users. It is not part of the *Arbitration Act*. 下面的对照表旨在方便使用者查考。该表不构成《仲裁法》的组成部分。

例 9. The Ministry has required that the report should provide a comparative study of the basic government procurement law, system and supervision and management of public procurement. 财政部要求这份报告应当对政府采购的基本法律、制度和公共采购监督管理进行比较研究。

例 10. UNODC further organized a regional legislative harmonization workshop for transposing the *Firearms Protocol* into national legislation, for countries of the Maghreb, held in Tunis in July 2017. Prior to the workshop, a preliminary assessment and comparative analysis of firearms legislation in States of the subregion was prepared by UNODC and presented to participants. 毒品和犯罪问题办公室进而于 2017 年 7 月在突尼斯为马格里布国家组织了一次关于将《枪支议定书》转换成国内立法的区域立法协调讲习班。在开办这次讲习班之前，毒品和犯罪问题办公室编写了一份该次区域诸国枪支立法的初步评估和比较分析并将其发给参加讲习班的学员。

例 11. The applicant submitted that the learned sentencing Judge fell into error on two discrete bases; first, by failing to take into account comparative sentences for like offences in determining the appropriate sentence to be imposed; and, secondly by failing to take into account and/or give any consideration, when imposing the maximum sentence permissible under the law, to relevant and applicable human rights instruments and precepts relating to the detention and imprisonment of detainees. 申请人呈述说，这位学识渊博的量刑法官在两个不同的基础上犯了错误；第一，在决定应判处的适当刑罚时，没有考虑同类罪行的比较量刑；第二，在判处法律允许的最高刑期时，没有考虑和 / 或顾及关涉羁押和监禁被羁押者的相关的和可适用的人权文书和准则。

例 12. We call on the WEF 2015 co-convenors, and in particular UNESCO, as well as on all partners, to individually and collectively support countries in implementing the *Education 2030 Agenda*, by providing technical advice, national capacity development and financial support based on their respective mandates and comparative advantages, and building on complementarity. 我们呼吁 2015 年世界教育论坛的共同召集机构，特别是联合国教科文组织，以及所有合作伙伴，根据各自职责和比较优势并利用它们的互补性，通过提供技术咨询、培养国家能力以及提供财政支持，各自或共同地支持各国实施《2030 年教育议程》。

comparatively [kəmˈpærətivli] *adv.*

例 13. The comparatively low adherence status continues despite the periodically expressed invitation by the Conference to States that have not yet done so to consider becoming parties to the *Firearms Protocol* and to fully implement its provisions. 尽管缔约方会议定期促请尚未加入《枪支议定书》的国家考虑成为其缔约方并充分实施其规定，加入该议定书的状态仍然比较差。

例 14. Classes still proceed through dialogue. This is much appreciated by students, who year after year report extraordinarily high levels of satisfaction with the pedagogical dimension of their law school experience. Comparatively few, however, use what law schools traditionally called with some pride the "Socratic method". 授课仍然通过对话进行。学生们对此非常赞赏，他们年复一年地报告说对法学院的教学特别满意。可是，较少有人采用法学院一直以来颇为自豪地称作"苏格拉底反诘法"的教学方法。

concur, incur, occur & recur

(1)

concur [kənˈkɜː] (concurring, concurred) *v.i.* ① to agree; to consent. In a judicial opinion, to agree with the judgement in the case (usu. as expressed in the opinion of another judge), or the opinion of another judge, but often for different reasons or through a different line of reasoning 同意，赞成；同意别人的意见或结论，但不一定是同一逻辑推理。在上诉审程序中，某法官的"同意意见"（concurring opinion），是指同意该案判决结果或其他法官的"不同意见"，但其论证推理可有所不同。② to happen at the same time 同时发生

例 1. The legitimacy of this Court ultimately rests "upon the respect accorded to its judgments". *Republican Party of Minn. v. White*, 536 U.S. 765, 793 (2002) (KENNEDY, J., concurring). 本院的正统地位最终取决于"对本院判决的尊重"。明尼苏达州共和党诉怀特，《美国判例汇编》第 536 卷第 765 页和第 793 页（2002 年）（肯尼迪大法官发表同意意见）。

concurrent [kənˈkʌrənt] *adj.* 同时的；并存的

例 2. The remaining question is, therefore, whether the court should stay the present proceedings pending the concurrent foreign proceedings between the aforesaid parties in the Mainland Court. 于是，剩下的问题就是：在上述当事人在内地法院提起的并存域外诉讼程序审结之前，本庭是否应当中止本案的诉讼程序。

concurrence [kənˈkʌrəns] *n.[U]* 同意；赞同

例 3. I also share the view to which Cumming-Bruce and Templeman, LJJ evidently inclined in their obiter observations that in such cases the unanimous assent of the shareholders is not enough to justify the breach of duty to creditors. The situation is really one where those conducting the affairs of the company owe a duty to creditors. Concurrence by the shareholders prevents complaint by them, but compounds rather than excuses the breach as against the creditors. 我也赞成上诉法院卡明—布鲁斯法官和坦普曼法官的观点，他们在附带意见中显然认为在这样的情况下，股东表示一致同意尚不足以证明违反对债权人承担的义务具有正当理由。具体情况其实是负责处理公司事务的人对债权人负有义务。股东的同意使债权人无法提出申诉，但却加剧侵害债权人的违约行为，而非为之提供辩解。

(2)

incur [inˈkɜ:] (incurring, incurred) v.t. to suffer or bring on oneself (a liability or expense)　招致；引起

incur 既有自己蒙受损失承担责任的意思，也有给别人招致损失责任的意思。

例 4. The Seller will be responsible for all costs incurred by the Buyer as a result of early or late deliveries. 卖方将承担买方由于提前或延迟交货而支出的所有费用。

例 5. What should students expect in exchange for the hundreds of thousands of dollars of debt they incur in student loans in order to receive a diploma from This Law School? 莘莘学子为了取得这所法学院的一纸文凭，背负几十万美元需要偿还的学生贷款，他们图的是什么呢?

例 6. If either Party delays, fails, or is unable to perform any obligations or responsibilities due to Force Majeure, such Party shall not be responsible for any loss or expenses suffered by or incurred to the other Party. 如果任何一方当事人由于不可抗力迟延履行、不履行或无法履行义务或职责，该当事人不负责赔偿对方遭受的或给对方招致的损失或费用。

例 7. Both sides will jointly commission one of the big 4 accounting firms to do financial and tax due diligence after signing the Term Sheet. The Local Co. and the investors will share the fees and costs incurred by such due diligence. 双方当事人将在签订条件文书之后共同委托四大会计师事务所之一进行财务和税务尽职调查。本地公司和投资人将分担尽职调查所支出的费用。

例 8. If any products or services fail to conform to the above warranties, the Seller, at the Buyer's option, will: (i) with respect to products, replace or repair the nonconforming products; (ii) with respect to services, re-perform all services necessary to correct any such nonconformity; or (iii) refund the purchase price of the nonconforming products or services and any related costs incurred by the Buyer. 如果任何产品或服务不符合上述保证，卖方将按照买方的选择：（ⅰ）对于产品，更换或修理不合格的产品；（ⅱ）对于服务，重新履行一切必要的服务，以纠正上述不符合要求之处；或者（ⅲ）退还不合格产品或服务的购买价款和买方支出的任何相关费用。

(3)

occur [əˈkɜː] *v.i. (formal)* (occurred, occurring) 发生；出现

动词 occur 有一个常用的句型：it occurs to sb. to do sth./that 想到，冒出……念头。

例 9. The jurisdiction and venue of this action within the Superior Court of the State of California for the County of San Diego is proper because the causes of action alleged herein, and many of the activities and conduct giving rise to the ensuing causes of action, substantially occurred in San Diego County, California. 加利福尼亚州圣迭戈县高级法院对本诉讼行使管辖权并作为审判地是适当的，因为本案所指称的诉讼原因，以及引起后续诉因的许多活动和行为实质上是在加利福尼亚州圣迭戈县发生的。

例 10. It never occurred to those kind-hearted people that greater leniency for such hardened criminals as Ted Bundy would have nothing but the opposite effect. 这

些善心人从未想到对泰德·邦迪这类心肠狠毒的罪犯心慈手软只会事与愿违。

例 11. Unless otherwise provided elsewhere in the *Purchase Agreement*, delivery will occur, and title and risk of loss will transfer, when: (i) with respect to product not incorporated into services, product passes into Buyer's storage facility; and (ii) with respect to product incorporated into services, the completed services have been accepted by Buyer. 除非《采购协议》在别处另有规定，货物交付以及所有权和灭失风险的转移的时间为：（ⅰ）对于没有被纳入服务的产品，在产品进入买方的仓储地点时；（ⅱ）对于被纳入服务的产品，在买方接受已经完成的服务时。

occurrence [əˈkʌrəns] *n.[C]* ① something that happens 事件；② the fact of something happening 发生

例 12. Violent crime has been an everyday occurrence in this neighborhood blighted by drugs. 毒品毁了这座社区，暴力犯罪在这儿成了家常便饭。

例 13. The Original Issuance Price shall be adjusted downward to reflect any decrease in the value of the Company resulting from the occurrence of any Material Adverse Effect. 原始发行价格应当向下调整，以便反映出由于发生严重不利事件导致公司价值降低。

例 14. As regards the existence of a fiduciary relationship owed by the directors to the appellants as shareholders, because in the present case the Parties had been engaged in hostile litigation for some time prior to the period in which the impugned conduct occurred, no such duty arose. 关于董事对提起上诉的股东负有的信托关系存在与否，因为在本案中，在受非议的行为发生的期间之前，双方当事人就已经进行了一段时间的敌对诉讼，因此没有产生这种信托义务。

例 15. The Affected Party shall orally notify the other Party as promptly as reasonably practicable after the occurrence of such event of Force Majeure and, in addition, shall provide the other Party with written notice of such event of Force Majeure within five (5) days after the occurrence of such event of Force Majeure. 发生上述不可抗力事件后，受影响方应当尽快口头通知对方当事人，除口头通知外，受影响方还应当在发生上述不可抗力事件后五（5）日内将上述不可抗力事件书面通知对方。

(4)

recur [riˈkɜː] (recurring, recurred) *v.i.* 反复出现，一再发生

recurrence [riˈkʌrəns] *n.[C,U]* 再次发生

recurrent [riˈkʌrənt] *adj.* = recurring 屡次发生的

recurring decimal *n.[C]* 循环小数

例 16. The dark side of human nature is a recurring theme throughout Alfred Hitchcock's films. 阿尔弗雷德·希区柯克的影片一再描写的主题是人性的阴暗面。

例 17. In an MNE group one of the enterprises may be suffering a loss, even a recurring one, but the overall group may be extremely profitable. 在一个跨国企业集团内，某一家企业可能遭受损失，甚至一再遭受损失，但整个集团却可能盈利甚丰。

例 18. *FAR Subpart* 13.303-5(d) provides that if, for a particular purchase above the micro-purchase threshold, there is an insufficient number of BPA's to ensure maximum practicable competition, the contracting officer must solicit quotations from other sources, and make purchases as appropriate, and establish additional BPA's to facilitate future purchases if recurring similar requirements are anticipated, qualified sources are willing to accept BPA's, and it is otherwise practical to do so. 《联邦采购条例》第 13 分编第 303－5 条（d）项规定：对于超过小额采购最低额度的某一特定采购，如果一揽子采购协议的数目不足以确保最大程度切实可行的竞争，则订约官员必须向其他来源征求报价，并酌情进行采购。如果预计以后会提出类似的要求，合格的货源也愿意接受一揽子采购协议，这样做也切实可行，订约官员就须制定额外的一揽子采购协议，以便促进未来的采购。

例 19. The architect and the engineer shall state in the accident report their opinion as to the cause of the subsidence and what remedial action in relation to the building has been done by them or should be done to prevent a recurrence of such accident. 建筑师和工程师必须在意外报告内说明他们关于沉降原因的意见，并须说明为防止再次发生沉降，他们对这座建筑物已经采取或认为应该采取的补救行动。

consent & consensus

(1)

consent [kənˈsɛnt] *n.[C,U] & v.i.* 同意

注意：动词 consent 是不及物动词，后面搭配介词 to，以名词或动词不定式作为宾语。

例 1. This Agreement may only be amended in whole or in part by the written consent of all the Shareholders. 只有经全体股东书面同意方可全部或者部分地修改本协议。

例 2. Neither Party shall assign or transfer this Agreement or any rights and obligations hereof without the prior written consent of the other Party, or without the approval of the relevant authorities if such approval is required by Applicable Laws. 未经对方当事人事先书面同意，或者，如果可适用的法律要求相关当局的批准而未获得该批准，当事人不得转让或者转移本协议或者本协议的任何权利或义务。

例 3. Without the prior written consent of AAA, BBB shall not at any time following the date hereof cause or permit BBB to merge, consolidate with, acquire, be acquired by or invest in any other person. 倘若事先未征得 AAA 的书面同意，BBB 在本协议签订日期之后的任何时候均不得促使或许可 BBB 兼并他人，与他人合并，收购他人，被他人收购或者对他人进行投资。

例 4. If all parties to any arbitral proceedings consent in writing and for so long as no party has withdrawn his consent in writing, an arbitrator may act as a mediator. 如果仲裁程序的全体当事人以书面形式表示同意而且只要没有任何当事人以书面形式撤回同意表示，仲裁员即可担任调解人。

在例 4 中，consent 同时以动词和名词的形式呈现。

例 5. The consent of the victim to the commission of a criminal offence against himself or herself or a right he or she possesses does not relieve the offender of criminal liability. 受害人同意犯罪人实施犯罪行为侵害受害人本人或受害人管有的权利，犯罪人的刑事责任不因受害人同意而免除。

例 6. Each Party shall use its best efforts to maintain the confidentiality of information concerning the Securities and cash in the Securities Account and RMB Special Account, and shall neither disclose such information to any third Party nor utilise such information, unless (1) the disclosure of such information is required by the Applicable Laws; (2) such information is obtained via other channels than the other Party; (3) the other Party has consented in writing to the disclosure of such information. Each Party shall ensure its representatives and employees to comply with the provisions of this clause. 各方当事人均应尽其最大努力对与证券账户和人民币专用账户中的证券和现金有关的信息保守秘密，不得向第三人泄露该信息，也不得利用该信息，除非（1）可适用的法律要求披露该信息；（2）经由对方当事人以外的其他途径获得该信息；（3）对方当事人已经以书面形式同意披露该信息。各方当事人均应确保自己的代表和雇员遵守本条的规定。

(2)

consensus [kənˈsɛnsəs] *n.[C,U]* 共识，一致的意见
consensual [kənˈsɛnʃuəl] *adj.* 经双方同意的（两厢情愿）；合意的

例 7. The decision to establish the Working Group on the Long-term Sustainability of Outer Space Activities, in particular, was very timely, due to the increasing number of space actors, spacecraft and space debris. Measures must be agreed in order to reduce the risks to space operations. There had also been progress towards consensus on a new multi-year workplan for the Working Group on the Use of Nuclear Power Sources in Outer Space. 特别是，由于空间活动者、太空船及空间碎片的数量越来

越多，设立外空活动长期可持续性工作组的决定因此是非常及时的。必须约定某些措施以减少空间操作所面临的各种风险。关于为在外层空间使用核动力源工作组制定一项新的多年工作计划，这次会议也取得了进展，与会者在这个问题上达成了共识。

例 8. Concerns over content are often accompanied by debates on whether history teaching should focus on transmitting a defined body of knowledge or on developing critical skills that allow students to compare interpretations and make informed judgements (Pingel, 2008). These debates are often particularly salient in conflict-affected countries where "facts" may be widely contested and a consensus difficult to establish. 对教学内容的担忧通常免不了这样的辩论，即历史教学是应当传播一批确定的知识，还是培养批判性技能，使学生能够对各种解释进行比较，并在了解背景情况后作出判断（平格尔，2008 年）。这种辩论在受冲突影响的国家和地区往往格外引人注目，在这些国家和地区，"事实"可能受到普遍质疑，人们难以达成共识。

例 9. People commit intentional homicide for many reasons and it is apparent that numerous different driving forces are at work when they do. But there is something of a consensus, both among scholars and the international community, that lethal violence is often rooted in contexts of paucity and deprivation, inequality and injustice, social marginalization, low levels of education and a weak rule of law. 人们由于许多原因故意杀人，人们实施这种犯罪的时候，显然有众多推动力量在起作用。但是，学者们和国际社会都一致认为，致命暴力的根源通常是匮乏与剥夺、不平等与不公正、社会边缘化、教育水平低下以及法治薄弱。

例 10. Although the Court's reasoning was limited by the scope of application of the *European Convention* and therefore cannot be considered to put forward a generally applicable principle, it gives an authoritative indication that consensual forms of surrender other than formal extradition cannot be automatically disregarded. 虽然欧洲人权法院的推理受到《欧洲人权公约》适用范围的限制，因此不能被看作提出

了一条普遍适用的原则，但该案的推理却提出了一条权威性意见，那就是不得自动否定正规引渡途径以外的合意引渡模式。

例 11. Other considerations were taken into account, in approaching those experiments. Resort to private law analogies is one of them. For example, the relation of the mandates, the analogy with the original *mandatum*, a consensual contract in Roman law; the roots of "trust" and "tutelage" in the *tutela* of Roman law (a sort of guardianship of infants); the English trust, to some extent a descendant of the *fideicomissa* of Roman law (in "fiduciary" relations). In any case, a new relationship was thereby created, in the mandates and trusteeship systems, on the basis of confidence (the "sacred trust") and, ultimately, of human conscience. What ultimately began to matter was the well-being and human development of the population, of the inhabitants of mandated and trust territories, rather than the notion of absolute territorial sovereignty. Those experiments were intended to give legal protection to newly-arisen needs of the "people" or the "population"; and the mandatory, tutor or trustee had duties, rather than rights.

探讨上述法律制度的尝试，还考虑到其他一些因素。采取私法类推就是其中一项因素。例如，用最初的"无偿委任制度（*mandatum*）"——罗马法的一种诺成合同——比拟委任统治的关系；"信托（*trust*）"和"监护（*tutelage*）"来源于罗马法的监护制度（*tutela*）（一种对未成年人的监护地位）；英文里的"trust"（"信托"），在一定程度上源于罗马法的"*fideicomissa*"（以"信托"关系）。不论属于何种情况，在信任（"神圣之信托"）的基础上，最终也是在人类良知的基础上，在委任统治和托管制度中创立了一种新的关系。民众的福祉和人的发展，委任统治地和托管地居民的福祉和人的发展，而不是绝对的领土主权概念，终于显示出重要意义。上述尝试是为了对"人民"或者"民众"产生不久的需求给予法律保护；委任统治国、监护人或者受托人承担义务，而不是享有权利。

参阅《元照英美法词典》：consensual contract 诺成合同；合意合同。（罗马法）仅需双方意思表示一致即可成立的合同，不需其他外在形式或象征性行为。

consequent & subsequent

(1)

consequent [ˈkɒnsikwənt] *adj.* happening as a result of a particular event or situation 由此引起的，

随之而来的

consequent 后面有时搭配介词 on 或 upon。

例 1. The forming of an "opinion" by the Director, which has the effect following the institution of an appeal of increasing a person's sentence, is inconsistent with the exercise of the judicial function which is constituted by the judicial act of imposing a penalty consequent upon conviction. 公诉处处长在提起增加对某人的量刑的抗诉之后形成某种具有效力的"意见"，这与因定罪而判处刑罚的司法行为所构成的行使司法职能发生矛盾。

例 2. No such waiver shall, however, extend to any subsequent or other default or impair any right consequent thereon except to the extent expressly waived in writing. 但是，上述放弃追究并不包括任何后来的或者其他的违约行为，亦不损害任何随之发生的权利，但是以书面形式明示放弃追究的除外。

consequently [ˈkɒnsikwəntli] *adv.* as a result 因此，所以

例 3. Consequently, it is communicated, in accordance with the calculation referred hereinabove, that on the day [insert the date] the success fee charged is [insert number] ([•]) Euros, corresponding to such period. 因此，依照本附件上文提到的计算方法，双方当事人约定，在此期限内，在［填入日期］日收取的成交费是［填入金额］欧元。

(2)

subsequent ['sʌbsikwənt] *adj.* (of an action, event, etc.) occurring later; coming after something else 随后的

例 4. Sometime later during the trial, the Crown sought to lead evidence of the relevant Corrective Services records establishing the fact that C and the present appellant had shared a cell at a time between the making of C's original statement to the arresting police and the making of his subsequent induced statement. 在庭审过程中晚些时候，公诉方试图诱致相关惩教机构档案证据，这些档案证明在 C 向执行逮捕的警察作出最初陈述到 C 作出后来的诱致陈述，其间的某个时候，事实上 C 与本案上诉人曾经被羁押在同一间牢房。

subsequent to sth. 在……之后

例 5. Where the value of the Mortgaged Property is diminished, the Mortgagor must on demand by the Lender restore the value of the Mortgaged Property or provide additional Security to compensate for the diminished value; provided that the Mortgagor shall have no such obligations to restore the value of the Mortgaged Property or provide additional Security if the aggregate outstanding Loan less the amount of Excess Cash does not exceed 65 per cent of the Value subsequent to such damage or infringement. 若抵押不动产的价值减少，抵押人必须根据贷款人的要求恢复抵押不动产的价值或者提供额外担保以弥补减少的价值；如果扣除超额现金的金额后，尚未偿还的贷款总额不超过损害或者侵害发生后抵押不动产价值的 65%，抵押人不承担恢复抵押不动产的价值或者提供额外担保的义务。

subsequently ['sʌbsikwəntli] *adv.* 后来，随后

例 6. Subsequently, AAA endeavored to resolve the dispute with BBB through multiple discussions and correspondence. 后来，AAA 通过多次讨论和通信，设法解决与 BBB 的纠纷。

例 7. The appellant's submissions, as they subsequently unfolded, moved away from any suggestion of impropriety on the part of the Crown Prosecutor, to a more generalized complaint which was put by learned senior counsel for the appellant in the following way. 上诉人的陈词就像后来表述的那样，不再暗指公诉人存在任何不正当行为，而是由代理上诉人的学识渊博的资深律师提出了如下更加泛泛的申诉。

consequential damages

consequential damages 在法律文件中经常和 indirect damages, incidental damages 并列，indirect damages 常被译成"间接损害"，incidental damages 常被译成"附带损害"。而 consequential damages 则不太好处理。

我们首先查看 *the dictionary by Merriam*-Webster 对 consequential 的解释：of the nature of a secondary result : indirect，https://www.merriam-webster.com/dictionary/consequential。

consequential 和 indirect 是同义词。

《布莱克法律词典》对 consequential damages 的解释是：Losses that do not flow directly and immediately from an injurious act but that result indirectly from the act.。

品味语义，似乎就是汉语中的"间接损害"。

《元照英美法词典》把 consequential damages 翻译成"间接损害"。解释是：由损害行为的某些后果所致的损害，而非由该行为直接导致的损害，即损害出于一般未预料到而与后果又有关的另一特殊情况的发生。这种损害有的可起诉，有的不能起诉。

consequential damages 和 indirect damages 似乎成了同义词。

笔者认为，在法规、合同等法律文件没有专门为 consequential damages 下定义，也没有司法判例专门说明 consequential damages 含义的情况下，可以有两种处理思路。一是类似于表示诉讼（如 action, suit, litigation, proceedings）或表示赋税的词（如 tax, duties, levies, impost, excise or withholding tax）并列的情形，因为中国与国外法律制度不同，汉语中并没有完全对应的词汇，有时将它们合并译成"诉讼"和"赋税"，不妨将前面几个表示损害的词译成"间接损害"，因为它们都与直接损害相对，可以笼统归并为间接损害。如果在实践中对这个词的理解发生争议，法律文件（尤其是协议）的管辖法律条款可以列明解释该词所依据的法律，如果管辖法律是中国法律，当事人可以提请最高人民法院发布司法解释或全国人大常委会作出立法解释。另一种是将 consequential damages 译成"引致损失"。参看下面的例句：

例 1. In no event shall any Finance Party be liable on any theory of liability for any special, indirect, consequential or punitive damages however arising and save only where such damages arise due to the sole and proximate cause of such Finance Party's gross negligence or wilful misconduct, the Company hereby waives, releases and agrees (for itself and on behalf of its affiliates) not to sue upon any such claim for any such damages, whether or not accrued and whether or not known or suspected to exist in its favor. 任何融资当事人无须根据任何责任理论承担任何特殊、间接、引致或惩罚性损害赔偿责任，无论该责任是如何产生的，但上述融资当事人的重大过失或蓄意玩忽职守是造成上述损害赔偿的唯一和直接原因的除外，公司特此放弃根据对于上述损害的赔偿请求权提起诉讼，公司同意（为公司本身和代表公司的关联机构）不提起上述诉讼，无论上述赔偿请求权是否属于应计债权、无论公司是否已经知道或怀疑存在有利于自己的上述赔偿请求权。

例 2. Except for the limited warranty provided in section 3.5(a) of this agreement, ABC grants no other warranties or conditions, express or implied, by statute, in any communication with distributor or customers, or otherwise regarding the products, their fitness for any purpose, their quality, or their merchantability. ABC neither assumes nor authorizes any other person to assume any other liabilities arising out of or in connection with the sale or use of any product. The remedies of the distributor or agent set forth herein shall be the only remedies available. Save as provided for by mandatory product liability law, ABC shall in no event be liable for any indirect, incidental or consequential damages, including without limitation lost revenues or profits, whether a claim for such damages is based upon warranty, contract, tort, common law, statute or otherwise. 除本协议第 3.5（a）条规定的有限保证以外，ABC 在与经销商或者顾客的沟通过程中或者在其他情况下，并未依照制定法作出有关产品、产品的适用性、产品的质量或者产品的适销性的其他明示或者默示的保证或者条件。ABC 既未承担也未授权他人承担由于销售或使用产品而产生的或者与销售或使用产品有关的任何其他责任。本协议所规定的经销商或经销商代理人的救济应当是其可资利用的唯一救济。除强制性产品责任法律规定的以外，ABC 不承担任何间接、附带或引致损害赔偿责任，包括但不限于收入或利润损失，无论关于上述损害赔偿的请求权是依据保证、合同、侵权、普通法、制定法抑或其他事由。

constitute & institute

(1)

constitute ['kɒnstitjuːt] *v.t.* 构成，组成；是，被看作

constitution [ˌkɒnstiˈtjuːʃən] *n.[C]* 宪法；章程；组成，构成；结构，构造

constitutional [ˌkɒnstiˈtjuːʃənəl] *adj.* 符合宪法（或章程）的，宪法（或章程）规定的

constitutionally [ˌkɒnstiˈtjuːʃənəli] *adv.* 依照宪法（或章程）

constitutional monarchy *n.[C,U]* 君主立宪制；君主立宪国

constitutionality [ˌkɒnstiˌtjuːʃəˈnæləti] *n.[U]* 合宪

unconstitutional [ˌʌnˌkɒnstiˈtjuːʃənl] *adj.* 违反宪法的

unconstitutionality [ˌʌnkɒnstitjuːʃəˈnæləti] *n.[U]* 违宪

例 1. Any Director or Alternate Director may participate in a meeting of the Directors or any committee of the Directors by means of conference telephone or other telecommunications equipment by means of which all persons participating in the meeting can hear each other speak and such participation in a meeting shall constitute being present in person at the meeting. 董事或替代董事可以借助使所有与会人能够听到对方发言的会议电话或者其他电信设备参加董事会议或任何董事委员会会议，董事或替代董事采用上述方式参加会议即为本人亲自出席会议。

例 2. The initial cost estimate should cover indirect costs such as security requirements, office furniture, and information technology equipment configuration, which do not constitute refurbishment or construction and are considered as associated costs. 初始成本估算应当包含间接开支，例如安保需要、办公家具以及信息技术设备配置，这些间接开支并不构成翻修或建造，但被视为相关成本。

例 3. The importance of including access to justice in the post-2015 development agenda is based precisely on the fact that access to justice constitutes a right that permits the fulfilment of other rights, be they civil, cultural, economic, political or social. 有必要将司法救助纳入 2015 年后发展议程，这恰恰是建立在这个事实基础之上，即司法救助构成了一项得以享有其他权利的权利，不论是公民、文化、经济、政治或社会权利。

例 4. The Supervisory Board shall be deemed to constitute a quorum if the members have been invited in writing or by cable under their last given address and not less than half the total members which it is required to comprise take part in the voting in person or by written vote. 如果已经按照监事最新提供的地址向监事会成员发送了书面或者电报邀请，而且所有必须出席会议的监事中有不少于半数的监事亲自或者通过书面方式参与表决，则应当视为监事会已经满足了法定人数的要求。

例 5. The environmental impact should be assessed and, on a case-by-case basis, specific arrangements to limit it should be envisaged. In any event this impact should not constitute a criterion for refusal of a marketing authorization. 应当评估药品对环境的影响，并且应当根据具体情况设想限制环境影响的特定安排。无论属于何种情况，环境影响都不应当构成拒绝办理销售许可的一项标准。

例 6. According to the constitutional provisions (Art. 44 Paragraph 1) family is based on the spouses' free consent to marriage. The *Family Code* stipulates in Art. 3 that marriage concluded before the civil status officer gives raise to the spouses rights and obligations provided for in the code. 根据宪法规定（第 44 条第 1 款），建立家庭的基础是配偶自愿同意结婚。《家庭法典》第 3 条规定，经婚姻登记官证明后缔结的婚姻赋予配偶该法典规定的权利和义务。

例 7. It is noted that the relevant legal environment for the proposed law may include (but not be limited to) the following constitutional and administrative laws: *Constitution of the PRC, Law on Legislation, Administrative Litigation Law, Administrative*

Supervision Law, Administrative Reconsideration Law, State Civil Servant Provisional Regulations, State Compensation Law, Administrative Penalties Law, Administrative Compulsory Law. 需要注意的是，拟制定的法律的相关法律环境可以包括（但不限于）下列宪法性法律和行政性法律：《中华人民共和国宪法》《立法法》《行政诉讼法》《行政监察法》《行政复议法》《国家公务员暂行条例》《国家赔偿法》《行政处罚法》《行政强制法》。

(2)

institute ['institju:t] *v.t.* to begin or start; commence 创立，开始，提起（诉讼等）；*n.[C]* 教研机构（例如：California Institute of Technology 加州理工学院）

institution [ˌinsti'tju:ʃən] *n.[C]* 机构；制度；*n.[U]* 开创，设立，制定

institutional [ˌinsti'tju:ʃənəl] *adj.* 机构的；制度的

institutionalize [ˌinsti'tju:ʃənəˌlaiz] *v.t.* 将……送到收容机构；使……制度化

例 8. The Government is determined to strengthen solidarity and social cohesion, by instituting a more effective and more flexible coordination between the various social policies (covering women, children and families). 政府决定加强团结和社会凝聚力，在（针对妇女、儿童、家庭的）不同社会政策之间建立更为有效和灵活的协调关系。

例 9. "Court", for the purposes of sections 6, 7, 8, 11(1), 55, 56 and 57, means the High Court, District Court, Magistrate's Court or any other court in which the proceedings referred to in those sections are instituted or heard. 第 6 条、第 7 条、第 8 条、第 11（1）条、第 55 条、第 56 条和第 57 条所称"法院"是指高等法院，区法院，治安法院或者可以向其提起或可以由其审理前述各该条文中所称的程序的任何其他法院。

例 10. Of the 41 cases in which indictments were issued and court proceedings instituted, 24 led to convictions and 15 to acquittals. One indictment was considered to constitute a violation of Article 209 of the *General Penal Code*. 在 41 起发布起诉书

和提起诉讼程序的案件中，24 起被定罪，15 起被宣判无罪。一项被起诉的罪行被认为触犯了《普通刑法典》第 209 条。

例 11. Full membership shall be restricted to state-supported development banks, financial institutions and government agencies and programs with strong interest in Micro, Small and Medium-sized Enterprises ("MSMEs") who meet established criteria as determined by the board of directors of the Corporation. 正式成员限于国家支持的开发银行、金融机构以及对满足公司董事会标准的微型、小型及中型企业（"中小企业"）具有浓厚兴趣的政府机构和项目。

例 12. The law can be a powerful way of organizing and coordinating a health system. It principally achieves this by assigning responsibilities and powers to particular institutions and individuals, establishing restraints on power and legal protection of rights, and providing for implementation and enforcement mechanisms. These institutional arrangements should give effect to the imperatives of government stewardship described above, including effective and equitable governance across all levels of government and across public and private sectors. 法律可以作为组织和协调卫生体系的一种有力方式。法律主要是通过下列方式做到这一点：将责任和权力分配给特定的机构和个人，确立对权力的约束和对权利的法律保护，以及规定实施和强制执行机制。这些体制安排应当实现上文描述的政府管理要务，包括在各级政府以及整个公营和私营部门有效和公平施政。

例 13. In this context, the Special Rapporteur has always emphasized that respect for the rule of law is fundamental in any functioning democracy and that the independence of the justice system has a central role to play as the institutional guardian of the enforcement of the rule of law. Equal access to justice and equality before the courts and tribunals are human rights that are essential aspects of the rule of law. 在这个背景下，特别报告员一直强调，尊重法治对于任何运行中的民主都非常重要，独立的司法系统作为执行法治的体制捍卫者发挥着重要作用。平等诉诸法律的机会以及在法院和法庭面前平等是人权，而这个人权是法治的基本方面。

例 14. By this legislation it was intended the granting of financial aid to NGO's with a view to improve the quality of social assistance services granted, as well as the increase of social solidarity by institutionalizing the partnership between the public administration and the civil society. 根据这部法律，为非政府组织提供财政援助的目的是提高社会援助服务的质量，并通过使公共管理机构和民间社会之间的伙伴关系实现制度化，增进社会团结。

construe & construction

(1)

construe sth. as sth. [kənˈstruː] *v.t.* 把······解释 / 理解成

put a construction on sth. 把······解释 / 理解成

misconstrue sth. as sth. [ˌmiskənˈstru] 把······误解成

注意：construe 的名词是 construction；construction 还有大家经常用到的义项：建造，构造，建筑物。

例 1. This Agreement is made under and shall be construed in accordance with the laws of the People's Republic of China. 本协议依照中华人民共和国的法律订立，并应当依照该法进行解释。

例 2. Any reference in this Agreement to a statute shall be construed as a reference to such statute as the same may have been, or may from time to time be, amended or re-enacted. 本协议中所称制定法应当被解释为所称的是可能已经修订或重新制定或者可能不时地修订或重新制定的制定法。

例 3. No provision of the *Trade Sanctions Reform and Export Enhancement Act of 2000* (Title IX of Public Law 106-387) shall be construed to limit or otherwise affect Section 2339A or 2339B of Title 18, *United States Code.* 对于《2000 年贸易制裁改革与促进出口法》（第 106–387 号公法第九编）任何规定的解释不应当限制或者以其他方式妨碍《美国法典》第 18 编第 2339A 条或者第 2339B 条。

例 4. Any provision of this Act held to be invalid or unenforceable by its terms, or as applied to any person or circumstance, shall be construed so as to give it the maximum effect permitted by law, unless such holding shall be one of utter invalidity or un-enforceability, in which event such provision shall be deemed severable from this Act and shall not affect the remainder thereof or the application of such provision to other persons not similarly situated or to other, dissimilar circumstances. 倘若本法某个条文的规定被判定无效或者无法强制执行，或者该条文在适用于某人或者某种情况的时候被判定无效或者无法强制执行，对于该条文的解释应当赋予其法律允许的最大效力，除非该条文被判定完全无效或者完全无法强制执行；在这种情况下，应当视为该条文可以与本法分离，本法其余条文的效力不受影响，该条文适用于不同地方的其他人或者其他不同情况的时候，它的效力亦不受影响。

例 5. STATUTORY CONSTRUCTION. Nothing in this section, or in any other law, shall be construed to limit the authority of the Attorney General or the Director of the Federal Bureau of Investigation to provide access to the criminal history record information contained in the National Crime Information Center's (NCIC) Interstate Identification Index (NCIC-III), or to any other information maintained by the NCIC, to any Federal agency or officer authorized to enforce or administer the immigration laws of the United States, for the purpose of such enforcement or administration, upon terms that are consistent with the *National Crime Prevention and Privacy Compact Act of 1998* (Subtitle A of Title II of Public Law 105-251; 42 *U.S.C.* 14611-16) and Section 552a of Title 5, *United States Code.* 法定解释。美国司法部长或者美国联邦调查局局长有权允许被授权执行或者实施美国移民法律的联邦机构或者官员为了执行或者实施美国移民法律，按照与《1998 年国家预防犯罪和保护隐私协议法》（第105–251 号公法第二编甲分编；《美国法典》第 42 编第 14611–16 条）和《美国法典》第 5 编第 552a 条的规定一致的条件，查阅国家犯罪信息中心（NCIC）州际识别索引（NCIC–III）中记载的犯罪记录信息或者查阅国家犯罪信息中心保存的其他信息。对于本条的任何规定或者其他法律的任何规定的解释不应限制美国司法部长或者美国联邦调查局局长的这种权力。

例 6. The Contractor and the sub-contractor(s), if any, shall have the status of an independent contractor vis-à-vis the Employer. The Contract Documents shall not be construed to create any contractual relationship of any kind between the Engineer and the Contractor, but the Engineer shall, in the exercise of his duties and powers under the Contract, be entitled to performance by the Contractor of its obligations, and to enforcement thereof. Nothing contained in the Contract Documents shall create any contractual relationship between the Employer or the Engineer and any subcontractor(s) of the Contractor. 承包人和分包人（如有）应拥有相对于雇主的独立缔约人身份。合同文件不应被解释为在工程师和承包人之间创设任何契约关系，但是工程师在依照合同行使其职责和权力时，应有权要求承包人履行义务，并且有权强制承包人履行义务。合同文件的规定不应在雇主或工程师与承包人的任何分包人之间创设任何契约关系。

例 7. The submission to the jurisdiction of the courts referred to in Clause 10.2 (English courts) shall not (and shall not be construed so as to) limit the right of any Finance Party to take Proceedings in any other court of competent jurisdiction nor shall the taking of Proceedings in any one or more jurisdictions preclude the taking of Proceedings in any other jurisdiction (whether concurrently or not) if and to the extent permitted by applicable law. 接受第 10.2 条所称法院（英格兰法院）管辖，不限制（而且不应被解释为限制）融资当事人在其他具有合法管辖权的法院提起诉讼的权利；在可以适用的法律允许的范围内，在一个或者多个管辖区域提起诉讼，不应排除在其他管辖区域提起诉讼（无论是否同时）。

例 8. All disputes between the Parties in connection with or arising out of the existence, validity, construction, performance and termination of this Agreement (or any terms thereof), which the Parties are unable to resolve between themselves, shall be referred to and finally settled by Beijing Arbitration Commission, The arbitration shall be held in Beijing in accordance with the Rules of Arbitration of such commission and language of arbitration shall be Chinese. 由本协议（或者本协议的任何条款）的存续、效力、解释、履行和终止所产生的双方当事人之间无法自行解决的所有纠纷，应当提请北京市仲裁委员会予以最终裁决。仲裁应依照北京市仲裁委员会的仲裁规则在北京市进行，仲裁活动所使用的语言为中文。

contemplate, contemplated, contemplation & contemplative

(1)

contemplate ['kɒntəmpleit] *v.t.* 考虑，打算，估量，盘算，预料，预计进行

contemplate doing sth.

contemplate 后面可加 what/whether/how 等疑问代词或疑问副词。

例 1. AAA could not be deemed by a court of competent jurisdiction to be unable to pay its debts within the meaning of the law of the jurisdiction in which it is incorporated, nor in any such case will it become so in consequence of its entering into this Agreement and/or exercising any rights and/or performing any obligation contemplated hereby. AAA 订立本协议和／或行使本协议规定的权利和／或履行本协议规定的义务，不会被有管辖权的法院视为无法偿还其成立为法人所在管辖区的法律规定意义上的债务，也不会因此变得无力偿债。

例 2. Any termination or expiration of this Agreement and/or any Agreed Order shall neither impair any rights of Customers granted to them in accordance with the provisions of this Agreement nor prevent Customers from delivering any Products in the future. Any sales rights and other rights and licenses granted by XYZ to the Company or any Ordering Entity under this Agreement shall be extended for the time period required to complete the activities of the Company or any Ordering Entity contemplated in this Article 27. 即使本协议及／或约定订单被终止或者期限届满，依照本协议的规定授予客户的权利不受影响，也不妨碍客户今后交付产品。XYZ 根据本协议授予公司或者订货实体的销售权利以及其他权利和许可应当顺延，顺延的时限为公司或者订货实体完成本协议第二十七条中预计进行的各项活动所需要的时间。

例 3. The Parties will use best endeavors to take all such actions as the other Party may reasonably request in connection with carrying out and effecting the intent and purpose hereof and all transactions and purposes contemplated by this Agreement. 双方当事人将尽其最大努力采取对方当事人可能合理要求的所有行动来完成和实现本协议的意图和宗旨以及本协议所预定的各项交易和目的。

例 4. Each Party will bear its own legal and other costs and expenses in connection with, the preparation, execution and completion of this Agreement and each of the transactions contemplated by this Agreement. 各方当事人自行负担本方为筹备、签署和完成本协议及本协议筹划的各项交易而支出的法律费用及其他费用。

例 5. Each Party agrees, at its own expense, on the request of any other Party, to do everything reasonably necessary for the purposes of or to give effect to this Agreement and the transactions contemplated by it (including the execution of documents) and to use all reasonable endeavors to cause relevant third parties to do likewise. 各方当事人同意，根据对方当事人提出的要求，由本方承担费用，采取一切合理必要的措施，以实现本协议的目的或者完成本协议和本协议筹划的交易（包括签署文件），并尽一切合理努力促使相关第三方亦复如此。

(2)

contemplated ['kɒntəmˌpleitid] *adj.* 预期进行的，预计进行的

例 6. According to the seasoned solicitor, the contemplated civil proceedings against the next-door neighbors should, though, be a last resort. 据这位老练的律师说，除非万不得已，不要想着跟隔壁邻居打官司。

(3)

contemplation [ˌkɒntəmˈpleiʃən] *n.[U]* 沉思

(4)

contemplative [kənˈtɛmplətiv] *adj.* 凝神沉思

106

context & pretext

(1)

context ['kɒntɛkst] *n.[C]* ① 背景，情境；② 上下文，语境

contextual [kən'tɛkstʃuəl] *adj.* ① 背景的，情境的；② 上下文的，与语境有关的

contextually [kən'tɛkstʃuəli] *adv.*

contextualize [kən'tekstʃuə͵laiz] *v.t.* ① 考虑……的情境或背景；② 将……置于上下文中考虑；结合语境理解……

例 1. Unless the terms or the context of this Agreement otherwise provide, the following capitalized terms in this Agreement shall have the meanings set forth below. 本协议中下列以楷体字显示的用语具有下文列明的含义，除非本协议的条款或语境另有规定。

例 2. References to any agreement or document herein shall be a reference to the same as from time to time varied in any manner whatsoever and any other agreements or documents from time to time executed supplemental or in addition thereto or in substitution therefor unless the context otherwise requires. 除非本协议的语境另有规定，本协议中所称之协议或文件指随时以各种方式变更的协议或文件以及随时签署的补充、附加或替代协议或者文件。

例 3. Unless the context otherwise requires or permits, references to the singular shall include references to the plural and vice versa and words denoting any particular gender shall include all genders. 除非上下文另外要求或允许，否则单数形式应包括复数形式，反之亦然，表示任何特定性别的词语应包含所有性别。

例 4. References herein to amounts in any currency shall, unless the context otherwise requires, include references to the equivalent in any other currency. 本《运营协议》中所称以任何货币计量的金额，除非上下文另有要求，应当包括以任何其他货币计量的等值金额在内。

例 5. We commit to developing more inclusive, responsive and resilient education systems to meet the needs of children, youth and adults in these contexts, including internally displaced persons and refugees. 我们承诺发展更加包容、更具反应力和复原力的教育系统，以满足这些局势下的儿童、青年和成人的需求，包括境内流离失所者和难民的需求。

例 6. There was a need for equitable and genuinely diverse geographic representation in the treaty bodies, to ensure that countries with different legal systems and regional, cultural, religious and political contexts were fairly represented and that those bodies were not dominated by representatives of the developed countries. 要确保公允地代表具有不同法律体系和区域、文化、宗教及政治背景的国家的利益，确保人权条约机构不会被发达国家的代表所控制，人权条约机构中各地域的代表必须实现公平和真正多样性。

例 7. "Loan" means, as the context requires, the lump sum loan made or to be made under the Facility or the principal amount outstanding at any time of that loan. "贷款"按照具体语境的要求，是指根据融资安排提供或将要提供的一次总付贷款，或者是指该贷款在任何时候尚未偿还的本金额度。

例 8. Any provision of the Agreement which by its context is intended to apply after termination of the Agreement will survive its termination. 根据本协议某个条款的上下文，该条款的目的是在本协议终止以后适用，则该条款将在终止协议以后继续有效。

(2)

pretext ['priːtekst] *n.[C]* 借口，托词

例 9. The occupying authorities in Crimea use multiple pretexts for persecution and discrimination against those who oppose annexation. Religion, political position and identity are the most frequently used ones. 克里米亚境内的占领当局采取各种借口迫害和歧视那些反对吞并的人。最常用的借口是宗教、政治见解和身份。

例 10. The Seller refused to pay damages on the pretext of his ignorance of any flooding history, which the Buyer claimed to be a flimsy pretext in that he had found a photograph the Seller posted on Facebook showing the very same property in poor condition immediately after a flood. 卖方借口不知晓房产以前被水淹过，拒绝支付损害赔偿金，但买方称这条借口站不住脚，因为他发现卖方曾经在脸书上贴出一张照片，显示一场洪水刚刚过后这座房产一片狼藉的样子。

例 11. It was disturbing that some Governments, in contravention of the *Vienna Declaration and Programme of Action*, were stifling the voices of human rights defenders, non-governmental organizations and journalists under the pretext of combating terrorism, violent extremism and separatism. 有些国家的政府借口打击恐怖主义、暴力极端主义和分离主义，违反《维也纳宣言和行动纲领》的规定，压制人权维护者、非政府组织和新闻记者的呼声，这种现象令人担忧。

counterpart & counterparty

(1)

counterpart ['kaʊntəpɑːt] *n.[C]* someone or something that has the same job or purpose as someone or something else in a different place 相对应的人或物

例如：During the Feb. 21−24 talks in Washington, the seventh round since February last year, the two sides further implemented the important consensus reached by Chinese President Xi Jinping and his U.S. counterpart, Donald Trump, during their December meeting in Argentina, said the Chinese delegation.

(2)

counterparty ['kaʊntə,pɑːti] *n.[C]* the other party to a financial transaction 对手方

counterparty 是金融、保险、法律领域的术语，根据 wikipedia 的解释，这个词从 20 世纪 80 年代开始广泛使用，特别是 1988 年的《巴塞尔资本协议》。

counterparty risk *n.[C]* 对手风险 / 交易对方风险

翻译英文合同尾部的 counterpart clause 的时候，经常遇到 copy、counterpart、duplicate、original 这几个词。例如：This agreement may be executed in one or more counterparts, each of which shall be deemed an original but which together will constitute one and the same instrument.

original 常被翻译成"正本"，而另外三个词常被译成"副本"。那么，它们是一个意思吗？如果不是，它们有什么区别呢？我们首先要梳理清楚它们的意思。

copy ['kɒpi] *n.[C]* ① something that is made to be exactly like another thing: 意思是复制品 / 复制件，根据具体语境，可以灵活处理。例如：This painting is only a copy, and the original is in the Louvre. 这幅画只是摹本，真品收藏在卢浮宫。② one of many books, magazines, records, etc that are all exactly the same 相当于汉语中的量词，根据它所修饰的词语，意思可以是一本、一份、一册、一部等。

original [əˈrɪdʒənəl] *n.[C]* a work of art or a document that is not a copy, but is the one produced by the writer or the artist 原物，原作，原文，原件

in the original 以原文。例如：I prefer to read it in the original.

adj. ① existing or happening first, before other people or things 原先的，原来的，最初的； ② completely new and different from anything that anyone has thought of before 独到的，有独创性的，有创意的； ③ an original work of art is the one that was made by the artist and is not a copy 例如，an original Vincent van Gogh painting 梵高真迹

original sin *n.[U]* 基督教的原罪

originality [əˌridʒəˈnæləti] *n.[U]* 独创性

duplicate ① [ˈdjuːpliˌkeit] *v.t.* to copy something exactly, or to repeat something in exactly the same way 复制，拷贝； ② [ˈdjuːpliˌkət] *adj.* [only before noun] exactly the same as something, or made as an exact copy of something = identical 例如：a duplicate key to the house 房子的备用钥匙 / 另配的钥匙； ③ [ˈdjuːpliˌkət] *n.[C]* an exact copy of something that you can use in the same way 根据具体语境，可以译成"副本"或"复制品 / 复制件"。

in duplicate 一式两份

duplication [ˌdjupliˈkeiʃən] *n.[U]*

切勿与下面的单词混淆：

duplicity [djuːˈplisəti] *n.[U]*

duplicitous [djʊˈplisitəs] *adj.*

这两个词的意思是"表里不一，口是心非，搞两面派，当面一套背后一套"。

《元照英美法词典》还将 counterpart 译成"副本"，并作了这样的解释：源于土地转让。有关土地转让的文件被制作多份，其中交由转让人执行的文本被称为"原件"（original），其余的文本则均被称为"副本"。后也被用作其他法律文件的副本。但现在多以"duplicate"或"copy"替代。

《元照英美法词典》将 duplicate 译成"原件复本"，并且作了这样的解释：指用一定的技术手段作成的与原件内容完全相同，而且通常是与原件同时作成的原件的复本。在原件丢失或毁损时，该复本可以替代原件作证据之用，与原件具有同样的法律地位和效力。因此，在这个意义上，它与 duplicate original 同义。在用作证据方面，它与纯粹的副本（copy）不同，后者适用最佳证据规则（best evidence rule），而 duplicate 不适用。

上面两项解释似乎有矛盾之处，前者说明 counterpart、copy、duplicate 是可以互换的同义

词。后者又指出 copy 与另外两者不同。其实不然，我们看看《元照英美法词典》对 best evidence rule 的解释：

best evidence rule 最佳证据规则。指为证明书面文件、录音录像或照片中的内容，当事人应当提供该书面文件、录音录像或照片的原件，除非该原件已丢失、毁损或因其他原因而无法提供。只有在原件已不存在或不可获得的情况下，相关的复印件、记录或证人证言等第二手的证据才可以被采纳。有时也称原始书证规则（original writing rule）。

可以看出，上文第二项解释中，copy 其实是指原件的复制件，而非副本。也就是采用扫描、打印、复印、拍照、抄录等技术手段制作的复制件。复制件必须与原件核对无误，方可作为证据采纳。例如，《民事事诉讼法》就有这样的规定：

第三百七十七条 当事人申请再审，应当提交下列材料：

（一）再审申请书，并按照被申请人和原审其他当事人的人数提交副本；

（二）再审申请人是自然人的，应当提交身份证明；再审申请人是法人或者其他组织的，应当提交营业执照、组织机构代码证书、法定代表人或者主要负责人身份证明书。委托他人代为申请的，应当提交授权委托书和代理人身份证明；

（三）原审判决书、裁定书、调解书；

（四）反映案件基本事实的主要证据及其他材料。

前款第二项、第三项、第四项规定的材料可以是与原件核对无异的复印件。

另外，美国的联邦证据规则的相关规定也可供我们参考：

Federal Rules of Evidence (https://www.law.cornell.edu/rules/fre)

Rule 1001. Definitions That Apply to This Article

In this article:

(a) A "writing" consists of letters, words, numbers, or their equivalent set down in any form.

(b) A "recording" consists of letters, words, numbers, or their equivalent recorded in any manner.

(c) A "photograph" means a photographic image or its equivalent stored in any form.

(d) An "original" of a writing or recording means the writing or recording itself or any counterpart intended to have the same effect by the person who executed or issued it. For electronically stored information, "original" means any printout — or other output readable by sight — if it accurately reflects the information. An "original" of a photograph includes the negative or a print from it.

(e) A "duplicate" means a counterpart produced by a mechanical, photographic, chemical, electronic, or other equivalent process or technique that accurately reproduces the original.

分析语义，可以看出，在这里 original 的意思是原件 / 原物，而 duplicate 的意思是复制件 / 复制品。而 counterpart 根据其使用的语境，既可以指原件 / 原物，也可以指复制件 / 复制品。

归纳一下，正本与副本是从登记备案的角度区分的。而副本与复制件是不同的概念，具有不同法律效力。复制件是与原件相对应的概念，强调制作过程的不同。

一种法律文书（比如合同）最初制作的时候，可以同时制作成一份或若干份，每一份可以称作 copy 或 duplicate，它们都是原件（original）。其中任何一份，相对于其他几份都是 counterpart。也就是说，如果具体语境没有指出 copy、counterpart、duplicate 是原件的复制件，copy、counterpart、duplicate 都可以是 original，也就是原始文件。

如果具体说明要从中选出一份或几份办理登记、备案、存档等手续，那么这一份或几份特定的文本可以称作正本，其余的几份称为副本，但它们的法律效力一般是相同的。

同样道理，一份合同的签字文本可以是一式两份（in duplicate），也可以有若干份（in any number of counterparts/copies），其中每一份（copy 或 duplicate copy）文本相对于另外的几份都是 "counterpart"。

根据具体语境，不妨将正本译成 the duly registered copy 或 the copy on file 或 the duly recorded copy。副本用 its counterparts 或 other copies 表示。

如果具体语境没有提到正本副本的区别，那么不妨将所有签字的 counterparts/copies/duplicates 译作 "文本"。

举例来说，下面这句话可以这样翻译：

This Agreement may be executed in any number of counterparts. Each counterpart constitutes an original of this letter agreement, and all together constitute one agreement. 本协议书可以任意数量的文本签署。每份文本均构成本协议书的原件，全部文本共同构成一份协议。

另外，请大家注意下面这几个关联词汇：

carbon copy *n.[C]* 复写本；一模一样的人或物

fair copy *n.[C]* a handwritten document that has been written neatly and correctly without scratch-outs and revisions. 例如：make a fair copy of sth. 把……誊写一遍

soft copy *n.[C]* a digital copy of a document, rather than a copy printed on paper

hard copy *n.[C]* a printed copy of a digital document, as opposed to a copy in electronic form

complimentary copy 图书的赠阅本

an autographed copy of a book 有作者亲笔签名的书

transcript ['trænskript] *n.[C]* 誊本

excerpt ['eksɜːpt] *n.[C] & v.t.* 摘录（的片段）

extract ['ekstrækt] *n.[C]* 摘录，例如：certified extract from a complaint 经过核证的诉状
摘录。

criminalize & decriminalize

(1)

criminalize [ˈkrimɪnəlaiz] *v.t.* to make illegal; to outlaw 规定……构成犯罪行为，使……负刑事责任

criminalization [ˌkrimɪnəlaiˈzeiʃən] *n.[C, U]*

例 1. The Committee on Economic, Social and Cultural Rights expressed concern over the Islamic Republic of Iran's criminalization of consensual same-sex sexual activity, where convicted persons could be subject to the death penalty. 伊朗伊斯兰共和国规定相同性别的人之间两厢情愿地发生性行为构成犯罪，可以将被定罪者处以死刑。经济、社会和文化权利委员会对此表示关切。

例 2. At the national level

88. The Special Rapporteur invites all States:

(a) To adopt and implement clear and comprehensive legislation that criminalizes the sexual exploitation and related sale and trafficking of children, recognizes their legal status as victims to access rights and services for their care, recovery and reintegration and ensures child-friendly judicial proceedings and remedies, including compensation;

在国家层面：

88. 特别报告员请所有国家：

(a) 通过并实施明确和综合的法律，追究对儿童的性剥削及相关买卖和贩运儿童行为的刑事责任，承认他们具有受害人的法律地位，使他们享受到关怀、康复和重返社会的权利和服务，并且确保关爱儿童的司法程序和救济，包括赔偿；

(2)

decriminalize [diːˈkrimɪnəlaiz] *v.t.* = legalize 使合法化

decriminalization [diːˌkrimɪnəlaiˈzeiʃən] *n.[U]*

例 3. Already having adopted a law that decriminalizes the possession of small amounts of marijuana, Bethlehem City Council approved a resolution Tuesday night urging the Pennsylvania Legislature to do the same. 伯利恒市议会已经通过了一项法律，规定持有少量大麻属于合法行为，而在星期二夜晚，伯利恒市议会又批准了一项决议，敦促宾夕法尼亚州议会也这样做。

例 4. There's a lot of confusion and misinformation about marijuana legalization and decriminalization. 关于大麻合法化和非刑事化有很多混乱和错误的信息。

curtail & entail

(1)

curtail [kɜːˈteil] *v.t.* 削减，限制

curtailment [kɜːˈteilmənt] *n.[C, U]*

例 1. The government is mindful of these concerns and, when taking counterter-rorism measures, tries to strike a fair balance with the classic fundamental rights of individuals that may be curtailed by these measures. 政府注意到这些关切，并且在采取反恐措施时尽量平衡这些措施与可能受到这些措施影响的个人典型的基本权利之间的关系。

例 2. In the case of statutory measures that could result in the curtailment of a fundamental right, the explanatory memorandum will clarify whether the intended measures are in accordance with the law, whether they serve a legitimate purpose and whether they are necessary in a democratic society. 就可能导致削弱基本权利的法规措施而言，解释性备忘录将要澄清预期措施是否与该法律一致，它们是否为某个合法目的服务，以及在民主社会中是否必要。

(2)

entail [kɜːˈteil] *v.t.* 使……必然，牵涉

例 3. The Court held that a trademark owner is entitled to oppose the release of genuine branded goods for free circulation. It is also entitled to oppose the "offering" or "putting on the market" of the goods while they have the Customs status "non-Com-munity goods", if such offering or sale will necessarily entail putting the goods onto the market in the EEC. It is not, however, entitled to oppose mere entry of the goods into the EEC under the "external transit" procedure or the Customs warehousing procedure. The onus is on the trademark owner to prove either that the goods have been released for free circulation or that there has been an offering or sale that necessarily entails their being put onto the market in the EEC. 承审法院认定，商标所有人有权反对为了让真实的有商标货物自由流通而将其放行。商标所有人还有权反对在货物具有"非共同体货物"的报关状态时将货物"报价"或者"投放市场"，如果这种报价或者销售必然使该批货物被投放到欧洲经济共同体市场。但是商标所有人无权反对货物依照"外部过境"程序或者海关仓储程序进入欧洲经济共同体。商标所有人承担举证责任，证明或者货物已经被放行，用于自由流通，或者已经进行了必然使货物被投放到欧洲经济共同体市场的报价或者销售。

例 4. However, benefits may not be realized if conditions in the host economy are not right. Moreover, services FDI may entail systemic, structural or contingent risks. 但是，如果东道经济的基本条件不成熟，就不可能实现应有的益处。另外，服务业的外国直接投资可能会带来系统、结构或偶发的风险。

例 5. Policy coherence means that the IIAs of a country should be consistent with its domestic economic and development policies. This entails creating a coherent national development approach that integrates investment, trade, competition, technology and industrial policies. 政策协调一致性是指一国的国际投资协定应当符合其本国经济和发展政策。这需要制订纳入投资、贸易、竞争、技术和工业政策的协调一致的国家发展方针。

例 6. Developing countries need to implement the treaty commitments they have assumed. Implementation entails completing the ratification process, bringing national laws and practices into conformity with treaty commitments, informing and training local authorities that actually have to apply the IIA, managing the disputes that arise under IIAs, and re-evaluating national investment policies in the light of national development strategies and past experience. 发展中国家需要履行他们所承担的条约承诺。履行承诺意味着需要完成批准进程，使国家法律和实践符合条约承诺，知会并培训实际执行国际投资协定的地方主管机构，管理国际投资协定下产生的争端，根据国家发展战略和过去的经验重新评价国家投资政策。

debar & disbar

(1)

debar [diˈbɑː] *v.t. (formal)* 禁止

现在分词是 debarring，过去式和过去分词是 debarred。

debar 常用的词组搭配是 debar sb. from (doing) sth.。

debar 的名词是 debarment [diˈbɑːmənt]。

例 1. The law debars insurance companies from denying coverage to people with "pre-existing conditions". 该法禁止保险公司拒绝为存在"既有病患"的人办理保险。

(2)

disbar [disˈbɑː] *v.t.* [usually passive] 取消……的律师执业资格

disbar 的现在分词是 disbarring，过去式和过去分词是 disbarred。

disbar 的名词是 disbarment [disˈbɑːmənt]。

例 2. A Connersville attorney accused of using client funds to pay for her children's school tuition and of repeatedly making false assertions to the Disciplinary Commission, among numerous other "criminal and dishonest" acts, has been disbarred. 康纳斯维尔的一位律师被指控挪用客户资金为自己的子女支付学费，并一再向纪律审裁委员会作虚假声明，她还犯下许多别的"具有犯罪性质的和不诚实的"行为，因此她已被取消律师执业资格。

delegate & relegate

(1)

delegate 和 delegation 是法律文件中使用频率很高的词汇，下面我们逐一讲解它们的常用
义项。

首先 delegate 是可数名词，意思是"代表"，与"representative"同义。与之相应，delega-
tion 也是可数名词，意思是"代表团"。

delegate ['dɛligət] *n.[C]* one who represents or acts for another person or group

delegation [ˌdɛli'geiʃən] *n.[C]* a group of representatives

例 1. Delegates highlighted improvements to their national legal frameworks and
mechanisms that allowed for States, individuals and legal entities to be compensated as
victims. 代表们着重介绍了对本国法律框架和法律机制的改进，这些改进使国家、
个人和法律实体能够以受害人身份获得赔偿。

例 2. Observations about the inhuman conditions on death row were made by delegates to the high-level panel discussion on the question of the death penalty held by
the Human Rights Council in March 2014. 人权理事会在 2014 年 3 月举行了死刑问
题高级别小组讨论会，代表们就死囚牢房的不人道状况发表了意见。

例 3. The Committee appreciates the constructive dialogue that took place between the delegation and the Committee, while noting that some questions were not
fully answered. 委员会赞扬代表团与委员会之间进行的建设性对话，同时指出仍
有一些问题没有详尽解答。

例 4. On the issue of the empowerment of women, the head of the delegation of

Trinidad and Tobago mentioned the increasing number of women in Parliament and in the Senate, noting that the presiding officers of the two houses were women. 关于增强妇女权能问题，特立尼达和多巴哥代表团团长提到在议会和参议院中有越来越多的女议员，他特别指出两院的议长都是妇女。

作为动词，delegate 有下面两个常用义项：

delegate ['dɛligeit] ① *v.t.* to choose someone to do a particular job, or to be a representative of a group, organization, etc. 委派或选举……为代表；固定搭配是 delegate sb. to do sth.。

例 5. In order to give the Buyer's personnel an opportunity to get acquainted with the Systems and to assist the Seller, the Buyer will delegate trained and experienced engineers to carry out a trial run on the Site. 为了使买方人员有机会熟悉系统及协助卖方，买方将选派训练有素且经验丰富的工程师前往现场进行调试。

② *v.t.* & *v.i.* 《布莱克法律词典》对名词 delegation 的解释是 "the act of entrusting another with authority or empowering another to act as an agent or representative"。我们可以看出动词 delegate 的第二个义项是：授权，委托。在翻译实践中，可以作为 delegate 的宾语的词汇不仅有 authority、power、right 等表示权利的词汇，还有 duty、obligation、responsibility、work 等表示义务的词汇，它的固定搭配是 delegate sth. to sb.。

例 6. Responsibility for preventing child abuse and providing victims with assistance is to be delegated to the municipal authorities. 应当指派市政当局履行防止儿童受虐待和为受虐待儿童提供救助的职责。

例 7. The Lender may delegate in any manner to any person any rights exercisable by the Lender under any Finance Document. Any such delegation may be made upon such terms and conditions (including power to sub-delegate) as the Lender thinks fit. 贷款人可以将其能够依据融资文件行使的任何权利按照任何方式授予任何人。贷款人可以按照其认为适当的条件进行授权（包括转授权的权力）。

例 8. The General Manager may delegate his duty to other staff and managers when it is necessary for him to do so. 总经理可以在必要时将其职责托付其他工作人员和经理。

例 9. The Lender hereby appoints the Facility Agent to act as its agent in connection with this Agreement and authorises the Facility Agent to exercise such rights, powers, authorities and discretions as are specifically delegated to the Facility Agent by the terms contained in Part A of *Schedule 9* together with all such rights, powers, authorities and discretions as are reasonably incidental thereto. 贷款人特此指定贷款事务代理人担任其与本协议有关的代理人，并且授权贷款事务代理人行使根据《附件9》A节所载条件专门委托贷款事务代理人行使的权利、权力、职权和裁量权，以及合理附带于这些权利的一切权利、权力、职权和裁量权。

例 10. Seller may assign its rights and delegate its obligations under this Agreement. Buyer's rights and obligations under this Agreement are personal in nature and shall not be transferable by assignment, delegation, operation of law, subcontract or otherwise without Seller's prior written consent and any attempt to do so shall be void. 卖方可以转让其根据本协议享有的权利并且可以转委其根据本协议承担的义务。买方根据本协议享有的权利和承担的义务属于个人性质，如事先未取得卖方书面同意，不得凭借转让、转委、法律的实施、分包或其他方式转让该权利和义务，凡试图转让该权利和义务均属无效。

例 11. The Coordinating Arranger may delegate any or all of its rights and/or obligations under the *Proposed Terms* to any of its affiliates (each a "Delegate") and may designate in writing to the Borrower any Delegate of it as responsible for the performance of any of its appointed functions under the *Proposed Terms*. 协调安排人可以将其在《拟议条款》项下的部分或全部权利和／或义务委托其关联机构行使（各该关联机构称为"代理行"），并且可以在给予借款人的书面文件中指定某个代理行负责履行《拟议条款》所规定的协调安排人的职能。

(2)

relegate ['rɛligeit] *v.t.* ① to give someone or something a less important position than before 降低……的地位或级别；② if a sports team is relegated, it is moved into a lower division 使球队降级

relegate 的固定搭配是 relegate sb./sth. to sth.。

relegation [,rɛli'geiʃən] *n.[U]*

例 12. Better-paid jobs require a minimum level of schooling while workers who are illiterate are more susceptible to exploitation. Lack of education relegates Nepali workers to low wage roles. 收入更高的工作要求工作者受过最起码的学校教育，而没有读写能力的工作者更容易遭受剥削。缺乏教育使尼泊尔工作者沦为低工资劳工。

例 13. Southampton fans may not welcome belt-tightening at the club, which narrowly avoided relegation this year and is among the league's lower-earning teams. 俱乐部今年勉强避免降级，目前是联赛收入较低的球队之一，但南安普敦队的球迷也许不欢迎俱乐部削减开支的做法。

例 14. The state's legislature and governor had been unable to agree to a budget for two years, prompting S&P and fellow rating agency Moody's to relegate the state's rating to the lowest possible investment grade. 该州的立法机关和州长两年来一直无法就预算达成一致，这促使标准普尔和同行评级机构穆迪将该州的评级下调到最低的投资级别。

deposit

deposit [di'pɒzit] *n.[C]* ① 保证金；② 存款；③ 沉淀物；沉积物；*v.t.* 存放，存储，寄存，寄托

deposit 作为名词的例子如下：

例 1. "London Business Day" means a day (other than a Saturday or a Sunday) on which commercial banks are open for general business including dealing in interbank deposits in London. "伦敦营业日"是指伦敦的商业银行对外办理一般业务（包括办理银行同业存款）之日（星期六和星期日除外）。

例 2. No loan may be made under this Subsection to finance any operation for the extraction of oil or gas. The aggregate amount of loans under this Subsection to finance operations for the mining or other extraction of any deposit of ore or other nonfuel minerals may not in any fiscal year exceed $4,000,000. 不得根据本款发放贷款资助任何开采石油或天然气的作业。根据本款规定发放贷款资助采矿或者其他开采任何矿砂或其他非燃料矿物的作业，此类贷款的总金额在任何财政年度不得超过四百万美元。

例 3. Subject to Paragraphs 5 and 6 below, the Bank agrees that any deposit into Trust Account No. 1 by AAA will be treated as a prepayment by BBB of amounts which fall due under the Loan Agreement, and any deposit into Trust Account No. 2 by CCC will be treated as a prepayment by DDD of amounts which fall due under the Loan Agreement. 根据下文第 5、6 段，银行同意，AAA 存入信托账户 1 中的任何款项均视为 BBB 偿还贷款协议下到期贷款的还款，CCC 存入信托账户 2 的任何款项均视为 DDD 偿还贷款协议下到期贷款的还款。

例 4. The Purchase Price shall be paid by the Purchaser to the Vendor's Solicitors as stakeholders in the following manner:

(a) upon execution of this Agreement, a sum of _____ only as deposit (hereinafter referred to as "*the Deposit*") representing ten per cent (10%) of the Purchase Price by way of a cashier's order or banker's draft from a financial institution acceptable to the Vendor, the receipt of which the Vendor hereby acknowledges;

买方应当按照下列方式向作为利害关系人的卖方律师支付购买价款：

（a） 自签署本协议时起，买方采用卖方可以接受的金融机构开具的银行本票或者银行汇票方式，支付占购买价款百分之十（10%）的总额为_____的保证金（以下统称为"保证金"），卖方收到上述保证金后应予确认；

deposit 作为动词的例子如下：

例 5. We have been further instructed by the Lender to remind the Borrower that under Clause 16 of the *Facility Agreement*, the Borrower shall deposit or shall procure all of its operation revenue to be deposited into the Account. 我们收到放款人进一步指示，要求我们提醒借款人，根据《贷款协议》第十六条，借款人应当将其所有营业收入存入相关账户或应当促致该收入存入相关账户。

例 6. Any appointment or revocation by a Director under this Article shall be effected by notice in writing given under his hand to the Secretary or deposited at the Office or in any other manner approved by the Directors. 董事根据本条指定或撤销替代人，应当向秘书发送经该董事亲笔签字的书面通知或者将该通知存放在办公室或者采用全体董事批准的其他方式。

例 7. In order to become a Limited Partner, a prospective member should deposit the $1,000,000 Capital Contribution plus $50,000 Administrative Expense Fee with the Escrow Agent by wire transfer. 要成为有限合伙人，潜在的合伙人应当以电汇方式向代管人交存一百万美元出资外加五万美元行政经费。

例 8. Funds must be deposited in bank accounts specified by the Board of Directors and remain under the exclusive control of the Company and may be used only for their lawful intended purpose. 资金必须存放在董事会指定的银行账户内，处于公司的专门控制之下，并且只能用于资金的合法预定用途。

例 9. For the purpose of this Article, any instrument deposited by a Regional Economic Integration Organization shall not be counted as additional to those deposited by member States of that Organization. 就本条而言，不应当在区域经济一体化组织的成员国交存的文书以外再记入该组织交存的任何文书。

deprave & deprive

这两个词拼写和读音都非常相似，意思却迥然不同，要格外注意。

(1)

deprave [diˈpreiv] *v.t.* 使……堕落

depraved [diˈpreivd] *adj.* 道德败坏的，恶毒的

depravity [diˈprævəti] *n.[U]* 行为败坏

《元照英美法词典》对 "depraved mind" 是这样解释的：depraved mind 堕落的思想。指
缺乏道德感和正直心，是最高等级的"恶意"，在二级谋杀罪（second-degree mur-
der）的定罪中指对他人生命漠不关心的心理状态。

According to *Black's Law Dictionary*, depraved-heart murder means a murder resulting from
an act so reckless and careless of the safety of others that it demonstrates the perpetrator's
complete lack of regard for human life.

根据《布莱克法律词典》的解释，存心邪僻的谋杀罪是指由罔顾和轻忽他人安全的行为
所导致的谋杀，该行为表明犯罪人毫不关心人的生死。

(2)

deprive [diˈpraiv] *v.t.* 剥夺，夺走

deprive 经常构成的词组是：deprive sb. of sth. / be deprived of sth.。

deprived [diˈpraivd] *adj.* 贫寒的，贫困的

deprivation [ˌdɛprəˈveiʃən] *n.[C usually plural; U]*

例 1. The social networking software in mobile phones is said to be one of the
culprits of sleep deprivation. 据说手机上的社交软件是导致人们睡眠不足的原因
之一。

例 2. Access to justice thus permits the fulfilment of all human rights, because without it, people are unable to claim their rights or challenge crimes, abuses or violations committed against them, which in turn can trap them in a vicious circle of impunity, deprivation and exclusion. 因此，司法救助让人们能够享有一切人权，因为没有司法救助，人们就无法主张其权利或与施加其身上的犯罪、虐待或侵犯行为相抗争，这反过来可能使他们陷入有罪不罚、剥夺和排斥的恶性循环。

例 3. Cross-sector policies and plans should be developed or improved, consistent with the overall 2030 Agenda for Sustainable Development, to address the social, cultural and economic barriers that deprive millions of children, youth and adults of education and quality learning. 为了消除导致千百万儿童、青年和成人丧失受教育和优质学习机会的社会、文化和经济方面的障碍，应当制定或改进跨部门的政策和计划，并使其与关乎全局的 2030 年可持续发展议程保持一致。

例 4. Early encouragement gives children a better start, improving their chances and maximising their development potential. This is particularly true for children from deprived environments, whose parents are unlikely to sufficiently understand the importance of encouraging education at an early age. 早期的鼓励可以改善儿童的机遇，最大程度地挖掘他们的发展潜力，从而给予他们更好的开始。对家境贫寒的儿童尤其如此，他们的家长未必充分理解早期鼓励教育的重要性。

例 5. The harsh conditions, persistent and extreme abuse, and trauma associated with sexual exploitation have been linked with a range of health-related problems. Physical abuse and deprivation, for example, can result in direct physical injury (e.g. bruises, contusions, cuts, burns), indirect physical injury (e.g. chronic headaches, dizziness), insomnia and disrupted sleep patterns, and in extreme cases homicide or suicide. 多种健康问题都与恶劣的条件、持续不断而且极其严酷的虐待以及与性剥削有关的创伤脱不开关系。例如，对肉体的虐待和剥夺会导致直接的身体伤害（如瘀伤、擦伤、割伤、灼伤）、间接的身体伤害（如慢性头痛、头晕目眩）、失眠和睡眠紊乱，在极端情况下，还会导致杀人或者自杀。

例 6. According to the Inter-American Commission on Human Rights, all persons deprived of liberty must receive humane treatment, commensurate with respect for their inherent dignity. This means that the conditions of imprisonment of persons sentenced to death must meet the same international norms and standards that apply in general to persons deprived of liberty. In this regard, the duties of the State to respect and ensure the right to humane treatment of all persons under its jurisdiction apply regardless of the nature of the conduct for which the person in question has been deprived of his liberty. 根据美洲人权委员会的看法，所有被剥夺了自由的人都必须获得人道待遇，这种待遇须与对他们固有尊严的尊重相称。这意味着被判处死刑者的监禁状况必须符合普遍适用于被剥夺自由者的国际规范和标准。在这方面，不论已导致该人被剥夺自由的行为具有何种性质，国家都有义务尊重和确保受其管辖的所有人员获得人道待遇的权利。

例 7. The international legal texts applicable to capital punishment and to detention do not address the specific concerns of prisoners on death row although some aspects have been dealt with in the case law of international human rights tribunals within the context of the prohibition of cruel, inhuman and degrading treatment or punishment and of arbitrary deprivation of liberty. 适用于死刑和监禁的国际法律文件并未涉及死囚犯的切身利害，不过，国际人权法庭在禁止酷刑和其他残忍、不人道或有辱人格的待遇或处罚和禁止任意剥夺自由方面的判例法已经涉及与死囚犯有切身利害的一些方面。

discriminant, discriminating & discriminatory

(1)

discriminant [disˈkriminənt] *adj.* serving to discriminate 起区分 / 判别作用的；*n.[C]* 可资辨别的因素；（数学术语）判别式，例如：discriminant function 判别函数，linear discriminant analysis 线性判别分析

(2)

discriminating [disˈkrimineitiŋ] *adj.* able to judge what is of good quality and what is not = discerning 有眼力的

例 1. The book, which is written in plain English rather than psychobabble, will appeal to discriminating readers. 这本书用通俗易懂的英文写成，没有使用让人摸不着头脑的心理学术语，有眼力的读者会对它感兴趣。

例 2. For a discriminating buyer, the community's family-friendly atmosphere is the real clincher. 这个社区适合居家的氛围会最终打动识货的买家。

(3)

discriminatory [diˈskriminəˌtɔːri] *adj.* treating a person or a group of people differently from other people, in an unfair way 歧视性的

例 3. Target 10.3. Ensure equal opportunity and reduce inequalities of outcome, including by eliminating discriminatory laws, policies and practices and promoting appropriate legislation, policies and action in this regard. 具体目标10.3。确保机会均等，减少结果不平等现象，包括取消歧视性法律、政策和做法，推动与上述努力相关的适当立法、政策和行动。

例 4. The Secondee agrees that she will act in a civil, co-operative and non-discriminatory fashion towards the Host's employees, visitors, donors, clients, volunteers and other contacts. 被借调人同意将以文明礼貌、乐于合作及非歧视性的方式对待接待单位的雇员、访客、捐赠者、客户、志愿者以及其他关系人员。

disproportionate & proportionate

proportional 和 proportionate 是同义词，proportionate 比 proportional 更正式，disproportionate 是 proportionate 的反义词。而 proportioned 与 proportional 和 proportionate 含义不同。下面结合例句学习这几个词。

(1)

proportionate [prə'pɔːʃənit] *adj.* 合乎比例的

proportional [prə'pɔːʃənl] *adj.* something that is proportional to something else is in the correct or most suitable relationship to it in size, amount, importance, etc. 合乎比例的

例 1. "Net Book Value" means, in relation to an asset, the amount equal to the original capitalized value less any depreciation incurred [including, for the avoidance of doubt, all depreciation for which a Service Recipient pays a proportionate share pursuant to Section 4,2(c)(ii)], in each case determined in accordance with *GAAP.* "账面净值"对于某项资产，是指该资产的原始资本化价值减去该资产发生的折旧［为避免产生疑问，包括服务接受者依照第4.2（c）（ii）条按比例分担的所有折旧］以后剩余的金额，原始资本化价值及折旧均依照《会计通则》确定。

例 2. As an entity treated as a partnership for tax purposes the Fund itself is not subject to tax. Instead, each Limited Partner will be required to take into account for each fiscal year, for purposes of computing his or her own income tax, his or her proportionate share of the items of taxable income or loss allocated to him or her pursuant to the *Limited Partnership Agreement*, whether or not any income is paid out to him or her. 作为一个出于税务考虑而被当作合伙组织的实体，本基金自身无须纳税。但每一位有限合伙人不论是否获得收益，需要为了计算他或她本人每一财政年度

的所得税，考虑依照《有限合伙协议》分派给他或她的应税所得或损失项目的相应份额。

例 3. There are two types of joint ventures in the PRC relevant to the Company: equity joint ventures (EJV) and cooperating joint ventures (CJV). In an EJV, profits and assets are distributed in proportion to the parties' equity holdings upon winding up. In a CJV, the parties may contract to divide profits and assets disproportionately to their equity interests. 在中国有两种与该公司有关的合资企业：股份制合资企业（"股份制企业"）和合作式经营企业（"合作经营企业"）。在股份制企业中，利润和资产在结业清理后即按照各方持股比例予以分配。在合作经营企业中，各方当事人可以通过订立合同，约定不按照其股权的比例分割利润和资产。

例 4. Where any person dies as the result partly of his own fault and partly of the fault of any other person or persons, and accordingly if an action were brought for the benefit of the estate under Section 20 the damages recoverable would be reduced under subsection (1), any damages recoverable in an action under the Act shall be reduced to a proportionate extent. 如任何人的死亡，部分原因是该人本人的过失，而部分原因是他人的过失，并若据此根据第 20 条为死者遗产的利益提出诉讼，可追讨的损害赔偿会根据第（1）款减少，则在根据该法而提出的诉讼中可追讨的任何损害赔偿，须按比例减少。

(2)

proportioned [prə'pɔːʃənd] *adj.* used to talk about how correct, attractive, suitable, etc. something is in its size or shape
proportioned 前面常常搭配副词用作定语修饰后面的名词，意思是"具有……比例或形状"。

例 5. It was a large, well-proportioned room, handsomely fitted up. 这是一间布局合理、陈设雅致的大屋子。

例 6. Few people can understand what the grotesquely proportioned figures in this abstract painting try to convey, and even fewer people dare to assert its meaninglessness. 没几个人看得懂这幅抽象画里面那些奇形怪状的人物想要传达什么意思，敢说这幅画毫无意义的人就更少了。

例 7. Since this medieval town became a tourist attraction, the otherwise quaint streets are thronged with generously proportioned tourists in their forties and fifties, posing for an Instagrammable photograph. 自从这个中世纪小镇成了旅游景点，本来古朴雅致的街道就挤满了体态臃肿的四五十岁的中年游客，摆好姿势拍网红照片。

(3)

disproportionate to sth. [ˌdɪsprəˈpɔːʃənət] *adj.* 与……不相称

例 8. One pressing concern regarding transfer pricing documentation is the risk of overburdening the taxpayer with disproportionately high costs in obtaining relevant documentation or in an exhaustive search for comparables that may not exist. 一个关于转让定价文件的最迫切问题是，获得相关文件或彻底搜索也许并不存在的参照对象，其过高的费用有可能让纳税人不堪重负。

例 9. I often stewed with righteous anger over physical punishments—my own or others'—especially when they seemed disproportionate to the crime. 我经常对自己或别人受体罚感到义愤填膺，尤其是体罚似乎与干的坏事不成比例的时候。

例 10. And knowing that the poor and minorities are disproportionately the victims of crimes, I'm loath to view the adversarial process of the law as class warfare by another name. 认识到受犯罪侵害的穷人和少数族裔特别多，所以我不想将抗辩式法律程序看成是阶级斗争的另一种说法。

例 11. That climate change and recurring natural disasters, including extreme weather events and drought, have a disproportionate impact on women. 气候变化和反

复发生的自然灾害，包括极端气候事件和旱灾，对妇女具有过度的影响。

例 12. *CoE*-ACFC recommended ensuring that the quality of education in minority language schools does not suffer as a result of a disproportionate focus on the promotion of the state language and that minority language schools are adequately prepared and resourced to implement effectively the education reform without negatively affecting the overall quality of education. 《保护少数民族框架公约》咨询委员会建议确保不会由于过度关注推广国家语言而令少数民族语言学校的教育质量受到影响，还要确保让少数民族语言学校做好充分准备、获得适足的资源，从而切实落实教育改革，不令整体教育质量受到负面影响。

dissolve & resolve

(1)

dissolve [diˈzɔlv] *v.t. & v.i.* 溶解；*v.t.* 解除，解散，终止；*v.t. & v.i.* 烟消云散

dissolution [ˌdisəˈluːʃən] *n.[U]* 解散

例 1. Either Party may at any time by notice in writing immediately terminate this Contract and/or any affected Deliverable under this Contract, if the other Party passes a resolution, or any competent court makes an order, that the other Party shall be dissolved or if a trustee in bankruptcy, liquidator, receiver, or manager on behalf of a creditor shall be appointed. 如果一方当事人通过决议，或者有管辖权限的法院发布命令，决定或饬令该当事人予以解散或者指定代表债权人的破产财产管理人、清算人、破产财产接管人或财务管理人，则对方当事人均可以随时借助书面通知立即终止本合同和／或本合同项下受影响的可交付货物。

例 2. If CCC becomes, or is likely to become, the subject of any bankruptcy, insolvency, liquidation, dissolution or any other similar resolution, plans to reach any reconciliation agreement with the creditor, is unable or likely unable to repay any debts due (collectively, the "Bankruptcy Incidents"), CCC shall immediately inform KKK of such facts. Without prejudice to the provision of Article 5.2.1, no Securities, cash or any other assets held by CCC for KKK shall constitute bankruptcy property of CCC. 如果 CCC 成为或有可能成为任何破产、无力偿还债务、清盘、解散或任何其他类似决议的对象，准备与债权人达成任何和解协议，无法或有可能无法偿还任何到期债务（统称"破产事件"），CCC 应当立即将此类事实通知 KKK。在不损害第 5.2.1 条的规定的情况下，CCC 为 KKK 持有的证券、现金和其他资产不构成 CCC 的破产财产。

(2)

resolve [ri'zɔlv] ① *v.t.* 解决，消除；② *v.i.* 决计，决心；（公司或社团）作出决议

resolution [ˌrɛsə'lu:ʃən] *n.[C]* ① 决议；决定，决心；② 解决

例 3. All disputes arising from the execution of or in connection with the Contract shall be settled through friendly consultation between both Parties. Such consultation shall ensure that said dispute(s) shall be resolved within a reasonable time, not exceeding one month after issuance by either Party of the registered letter indicating the nature of the dispute. 因履行本合同而产生的或者与本合同有关的所有纠纷应当由双方当事人友好协商解决。友好协商应当保证上述纠纷在合理时间内得到解决，但从任何一方当事人发出说明纠纷性质的挂号信函之后不得超过一个月。

例 4. Any dispute that cannot be resolved through friendly consultations within 90 days shall be submitted to the China International Economic and Trade Arbitration Commission for final settlement in accordance with its Arbitration Rules. 无法在 90 日内通过友好协商得到解决的争端，应当提交中国国际经济贸易仲裁委员会，依照该委员会的仲裁规则予以最终裁决。

例 5. In the event of any over-purchase of Securities by mistake, such mistake shall be resolved according to the procedure stipulated in the separate arrangement. In addition, any transaction erroneously caused by one Party shall be resolved by negotiation between relevant parties, provided, however, the Bank shall apply for non-transactional transfers (if applicable) when depository and clearing company so requires. The Party causing the mistaken transaction shall take responsibilities in accordance with this Agreement. 如果由于错误而过量购买证券，应当按照单独协议中规定的程序解决上述错误。此外，一方当事人错误地导致的交易，应当由相关当事人协商解决，但是托管机构和结算公司要求非交易过户时，银行应当申请非交易过户（倘若可以非交易过户）。导致错误交易的当事人应当依照本协议承担责任。

例 6. In event of Force Majeure, the Parties shall immediately consult with each other to find a fair resolution and use all their reasonable efforts to minimize the consequences caused by the Force Majeure. 如果发生不可抗力，双方当事人应当立即进行协商，寻求公平的解决之道，并付出它们的一切合理努力，将不可抗力造成的后果减少到最低限度。

例 7. A cumulation interaction may occur not only with respect to substantive provisions in the same agreement, but also with respect to dispute resolution provisions. For example, some IIAs include an investment chapter with an investor–State resolution mechanism that is cumulative to the more general dispute resolution mechanism in the agreement. The issue may arise as to whether disputes concerning other chapters of the agreement may be brought under the investor–State dispute resolution mechanism. "累积型"的相互作用不仅发生于同一协定的实质性条款中，也发生于争端解决条款中。例如，有些国际投资协定在投资一节中规定了投资者与国家之间争端的解决机制，与协定中一般争端解决机制是重叠的。可能产生的问题是，涉及协定其他章节的争端能否提交投资者与国家争端解决机制。

例 8. The Board of Directors may resolve from time to time to expand, reduce or amend the scope and scale of the Company's business as appropriate in accordance with the development of the Company and market demands, taking into consideration the Company's business strategy and financing abilities and subject to any approval required under Chinese Law. 董事会可以在适当情况下，按照公司的发展情况和市场需求，虑及公司的经营战略和融资能力，不定时地作出决议，扩大、缩减或修正公司的经营范围和经营规模，上述决议应当取得中国法律所要求的批准。

例 9. Resolutions of the Supervisory Board are taken with the simple majority of the votes unless otherwise provided by law. If there is equality of votes the Chairman shall have the casting vote pursuant to § § 29 (2) and 31 (4) of the *Co-determination Act*; a second poll within the meaning of these provisions can be demanded by any member of the Supervisory Board. 监事会采用简单多数表决方式作出决议，除非法律另有规定。如果赞成票数与反对票数相同，监事会主席可以根据《共同决策法》第 29（2）条和第 31（4）条的规定，作出决定性表决；监事会成员均可要求进行上述条款所规定的第二轮投票。

due & undue

(1)

due [dju:] *adj.* ① just, proper, regular, and reasonable 应有的，正当的； ② 预计的，预期的；

③ immediately enforceable; owing or payable; constituting a debt 欠债的，到期应付的

due *adv.* = directly （指方向）正对着

dues [dju:z] *n.[PL]* 会费

give sb. his due / give the devil his due 说句公道话，实事求是地讲

例 1. The Purchaser has the right to set off against payment of the Purchaser Price due to the Vendors any amounts due or claimed to be due to the Purchaser or the Company from the Vendors. 买方有权以卖方应当付给（或者买方声称卖方应当付给）买方或者对象公司的款项抵消买方应当付给卖方的购买价款。

例 2. Royalties due to First Nations are calculated in accordance with the terms and conditions outlined in each lease and the *Indian O&G Regulations*. IOGC is responsible for collecting oil and gas royalties on behalf of First Nations for all oil and gas produced from First Nations reserve lands. 应当付给原住民的使用费按照各该租约以及《印第安人油气管理条例》载明的条件计算。印第安人油气事务署负责代表原住民就原住民保留地上生产的所有油气收取油气使用费。

例 3. Any payment which is due to be made on a day that is not a business day shall be made on the next business day in the same calendar month (if there is one) or the preceding business day (if there is not one). 应当支付款项的日期如果不是营业日，那么该笔款项应当在同一公历月份的下一个营业日支付（如果下一个营业日与应当支付该款项的日期处于同一月份）或者前一个营业日（如果下一个营

业日与应当支付该款项的日期不处于同一月份）。

例 4. The environmental assessment process under *CEAA* is not an approval process; it only determines if, with due regard for mitigation measures, a project's environmental impacts can be reduced to the point where the project should be permitted to proceed. 《加拿大环境评价法》规定的环境评价程序并非审批程序；这套程序仅仅确定，在妥善考虑减轻环境影响的措施后，某个项目的环境影响能否降低到一定程度，使这个项目得以继续。

例 5. The Committee requests the State party to respond to the concerns expressed in the present concluding comments in its next periodic report under Article 18 of the *Convention*. The Committee invites the State party to submit its seventh periodic report, which is due in February 2007, and its eighth periodic report, due in February 2011, in a combined report in 2011. 委员会请该缔约国在其下一次报告中，依照《公约》第 18 条的规定对本结论意见所表达的关切作出答复。委员会请该缔约国在 2011 年合并提出其第七次定期报告（原定于 2007 年 2 月提交）和第八次定期报告（原定于 2011 年 2 月提交）。

例 6. In the event of termination under Section 8(a), all sums payable by Client to AAA under this Agreement shall become immediately due and payable. 如果 AAA 根据第 8(a) 条终止许可，则客户根据本协议应当付给 AAA 的所有钱款立即成为到期应付款。

例 7. Any Financial Indebtedness of the Borrower is not paid when due nor within any originally applicable grace period. 借款人没有在其负担的金融债务的到期日，也没有在最初适用的宽限期内偿还该债务。

例 8. X Bank shall contact relevant parities to collect any dividend and interests of the Securities due and unpaid. If any company that needs to pay any dividends or interests is likely to refuse or delay to pay such dividends or interests of any Securities,

X Bank shall promptly notify Y Bank as soon as possible. X 银行应当与相关当事方联系，以便收取到期未付的证券红利和利息。如果必须支付红利或者利息的公司有可能拒绝支付或者迟延支付证券的红利或者利息，X 银行应当尽快及时通知 Y 银行。

例 9. Both Parties shall jointly source potential underlying investment managers for the Product (each an "Investment Manager"). Although Party B shall be primarily responsible for the delivery of investment due diligence with respect to each potential Investment Manager ("IDD"), both Parties shall jointly conduct such IDD. 双方当事人应当共同为约定产品探求若干潜在的基础投资管理人（均称为"投资管理人"）。虽然应当由乙方主要负责完成对每一位潜在投资管理人的投资状况尽职调查（"投资状况尽职调查"），但是双方当事人应当共同开展此项调查。

例 10. Vendor shall make due arrangements for inspections requested by the Customs authorities and other applicable government agencies. 销售商应当为海关当局和其他相关政府机关要求的检验做好妥善的安排。

例 11. Prior to the expiration of such period the Parties shall agree on price changes, whereby due consideration shall be given to changes in market conditions, currency fluctuations and/or costs. As long as the Parties have not agreed upon revised prices, the then current prices shall further apply. 在上述期间届满之前，双方当事人应当对市场状况、货币波动及／或成本的变化给予应有考虑，由此就价格变动达成协议。只要双方当事人尚未就修订价格达成合意，当前价格应当继续适用。

例 12. If one Party suffers loss due to the misconduct of the other Party, the Party shall get compensated from the other Party in accordance with the terms of this MOU and law. 如果一方当事人由于对方的不法行为而遭受损失，对方当事人应当依照本备忘录载明的条件和法律的规定对遭受损失的当事人给予赔偿。

例 13. There are several reasons why developing countries, on average, remain more restrictive to FDI in services than developed ones. It is partly due to the particular nature of services. 发展中国家与发达国家相比对于服务业外国直接投资的限制程度平均较高。这有若干原因，其中部分原因是服务业的特殊性质。

例 14. Biological medicinal products similar to a reference medicinal product do not usually meet all the conditions to be considered as a generic medicinal product mainly due to manufacturing process characteristics, raw materials used, molecular characteristics and therapeutic modes of action. 与某种参照药品类似的生物药品通常不能满足被视为通用名称药品的全部条件，这主要是制造工艺的特点，所使用的原材料，分子特征以及行为治疗模式所致。

例 15. Enterprises should, within the framework of laws, regulations and administrative practices in the countries in which they operate, and in consideration of relevant international agreements, principles, objectives, and standards, take due account of the need to protect the environment, public health and safety, and generally to conduct their activities in a manner contributing to the wider goal of sustainable development. 企业应在经营所在国法律框架、规章和管理做法框架内，并考虑到相关国际协定、原则、目标和标准，适当顾及环境保护、公共健康和安全需求，一般应以有助于更广泛的可持续发展目标的方式开展其活动。

例 16. BITs and other international instruments for the protection of foreign investment virtually always contain provisions prohibiting the taking of foreign investors' assets by public authorities, except if done for a public purpose, on a non-discriminatory basis, against payment of compensation, and, in many cases, with due process of law. 双边投资条约和其他保护外国投资的国际文书几乎总是载有禁止公共当局占取外国投资者资产的规定，为公共目的、基于不歧视原则、作出相应赔偿付款以及在许多情况下通过正当法律程序所为者例外。

(2)

undue [ʌnˈdjuː] *adj.* 过度的；不当的

unduly [ʌnˈdjuːli] *adv.*

例 17. Each State Party shall grant the body or bodies referred to in Paragraph 1 of this Article the necessary independence, in accordance with the fundamental principles of its legal system, to enable the body or bodies to carry out its or their functions effectively and free from any undue influence. 各缔约国均应当根据本国法律制度的基本原则，赋予本条第一款所述机构必要的独立性，使其能够有效地履行职能和免受任何不正当的影响。

例 18. If Documentation supplied by XYZ hereunder fails to conform to this warranty, XYZ shall provide new and warranty compliant versions of the Documentation to Ordering Entity or its Customers without undue delay. 如果 XYZ 根据本协议提交的文献不符合此项保证，XYZ 应当向订货实体或者订货实体的客户提供新的和与保证相符的文献版本，不得无故拖延。

effective & efficient

注意辨别 effective 和 efficient：effective 强调有效果、起作用。efficient 强调有效率，不浪费。

(1)

effective [iˈfɛktiv] *adj.* ① successful, and working in the way that was intended 有效的，起作用的，灵验的，奏效的； ② if a law, agreement or system becomes effective, it officially starts 生效的； ③ real rather than what is officially intended or generally believed 实际上的

effectively *adv.* ① in a way that produces the result that was intended 有效； ② used to describe what you see as the real facts of the situation = in fact 实际上

effectiveness *n. [U]*

ineffective [ˌiniˈfɛktiv] *adj.* something that is ineffective does not achieve what it is intended to achieve 无效果的；不起作用的；不奏效的（注意 ineffective 构成的词组搭配：be ineffective in doing sth.。）

ineffectively *adv.*

ineffectiveness *n. [U]*

例 1. A notice or other document may be served on a person by any effective means. 通知或其他文书可以借助任何有效的手段送达个人。

例 2. There was little evidence that these policies, which had been pursued for many years, had been effective. 几乎没有证据可以证明这些已经施行多年的政策取得了成效。

例 3. This carelessly written lease has proved ineffective in protecting the interest of the landlord. 这份措辞粗心大意的租约没有起到保护房东权益的作用。

例 4. Information and communication technologies (ICTs) must be harnessed to strengthen education systems, knowledge dissemination, information access, quality and effective learning, and more effective service provision. 必须利用信息通信技术来加强教育系统、知识传播、信息获取、学习质量和效果，并提供更加有效的服务。

例 5. The Company's obligations under this Paragraph shall be effective whether or not the *Facility Agreement* is signed or drawn. 无论《贷款协议》签订或拟定与否，贵司均应承担本节所规定的义务。

例 6. Except as otherwise provided herein, no proposed modification of or addition to the terms of this Agreement shall be effective as against Buyer until such modification or addition has been countersigned on behalf of Buyer. 除非本协议另有规定，对本协议进行的修改或补充只有在买方代表会签后才能对买方发生效力。

例 7. We recommend improving aid effectiveness through better coordination and harmonization, and prioritizing financing and aid to neglected sub-sectors and low income countries. 我们建议通过更好地协调和统一来改善援助的效益，并优先向受忽视的分部门和低收入国家提供资金和援助。

例 8. Should an individual provision of this Agreement be or become ineffective or unenforceable for reasons beyond the Parties' control, including by force of Law, the Parties shall modify this Agreement to replace the ineffective or unenforceable provision. 假若由于法律规定等超出双方当事人控制范围的原因，本协议的某个条款无效或者无法执行，或者成为无效条款或者无法执行条款，双方当事人应当修订本协议，替换无效的或者无法执行的条款。

例 9. Where in any arbitral or legal proceedings, a Party asserts the existence of an arbitration agreement in a pleading, statement of case or any other document in circumstances in which the assertion calls for a reply and the assertion is not denied, there shall be deemed to be an effective arbitration agreement as between the Parties to the proceedings. 凡在任何仲裁程序或法律程序中，一方当事人在状书、案情陈述或其他文书中声明存在仲裁协议，对方需要对该声明作出答复，但又未对该声明予以否认，在这种情形下，应当视为上述程序的双方当事人之间存在有效的仲裁协议。

例 10. Given that the school board administers the only two schools for lower vocational education in Aruba and the pupil concerned was unable to pursue her studies at either of these two schools, she had been effectively excluded from education. The court ruled that this violated the right of the person concerned to education and was therefore unlawful. 鉴于教育委员会管理着阿鲁巴仅有的两所提供低端职业教育的学校，被开除的女学生无法在这两所学校之中的任何一所求学，她实际上已被排斥于受教育对象之外。法院裁定这种做法侵犯了这名女学生的受教育权利，因此属于违反行为。

effective、 effectual、efficacious 是同义词，ineffective、ineffectual、inefficacious 分别是它们的反义词。

effectual [i'fɛktʃuəl] *adj.* producing the result that was wanted or intended

ineffectual [ˌini'fɛktʃuəl] *adj.* not having the ability, confidence, or personal authority to get things done

efficacious [ˌɛfi'keiʃəs] *adj.* working in the way you intended

inefficacious [ˌinɛfə'keiʃəs] *adj.*

efficacy ['ɛfikəsi] *n.[U]* the ability of something to produce the right result = effectiveness

例 11. In relation to an arbitration to which this Act applies, the Court shall have the following powers for the purpose of ensuring that any award which may be made in the arbitral proceedings is not rendered ineffectual by the dissipation of assets by a Party. 对于适用本法的仲裁案件，为确保在仲裁程序中作出的仲裁裁决不会由于

一方当事人浪费财产而无法执行，高等法院应当享有下列权力。

例 12. This TCM expert had explained its properties and said that small doses of it to be very efficacious in whooping cough and asthma. 这位中医专家解释了这味中药的药性，说少许药量就能非常有效地治疗百日咳和哮喘。

例 13. As noted above, the efficacy of the challenge mechanism relies on Parties or their counsel being willing to apply to disqualify an arbitrator and on an effective procedure when they do so. 如前所述，回避制度的实效取决于当事各方或其顾问是否愿意提出取消仲裁员资格的申请，以及他们在有此意愿的情况下，有无有效的程序可用。

(2)

efficient [ɪˈfɪʃənt] *adj.* if someone or something is efficient, they work well without wasting time,
    money or energy 效率高的

efficiency [ɪˈfɪʃənsi] *n.[C,U]* 效率，效能

inefficient [ˌɪniˈfɪʃənt] *adj.* not using time, money, energy etc in the best way 效率低下的

inefficiency [ˌɪniˈfɪʃənsi] *n.[C,U]*

例 14. The Seller guarantees that qualified technical personnel shall be dispatched in due time to provide professional, correct and efficient Information Service and Training. 卖方保证及时派遣合格的技术人员提供专业、正确而且高效的信息服务及培训。

例 15. If Supplier develops any products that are more efficient or less expensive than the comparable Products available under this Agreement, ABC will have the right to substitute the newer products at the same price as the comparable Products for all subsequent purchases under this Agreement. 如果供货商开发的产品比本协议项下可以获得的类似产品更有效率或价格更低廉，ABC 将有权在今后本协议项下的所有采购中，按照与类似产品相同的价格，购买较新的产品。

例 16. The staffing levels in the courts were being reinforced to that end. Once they are fully functional, the restructuring is expected to improve the efficiency of the justice system, particularly given that the new units in the largest courts will be equipped with a case management database. 为此正在加强法院的人事编制。一旦法院工作人员能够充分履行职责，改组工作预计会改进司法系统的效率，特别是考虑到将为最大的法院内的新部门配备一个案件管理数据库。

例 17. With a view to reforming the legal and judicial system to make it more efficient, accessible and accountable, the Government had established a legal and justice sector reforms commission, tasked with making appropriate recommendations, as well as a human rights commission to investigate human rights violations and propose measures to prevent human rights abuses. 为了改革法律和司法系统，使之更有效率、更加便民、更负责任，政府成立了一个法律和司法部门改革委员会，负责提出适当的建议。政府还成立了一个人权委员会，负责调查侵犯人权事件，并提出防止侵犯人权的对策。

efficient 和 effective 有时连用，表示有效率和有成效。

例 18. The efficient and effective implementation of the rights of indigenous peoples requires States to develop an ambitious programme of reforms at all levels to remedy past and current injustices. 既有效率也有成效地落实土著人民权利，要求各国在各个层面制定有胆识的改革方案，纠正以往和目前的不公正现象。

例 19. Effective and efficient labor policies and legislation ensure that every individual has the opportunity to practise a freely chosen occupation, in a safe, healthy, and productive work environment. 有效果而且有效率的劳动政策和劳动法律确保每一个人都有机会在安全、有益健康和富有成效的工作环境中从事自主选定的职业。

例 20. To implement the *Convention* effectively and efficiently, the Minister of Economic Affairs, Social Affairs and Culture decided to set up the Centro di Desaroyo di Hende Muhe (Center for Women's Development, CEDEHM). 为有成效且有效率地执行《公约》，经济事务、社会事务和文化部长决定设立妇女发展中心（Centro di Desaroyo di Hende Muhe，CEDEHM）。

embargo & embark

embargo [imˈbɑːgəʊ] *n.[C] & v.t.* 禁运

例 1. Force Majeure 不可抗力： Neither Party shall be liable for a delay in its performance of its obligations and responsibilities under this Agreement due to causes beyond its control such as, but not limited to, war, strikes or lockouts, embargo, national emergency, insurrection or riot, acts of the public enemy, fire, flood or other natural disaster, provided that said party has taken reasonable measures to notify the other in writing of the delay and its anticipated duration. Failure of subcontractors and inability to obtain materials shall not be considered as force majeure delays. 任何一方当事人由于非其所能控制的因由，例如，但不限于战争、罢工或关闭工作场地、禁运、国家紧急状况、暴动或骚乱、公敌的行为、火灾、洪水或其他自然灾害，延迟履行其根据本协议承担的义务和职责，只要该当事人已经采取合理的措施，将发生的延迟及其预计持续时间以书面形式通知对方，该当事人无须对该延迟承担责任。分包人不履约以及无法获得物料不应当被视为不可抗力导致的延迟。

embark [imˈbɑːk] *v.i.* 上船，登机，搭车
embark on/upon sth. = to start something new or important 开始，着手做
embarkation [ˌembɑːˈkeiʃən] *n.[U]*
反义词：disembark [ˌdisˌimˈbɑːk] *v.i.* 下（船、飞机、车）
disembarkation [ˌdisˌim.bɑːˈkeiʃən] *n.[U]*

例 2. Before you embark on a process of formal proceedings, always bear in mind that any such dispute must be disclosed to a future buyer of your property, which could blight a prospective sale in the future. 在您启动正式法律程序之前，请始终牢记：

今后有人要购买您的物业，就必须向他披露此类纠纷，这会破坏将来预期的销售。

例 3. Before you embark on either claim, it is advisable to get specialist advice relevant to your specific circumstances to avoid having your complaint dismissed and end up having to appeal. 在您提出任何一项赔偿请求之前，最好就您的具体情况征求相关的专家建议，以免您的投诉被驳回，最终还得提起上诉。

evidence, evident, evidential & evidentiary

(1)

evidence [ˈɛvidəns] *n.[U]* 证据； *v.t.* to provide evidence for 证明

作为名词，evidence 是不可数名词，中文"一件证据"可以译为 a piece of evidence 或 an item of evidence。

例 1. However, no evidence for the lump sum compensation payment was provided by the Company. The lack of proper evidence on this subject matter may suggest the Company was not in compliance with the Chinese Labor Law. 但是，XX 公司没有提供证明其一次性支付了上述补偿金的证据。关于这个问题缺乏适当的证据可能表明 XX 公司没有遵守中国劳动法。

例 2. The legal advisor is entitled to be present when statements are taken from the victim at all stages of the investigation of the case, and also has the right to attend all court hearings in the case, and to make statements, up to a certain point, in court. He or she also has the right of access to evidence in the case. 在案件调查的各个阶段，录取受害人的陈述时，法律顾问有权在场。法律顾问还有权参加该案的所有庭审，并在法庭上进行一定程度的陈述，有权取证。

例 3. There is no positive evidence that indicates that the subject imports have had a significant negative effect on domestic prices, as is also required the Article 3.2 of the *WTO Antidumping Agreement*. Indeed, there is no evidence presented to show that there has been a significant price undercutting by the subject imports as compared with domestic prices. 没有直接证据可以证明涉案进口产品对国内物价产生了显著的消极影响，而这种消极影响也是《世贸组织反倾销协定》第3.2条规定的条件。

实际上，商务部没有提供证据证明与国内物价相比，涉案进口产品采取过明显的降价行为。

例 4. Prior to fulfilling orders for such Products, AAA shall be entitled to request and receive documentary evidence of all such outstanding purchase orders and an accounting of Distributor's existing inventory of Products. 在完成上述必需产品的订单之前，AAA 有权要求和接收上述所有未交货订单的书面证据和一份经销商现有产品库存的账目。

例 5. Any notices of default or termination of this Agreement provided for hereunder shall be in writing and shall be sent by registered mail addressed to the other Party at its address here in above set forth or at such other address as the other Party shall have theretofore designated in writing. The date of giving any such notice of default or termination mailed by registered mail shall be the date on which such envelope was deposited, and the Post Office receipt showing the date of such deposit shall be prima facie evidence of these facts. 本协议规定的违约通知或者解约通知应当采用书面形式，并应通过挂号信函方式发送至上文规定的对方当事人的地址或者对方当事人此前以书面形式指定的其他地址。采用挂号邮件方式发送上述违约通知或者解约通知的日期，应当为挂号信的信封载明的日期，显示载明日期的邮局收据应当是上述事实的表面证据。

例 6. Any certification or determinations by a Finance Party hereto of a rate or amount under any Finance Document to which it is a Party is, in the absence of manifest error, conclusive evidence of the matters to which it relates. 本协议的融资当事人关于其作为一方当事人的融资文件项下费率或金额的证明或决定，如果没有明显错误，应当是与该证明或决定有关事项的确证。

例 7. Contractor will maintain books, records, documents and other evidence pertaining to costs, charges, fees and other expenses to the extent and in such detail as will properly evidence all costs for labor, materials, equipment, supplies and work, and other costs and expenses of whatever nature for which reimbursement is claimed under the provisions of this Agreement. 承包商应当保持有关成本、收费、费用和其他开支的账簿、记录、文件和其他证据，其范围和细节可以适当地证明根据本协议可以主张的劳动力、材料、设备、供货和作业的所有成本，以及其他各类费用和开支（例句中第一个 evidence 是名词，第二个 evidence 是动词。下面的例句中，evidence 是动词）。

例 8. "Real Estate Ownership Certificate" means the Real Estate Ownership Certificate issued in respect of the Land and the Building(s) evidencing the ownership of the Building(s) by the Mortgagor, a copy of which is contained in Schedule 2. "地产所有权证书"是指有关土地和建筑物的地产所有权证书，证明抵押人对建筑物享有的所有权，地产所有权证书的复印件收录在本协议的附件二内。

例 9. For the purpose of better evidencing the date on which the Initial Term commences, Landlord and Tenant shall execute an addendum to this *Lease* setting forth the Commencement Date and the expiration date of the Initial Term. 为了更清楚地表明初始期限开始的日期，出租人和承租人应当签署一份《租约》的附件，载明初始期限的开始日期和截止日期。

例 10. Furthermore, instead of respecting the limits of fair competition, the Respondent Party launched in the market a line of products that clearly reproduces each specification, characteristic, configuration and design of the famous HONDA GX engines, as evidenced by the pictures attached to the complaint (Doc. 13 of the complaint) and the technical expert report included in the records of the criminal writ of prevention previously filed by the Appellant Petitioner (Doc. 22 of the complaint). 此外，被上诉人并未遵守公平竞争限制措施，反而在市场上推出系列产品，该产品明显复制著名的 HONDA GX 型发动机的每一项规格、特征、结构和设计，附于起诉状的图片（起诉状的第 13 号书证）以及此前上诉人对之提出刑事防止令的法院的案卷中收录的技术专家报告（起诉状的第 22 号书证）可以证明这一点。

(2)

evident [ˈɛvidənt] *adj.* 明显的，显而易见

例 11. Agreements adopting a services-based approach allow addressing the specificities of services FDI. However, this approach requires a determination of whether an investment is a services or a non-services investment, which is sometimes difficult, even for statistical agencies. Such difficulties are also evident in the *GATS*, e.g. in the context of "services related to manufacturing consulting" or "services incidental to manufacturing". 采用基于服务方法的协定允许处理服务业外国直接投资的特定具体问题。但是，采用这种方法需要确定一项投资是服务投资还是非服务投资，而有时很难做到这一点，即使对于统计机构来说也是困难的。这种困难在《服贸总协定》中也可以看到，例如在涉及"制造业咨询服务"或"从属于制造业的服务"时。

(3)

evidential [ˌɛviˈdɛnʃəl] *adj.* of, relating to, relying on, or constituting evidence 证据的；与证据有关的；依赖证据的；构成证据的

例 12. According to *The Civil Procedure Law of the People's Republic of China* currently in effect, a duly notarized copy of the Real Estate Ownership Certificate shall, in the absence of evidence to the contrary, be of equivalent evidential value to that original certificate issued by relevant governmental agencies. 根据现行《中华人民共和国民事诉讼法》的规定，如无相反证据，经过依法公证的房地产权证副本与有关政府部门核发的该证原件具有同等法律效力。

(4)

evidentiary [ˌɛviˈdɛnʃəri] *adj.* ① having the quality of evidence; constituting evidence; evidencing. 具有证据特质的；构成证据的；起证明作用的；② pertaining to the rules of evidence or the evidence in a particular case 与证据规则或具体案件中的证据有关的

例 13. States Parties shall, subject to their domestic law, endeavor to expedite extradition procedures and to simplify evidentiary requirements relating thereto in respect of any offence to which this Article applies. 对于本条所适用的任何犯罪，缔约国应当在符合本国法律的情况下，努力加快引渡程序并简化与之有关的证据要求。

例 14. Dissatisfaction has been expressed by some members of the United States Congress with the operation of positive comity, because it is considered not to have led to improved market access for United States exports so far. United States business people have also alleged that there have been delays in investigations by the European Commission and that there are insufficient powers to compel the discovery of documents, as well as that evidentiary standards are too high. 一些美国国会议员对积极礼让的效果表示不满，因为他们认为，积极礼让至今为止没有使美国出口的市场准入得到改进；美国工商界人士还声称，欧盟委员会拖延调查，也没有充分的权力来强制提供材料，并声称证据标准太高。

例 15. With regard to illicit enrichment, one speaker raised the issue of the evidentiary challenges encountered in demonstrating that the enrichment was beyond the suspect's lawful income and suggested that it might be necessary for prosecutorial authorities to pursue the establishment of links to other criminal activities in related cases. 关于非法敛财，一名发言者提出了在证明所涉财物并非嫌疑人合法收入上遇到的取证困难，建议检察机关可能必须在相关案件中设法确定与其他犯罪活动之间的联系。

evolve, devolve, involve & revolve

(1)

evolve [i'vɒlv] *v.t.* & *v.i.* ① 进化，演化；② 逐步发展，演变

例 1. Piltdown Man proved to be a paleoanthropological hoax and cast a shadow on the theory that humans evolved from apes. 最终证明皮尔当人是古人类学领域的一场骗局，这给人类从猿进化而来的理论蒙上了阴影。

例 2. Some insects have evolved camouflage. For example, a flower mantis has wings that are shaped like petals. 有些昆虫逐渐学会了伪装，比如花螳螂长着花瓣形状的翅膀。

例 3. In addition, ethical standards, which by nature evolve with practical reality usually lack explanatory contents about their practical implications. 另外，操守标准本质上会随着现实的发展而演变，但又往往缺乏关于其实际影响的解释性内容。

例 4. There is often a dearth of care literacy, or understanding the ageing process and how it evolves, frailty, what caregiving entails, where to turn for services and information that can be of assistance, and how to monitor and improve the quality of care. 往往不具备基本护理知识，不明白衰老过程及其如何演变，不了解衰弱，不清楚照料别人需要做哪些工作，不知道向哪里寻求可能有帮助的服务和信息，不懂得如何监督和改进护理的质量。

例 5. TCEs were dynamic and constantly evolving due to changing circumstances, for example, climate change and the interests of the beneficiaries. The Delegation would expand with practical examples of TCEs that had evolved over time in East Africa during informals. 由于环境不断发生变化，例如，气候变化和受益人的利益，传统文化表现形式充满活力而且不断发展。代表团将在非正式会议期间利用东非地区不断发展的传统文化表现形式的实例做进一步论述。

例 6. The Special Rapporteur on torture and other cruel, inhuman or degrading treatment or punishment concluded "that there is an evolving standard whereby States and judiciaries consider the death penalty to be a violation per se of the prohibition of torture or cruel, inhuman or degrading treatment ... The Special Rapporteur is convinced that a customary norm prohibiting the death penalty under all circumstances, if it has not already emerged, is at least in the process of formation." 酷刑和其他残忍、不人道或有辱人格的待遇或处罚问题特别报告员得出的结论是"各个国家和司法机关根据逐步变化的标准认为死刑本身就违反了禁止酷刑和其他残忍、不人道或有辱人格的待遇或处罚……特别报告员相信，一项禁止在任何情况下使用死刑的习惯准则，即使还未出现，至少正在形成中。"

evolution [ˌiːvəˈluːʃən, ˈɛvəluːʃən] n.[U] ① 进化，演化；② 发展，演变

evolutionary [ˌiːvəˈluːʃənri, ˌevəˈluːʃəneri] adj. ① 进化的，演化的；② 渐进的，演变的

注意 evolutionary 与 revolutionary 的区别。

revolutionary [ˌrevəˈluːʃənri] adj. 革命性的

(2)

devolve [diˈvɒlv] v.t.& v.i. (formal) to transfer (rights, duties, or powers) to another or to pass
   (rights, duties, or powers) by transmission or succession （财产、权利、责任）转移

sth. devolve on/upon sb. / devolve sth. to sb. 将……移交或下放给某人

devolution [ˌdiːvəˈluːʃən] n.[C,U] the act or an instance of transferring one's rights, duties, or
   powers to another; the passing of such rights, duties, or powers by transfer or succession

例 7. The due diligence shall devolve upon a competent solicitor equipped with relevant expertise. 尽职调查任务由一名具备相关专长的称职律师负责。

例 8. Various government tasks, such as youth care, work and income and care of the elderly and long-term sick people have devolved to the municipal authorities, since they are closest to the people, and can provide customised services with less red tape and at lower cost. 由于市政当局最贴近民众，能够以较少的繁文缛节和较低的成本提供个性化服务，政府的各项任务，例如关爱青少年、工作和收入以及护理老年人和长期患病者，已经被移交市政当局。

(3)

involve [in'vɒlv] *v.t.* ① if an activity or situation involves something, that thing is part of it or a result of it 需要，包括；② to include or affect someone or something 牵涉，涉及，包含，包括；③ to ask or allow someone to take part in something 让……参与；④ take part actively in a particular activity 积极参与

involve 经常构成这样的词组搭配：involve sb./oneself in (doing) sth.。

involvement [in'vɒlvmənt] *n.[C,U]*

involve 在法律文件中使用频率相当高，翻译的时候要结合语境仔细体会，不要拘泥词典列出的译法。

例 9. According to the Act, closing a merger involves drafting a certificate of merger and filing it with the secretary of state. 根据这部法律的规定，完成合并需要起草一份合并证明书并将该证明书提交州务卿备案。

例 10. You would be well advised to avoid getting involved in a long-running legal dispute with this company. 明智的做法是避免卷入与这家公司的漫长法律纠纷。

例 11. Nowhere does the article mention the names of persons involved. 这篇文章并未提及相关人员的姓名。

例 12. Most rookies don't realize the amount of effort involving in drafting a legal document. 大多数新手没有认识到起草法律文件得付出多少心血。

例 13. The Ministry of Education is involved in an ongoing process of bringing educational standards in line with modern pedagogic practices such as mandating gender equality, broadening humanistic curricula and promoting scientific and technological studies, along with upgrading teacher status. 教育部参与不断提高教育水平的进程，使其符合现代教学实践，例如，除提高教师地位外，还规定性别平等、扩大人文课程和促进科学技术研究。

例 14. Contractor agrees that it shall not make any public announcements with respect to its involvement in the Work without the prior written consent of Owner. 承包人同意，事先未征得所有人的书面同意，承包人不应公开宣布自己参与工作。

例 15. The State Party is making genuine efforts to further involve civil society in the process of articulating its periodic reports to all the human rights committees. 缔约国正在一丝不苟地作出努力，以求进一步让民间团体参与向各个人权委员会清楚表述本国定期报告的流程。

例 16. Both Parties agree that emergency implementation of all or part of the *Disaster Recovery Plan* may involve emergency acquisition of certain equipment that may be readily available for demand. 双方当事人同意，紧急执行所有或部分《灾后恢复计划》可能包括紧急获取某些可随时满足需要的设备。

例 17. Singapore reported that capital punishment was available for murder, offences involving firearms and drug trafficking. It said that the death penalty had deterred major drug syndicates from establishing themselves in Singapore. 新加坡报告称，可以对谋杀、涉及枪支的犯罪和贩卖毒品判处死刑。新加坡称，死刑震慑了主要的毒品辛迪加，使其无法在新加坡立足。

(4)

revolve [ri'vɔlv] *v.t. & v.i.* 旋转，环绕，围绕

revolve around sb./sth. 以……为中心 / 主题；围绕……旋转

例 18. According to Copernicus, planets revolve around the Sun which is located at the center of the universe. 根据哥白尼的观点，太阳位于宇宙的中心，行星绕着太阳旋转。

例 19. In November 2012 the Court heard a case in interim injunction proceedings that revolved around a school board that had expelled a pregnant schoolgirl. 2012 年 11 月，法院审理了一起适用临时禁制令程序的案件，这起案件的争议点是一个教育委员会开除了一名怀孕的女学生。

同源词汇：
revolution [ˌrɛvəˈluːʃən] ① n.[C] 剧变，变革

例 20. Pixar Animation Studios brought a revolution in animation film industry. 皮克斯动画工作室给动画行业带来了一场剧变。

② n.[C,U] 政治性革命

例 21 The Storming of the Bastille signaled the outbreak of the French Revolution. 攻占巴士底狱标志着法国大革命爆发。

③ n.[C,U] 旋转，环绕

例 22. Engine speed can be measured in revolutions per minute (RPM). 可以用每分钟转数来测量发动机的速度。

revolutionize [ˌrɛvəˈluːʃənaiz] v.t. to completely change the way people do something or think about something: 引起革命性剧变
revolutionary [ˌrɛvəˈluːʃənri] adj. 革命性的；n.[C] 革命者

expatiate, expiate, expiration, expatriate & repatriate

(1)

expatiate on/upon sth. [ik'speiʃieit] *(formal)* 滔滔不绝地谈论；长篇大论地描写

例 1. And now the public being invited to the purchase of minor objects, it happened that the orator on the table was expatiating on the merits of a picture, which he sought to recommend to his audience: it was by no means so select or numerous a company as had attended the previous days of the auction. 眼前出卖的都是些次要的货色。桌子上面的演说家正在把一张图画推荐给各位买客，一味地称扬它的好处。那天到的人很杂，也远不如前几天拥挤。

注意：动词 expatiate 后面搭配的介词是 "on/upon"。

(2)

expiate ['ɛkspieit] *v.t.* 赎罪
expiation [ˌɛkspi'eiʃən] *n.[U]*

例 2. He expiated his sin of recreational hunting wildlife by becoming a veterinarian. 他当了兽医，借此补赎自己猎杀野生动物取乐的罪过。

(3)

expiration [ˌɛkspə'reiʃən] *n.[U]* a coming to an end; a formal termination on a closing date 期满，到期
注意：expiration 是美式英语，在英式英语中对等的词汇是 expiry。

例 3. All such insurance policies shall require the insurance carrier to notify Owner at least thirty (30) days prior to any expiration or termination of, or material change to, the applicable insurance policy. 上述所有保险单应当要求保险人在相关保单到期或被终止或发生重大变更之前至少三十（30）日将此情况告知所有人。

例 4. Upon the Expiration Date or termination of the Agreement, Distributor agrees to cease all display, advertising and use of any and all Marks. 自本协议到期日起或在本协议被终止后，经销商同意停止对于所有标记的一切展示、广告宣传和使用。

(4)

expatriate [ɛksˈpeitriət] *n.[C]* 侨民； *adj.* 侨居国外的； *v.t.* 侨居国外

expatriation [eksˌpætriˈeiʃən] *n.[C,U]* 旅居国外

expat [ˌɛksˈpæt] *n.[C] (informal)* = an expatriate

例 5. Asian cities now account for eight of the 10 most expensive places for expatriates to live, according to new research, up from seven in 2018. 根据最新研究，在侨民生活成本最高的十个城市中，亚洲城市从 2018 年的七个增加到如今的八个。

(5)

repatriate [riːˈpeitrieit] *v.t.* 遣返，将……遣送回国；将利润、资金调回本国

repatriation [ˌriːpætriˈeiʃən] *n.[U]*

例 6. U.S. President has called on America's allies to repatriate their citizens and try them at home. 美国总统已经呼吁美国的盟国将本国公民遣返并在本国对他们进行审判。

例 7. In 2017, the QIA was forced to repatriate more than $20bn in overseas deposits to stabilize the domestic financial sector after Saudi Arabia, the United Arab Emirates, Egypt and Bahrain cut diplomatic and transport links with the gas-rich state. 2017 年，沙特阿拉伯、阿拉伯联合酋长国、埃及和巴林切断了与这个蕴藏丰富天然气资源的国家的外交和运输联系以后，卡塔尔国家投资公司被迫把逾二百亿美元的海外存款汇回本国，以便稳定国内的金融业。

extent & extant

extent [ik'stent] *n.[C]* 规模；范围；程度；限度

注意区分 extent 与 extant。

extant [ik'stænt] *adj. (formal)* still existing in spite of being very old 现存的，留存下来的

extent 是法律文件中使用频率极高的词汇，常用于 to some extent, to the extent that 这样的
短语。

例 1. All decisions relating to the extent and mode of travel and other reimbursable expenses should be made with concern for efficiency and economy. 有关差旅范围和方式以及其他可报销费用的所有决定应当注重效率和节约。

例 2. Contractor, including its staff, shall view and process Owner Personal Data only on a need-to-know basis and only to the extent necessary to perform this Agreement or Owner's further written instructions. 承包商（包括承包商的工作人员）应当仅在必要的时候，而且仅以履行本协议或业主的其他书面指示为目的，查阅和处理业主的个人资料。

例 3. Whenever possible, each provision of this Agreement shall be interpreted in such manner as to be effective and valid under applicable law, but if any provision of this Agreement or the application of any such provision to any Party or circumstance shall be held to be prohibited by, illegal or unenforceable under applicable law or rule in any respect by a court of competent jurisdiction, such provision shall be ineffective only to the extent of such prohibition, illegality or unenforceability, without invalidating the remainder of such provision or the remaining provisions of this Agreement. 凡有可能，应当采用使本协议各条款依照相关法律具有效力的方式，对这些条款

进行解释，但是如果本协议的任何条款或者任何条款针对任何当事人或情势的适用，被具有合法管辖权的法院依照相关法律判令禁止、判定为在任何方面违反法律或无法执行，该条款仅在被禁止、被判定违法或无法执行的范围无效，该条款的其余部分或者本协议的其余条款的效力不受影响。

例 4. For Contractor's Worker(s) performing services for the Owner in jurisdictions outside the United States, in the event that local law does not permit background or criminal conviction screening to the extent required under this Sub-paragraph 2.2, the Contractor shall perform such required checks to the extent permissible under local law. 对于在美国以外的司法管辖区域内为业主履行服务的承包商的工人，如果当地的法律不允许本附件第 2.2 条所要求的背景核查或犯罪记录调查，承包商应当在当地法律允许的范围内开展上述核查。

例 5. To the fullest extent permitted by applicable law, Contractor shall defend, indemnify and hold harmless Owner, and its respective officers, directors, employees or agents from and against any and all claims, damages, losses and expenses, including attorney's fees, made or incurred by a third party and arising out of, related to, or resulting from the Work by Contractor, it agents, servants or employees. 在可适用的法律允许的最大限度内，承包商应该维护业主、业主的高级职员、董事、雇员或代理人的利益，给予其赔偿，使其免于负担由承包商、承包商的代理人、服务人员或雇员履行的工作造成的、与之有关的或由其引起的第三人所提出的或第三人所招致的任何和所有索赔、损害、损失和费用，包括律师费在内。

例 6. WHEREAS the Parties have held preliminary discussions on a future Co-operation, this Letter of Intent aims to reflect the Parties' present intentions in respect of certain matters to be addressed during the future. This Letter of Intent does not contain all of the material terms underlying the proposed Co-operation and is only binding to the extent specified in Section 7 hereof. 鉴于双方当事人已就未来合作事宜进行初步洽谈，本意向书力求反映双方当事人目前对于今后需要解决的某些事务具有的意向。本意向书并不包含构成拟进行的合作事宜的所有实质性条件，本意向书仅在其第 7 条明确规定的范围内具有约束力。

例 7. No such waiver shall, however, extend to any subsequent or other default or impair any right consequent thereon except to the extent expressly waived in writing. No waiver of any provision of this Agreement shall constitute a waiver of any other provision, whether or not similar, nor shall any waiver constitute any continuing waiver. 但是，上述放弃追究并不包括任何后来的或者其他的违约行为或者损害任何随之发生的权利，但是以书面形式明示放弃追究的除外。放弃本协议的任何条文不构成放弃本协议任何其他条文（不论这些条文是否相似），任何放弃也不构成任何持续放弃。

例 8. If any term, condition or obligation under this Agreement is or becomes, for any reason, wholly or partially invalid or unenforceable, such term, condition or obligation shall be enforced to the extent that it is legal and valid and/or replaced by legal, valid and enforceable term that reflects the purpose that the Parties intended with the invalid or unenforceable term best and the remaining terms, conditions and obligations shall continue to be valid and enforceable and shall be enforced, unless such enforcement is in manifest violation of the present intention of the Parties as reflected in this Agreement. 如果本协议之下的任何条款、条件或义务不论由于何种原因而全部或部分无效或无法执行，应当在该条款、条件或义务合法而且有效的范围内执行该条款、条件或义务，或者利用合法、有效和可以执行的条款来取代这些无效或无法执行的条款，以便最好地体现双方当事人原本打算利用该无效或无法执行的条款所欲实现的目的。其余的条款、条件和义务应当继续有效和可以执行而且应当得到执行，除非执行这些条款，条件和义务明显违反本协议所反映的双方当事人的当前意图。

例 9. The Law 346/2002 on insurance for labor accidents and professional diseases grants social protection to employed women, in the same extent as men, against the following categories of vocational risks: loss or diminution of labor capacity and death following labor accidents and professional diseases. 关于劳动事故和职业病的第 346/2002 号法律为女性雇员提供与男性雇员相同的社会保护，以防她们遭到以下类别的职业风险：丧失或减少劳动能力以及因劳动事故和职业病死亡。

facility & facilitate

(1)

facilitate [fəˈsiliteit] *v.t.* 有助于；促成，促进；便利；协助

例 1. To further enhance the quality of information collected and facilitate the process for States, the Secretariat also organized an expert group meeting in March 2007 to discuss the review of implementation, in particular information-gathering. 为了进一步提高所收集信息的质量并促进各国的信息收集工作，秘书处于 2007 年 3 月组织了一次专家组会议，讨论实施情况审查的问题，特别是信息收集问题。

例 2. To mobilize and facilitate the participation of United States private capital and skills in the economic and social development of less developed countries and areas, and countries in transition from nonmarket to market economies, thereby complementing the development assistance objectives of the United States, there is hereby created the Overseas Private Investment Corporation (hereinafter called the "Corporation"), which shall be an agency of the United States under the policy guidance of the Secretary of State. 为了动员和方便美国私人资本和技艺参与不发达国家和地区以及从非市场经济向市场经济过渡的国家的经济和社会发展，从而补充美国的开发援助目标，特此设立海外私人投资公司（以下称为"海外私投公司"），该公司是美国的一个机构，接受国务卿的政策指导。

例 3. The BORROWER undertakes to inform the BANK of the measures taken to seek damages from the persons responsible for any loss resulting from any such act; and to facilitate any investigation that The BANK may make concerning any such act. 借款人承诺向银行通报借款人采取哪些措施就上述行为所造成的任何损失，向

有关责任人员寻求损害赔偿，以及采取了哪些措施为银行可能对上述行为开展的任何调查创造便利条件。

例 4. *Kyoto Protocol* sets flexibility mechanisms to facilitate the countries committed and obliged by the protocol to comply with the greenhouse gas emission reduction. These flexible mechanisms are the CDM-Clean Development Mechanism and the JI or Joint Implementation. 《京都议定书》确立了有助于承担减排义务的国家 / 地区遵守减少温室气体排放义务的灵活性机制。这些灵活性机制包括清洁发展机制（CDM）和联合执行机制（JI）。

例 5. Oversight by legislative/governing bodies, being the main stakeholders in capital/refurbishment/construction projects, should not be underestimated. It is essential that these major investments — for both the organizations and Member States — be closely monitored and that clear reporting mechanisms be established throughout their execution, that look at their progress and the achievement of expected benefits. Close oversight by governing bodies would escalate the importance of the project, provide better discipline and motivation on the part of senior management, and facilitate timely decision-making by governing bodies for a successful project. 作为基建 / 翻修 / 新建项目的主要利益攸关方，立法 / 理事机构的监督不应该被低估。必须对这些重大投资（对于各组织和会员国而言）进行密切监督，必须建立整个执行期内的明确报告机制，必须审查预期惠益的实现进度，这一点极其重要。理事机构的密切监督将会逐步提高项目的重要性，为高级管理层带来更好的纪律和动机，并且推动理事机构为项目取得成功作出及时决策。

(2)

facility [fəˈsiliti] *n.[C]* 机构，设施；便利

facility 一般意思是设施、场所、机构。在贷融资类法律文件中，facility 的意思是提供融资便利的安排，可以根据具体语境，把它翻译成 "贷款" 或其他名目。

例 6. The Real Estate Property and its facilities are in good condition and repair, and are adequate for the uses to which they are being built, and none of it is in need of maintenance or repairs except for ordinary, routine maintenance and repairs that are not material in nature or cost. 对象公司不动产及其设施状况良好, 适合其预定用途, 除在性质或者费用方面无关紧要的正常例行维护和修缮外, 无须其他维护或者修缮。

例 7. If all the directors of the Corporation consent thereto generally or in respect of a particular meeting, a director may participate in a meeting of the board or of a committee of the board by means of such conference telephone or other communications facility as permit all persons participating in the meeting to hear each other, and a director participating in such a meeting by such means is deemed to be present at the meeting. When a meeting is held by conference telephone or other communications facility as aforesaid, the chair of the meeting shall confirm the presence or absence of each director orally and confirm to the other directors present whether or not a quorum has been established. At meetings held by conference telephone or other communications facility as aforesaid, every question shall be decided by an oral poll taken by the chair of the meeting and recorded by the secretary thereof and in the case of an equality of votes, the chair of the meeting shall have a second or casting vote. 如果公司的全体董事同意所有会议一律采用会议电话或能够让所有与会者听到对方发言的其他通信手段举行, 或者同意某一次特定会议采用以上方式举行, 董事可以借助上述方式参加董事会的会议或者董事会下设委员会的会议, 借助上述方法参加会议的董事被视为亲自出席会议。借助前述会议电话或者其他通信手段举行会议时, 会议主席应当以口头方式确认每一位出席或缺席的董事, 并且向其他出席会议的董事确认是否达到法定人数。在借助前述会议电话或其他通信手段举行的会议上, 会议主席应当采用口头投票方式决定每一个问题, 并由会议书记加以记录, 如果赞成与反对的票数相当, 会议主席应当进行第二次投票或进行决定性投票。

例 8. Finally, there are fundamental concerns as regards due process, transparency and the proper functioning of the procedures: not only are investment disputes usually conducted behind closed doors (doors also closed to affected stakeholders), but also not all of the arbitration facilities maintain public registries of claims, thus making it virtually impossible to have precise information about the number and nature of ongoing cases (see also UNCTAD 2004b and 2005e). 最后，在正当程序、透明度以及程序的正常运转等方面，也存在一些根本关切。不仅投资争端解决通常不公开进行（对受影响的利益相关者也不公开），而且并非所有的仲裁机构都对诉讼主张保存公开的记录，这使得事实上难以获得有关案件数额和性质的确切信息（又见贸发会议 2004b 和 2005e）。

例 9. This Agreement sets out the terms and conditions upon which the Lender will make available to the Borrower a loan facility of up to XXX USD (the "Facility"). The Facility shall be applied towards general corporate purposes. 贷款人将向借款人提供一笔最高额度为 XXX 美元的融通贷款（"融通贷款"）。本协议载明贷款人提供融通贷款所依据的各项条件。融通贷款应当被用于实现一般公司目的。

例 10. "Term Loan Facility Agreement" means the USD term loan facility agreement signed or to be signed by the Project Company as the borrower, the Company as lender, the Bank as facility agent and security agent and XYZ as the account bank for the granting of the Loan Facility; "定期贷款安排协议"是指项目公司、XX 公司、XX 银行和 XYZ 签订或者将要签订的额度为 XXX 美元的定期贷款安排协议，其中，项目公司作为借款人，XX 公司作为贷款人，XX 银行作为贷款安排代理人和担保代理人，XYZ 作为提供贷款安排的账户银行。

finalize & formalize

(1)

finalize [ˈfaɪnəlaɪz] *v.t.* to finish the last part of a plan, business deal, etc. 最后确定

finalization [ˌfaɪnəlaɪˈzeɪʃən] *n.[U]*

例 1. In 2017, the Working group finalized its report to the Subcommittee, including conclusions. 工作组在 2017 年最后完成了提交小组委员会的报告(包括结论)。

例 2. A new strategy for the MOST Programme is being finalized which will embrace a fresh perspective to recast core activities, by and within regions, in line with the criteria of relevance to current challenges, efficiency and high-level visibility for enhanced and sustained impact. 社会变革管理计划的一项新策略正在最终确定中，这项新策略按照与当前挑战的相关性、效率和高度透明的评判标准，以全新的视角，不仅按照不同地区重新安排核心活动，还重新安排各该地区内部的核心活动，以求使计划产生更大和持久的影响。

例 3. At the relevant time, having been advised by lawyers and accountants, both Parties were endeavouring to finalize the settlement of their differences. 当时，经律师和会计师建议，双方正在努力最终解决分歧。

例 4. The technical specifications need to be comprehensive and finalized at the time of commencement of the procurement proceeding. 在采购程序开始的时候，技术规范必须内容全面且最终确定。

例 5. The Developer has chosen to work with XXX Architecture, the original architectural firm that designed the Phase I of the Project, to update and finalize all the architectural plans for the 16 units. 开发商已经选择聘请最初设计项目一期的XXX建筑师事务所更新并审定16套别墅的所有建筑图纸。

例 6. At the time of finalization of the present report, the Government still had not shared the latest draft, which was reportedly nearly ready for submission to the Council of Ministers, prompting labor rights activists to join the latest protests against both the law on associations and non-governmental organizations and the trade union law. 在完成本报告的时候，柬埔寨政府仍然未就最新的法律草案与其他方面进行协商，据称这部最新草案几乎准备好提交部长理事会，这促使劳工权利积极分子加入了最近针对社团和非政府组织法和工会法的抗议活动。

例 7. In May 2015, it held an expert workshop to review the updated draft. The experts validated the annotations; the revised annotated code was to be finalized in Khmer and English in July 2015. 2015 年 5 月，人权高专办举办了一次专家研讨会，对经过最新修订的草案进行复审。与会专家认可了法律草案的注释；经过修订的高棉语和英语法典注释本将于 2015 年 7 月定稿。

例 8. A victim assistance protocol is being finalized, outlining the roles and responsibilities of key actors for the effective referral, provision and monitoring of the quality of services provided. 一份受害人援助协议正在最终定案，该协议扼要规定了主要行动方在有效移案、提供服务和监督所提供服务的质量方面起到的作用和承担的责任。

例 9. The delegation informed Costa Rica that Trinidad and Tobago had ratified the *Arms Trade Treaty* at an early stage, and was currently in the process of finalizing its implementation. 特立尼达和多巴哥代表团告知哥斯达黎加：特立尼达和多巴哥已经初步批准《武器贸易条约》，目前正在最后确定该条约的执行事宜。

(2)

formalize ['fɔːməlaiz] *v.t.* to make a plan, decision, or idea official, especially by deciding and
clearly describing all the details 正式确定

formalization [ˌfɔːməlaiˈzeiʃən] *n.[U]*

例 10. The Policy is aimed at structuring, formalizing and promoting cooperation
between the various agencies and disciplines active in reproductive health care. 这项
政策的目的是构建、正式确立和促进在生殖保健方面发挥积极作用的机构和学
科之间的合作。

例 11. Prior learning recognition helps people formalize their knowledge and experience (gained at work or elsewhere) so that it can be recognized. 承认原有学历有
助于人们使自己（在工作中或其他地方获得的）知识和经验合乎规范，使之可
以得到认可。

例 12. Other countries, such as Afghanistan, Bahamas and Colombia, have expressed a commitment to formalizing their engagement with stakeholders such as civil
society in their implementation efforts. 其他国家，例如阿富汗、巴哈马和哥伦比亚，
则承诺将它们与民间社会等利益攸关方合作落实可持续发展目标的工作正规化。

例 13. Mexico recognized the challenge of institutionalizing mechanisms for participation and the joint creation of public policies, and proposed as a solution the formalization of mechanisms for civil society participation. 墨西哥认识到将参与和共同
制定公共政策机制形成制度是一项艰巨任务，它提议将民间社会参与机制正规
化作为解决办法。

例 14. The adoption of regulations and agreements have formalized care work
and limited the expansion of private markets by requiring that migrant domestic workers pass a license examination to receive temporary residency and instituting salaries
and benefits similar to those of national care workers. 已通过多项法规和协议，将

护理工作正规化，限制私营市场扩张，要求移民家政工人通过护理证考试才能获得临时居留权，同时对移民家政工人的薪金和福利作出与本国护理工类似的规范。

例 15. Further, it is important that the receiving country open an investigation, in the course of which it prepares a mutual legal assistance request to formalize the transmission of information and complement the information received. 进一步讲，接收国必须开始调查，在调查过程中，接收国准备相互法律援助请求，使提供信息成为正式安排，并补充已经收到的信息。

foresee

foresee [fɔːˈsiː] *v.t.* 预见，预知，预料

注意：foresee 的现在分词、过去式和过去分词分别是：foreseeing、 foresaw、 foreseen。

foreseeable [fɔːˈsiːəbl] *adj.* 可以预见的

foreseeability [fɒˌsiːəˈbilәti] *n.[U]* 可预见性

unforeseeable [ˌʌnfɔːˈsiːəbl] *adj.* 无法预见的

unforeseen [ˌʌnfɔːˈsiːn] *adj.* 未预见到，出乎意料的

例 1. However, note that it is difficult to draw up an exhaustive list of breaches that will allow termination as it is hard to foresee all possible future outcomes at the time of entering into a contract. 但要注意：由于在订立合同时难以预见未来可能出现的所有结果，因此很难详尽无遗地列出可能导致终止合同的各种违约情形。

例 2. Affected Parties are required to take reasonable steps to avoid or mitigate the force majeure event and its consequences, although there is no requirement for a force majeure event to be unforeseeable. 虽然并没有要求不可抗力事件是无法预见的事件，但受其影响的各方仍须采取合理的步骤来避免或减轻不可抗力事件及其后果。

例 3. Such a globalized perspective of the entirety of the refurbishment/construction needs across the system in times of a global financial crisis, that is also affecting the contributions of major contributing Members States, will help all Member States to plan better in the long term and to foresee and respond more effectively to incoming demands for refurbishment/construction funding. 金融危机也影响到主要缴费会员国的缴费活动，而借助于这种全球化的视角对全球金融危机时代联合国系统内

全部翻修／新建需求进行审视，将有助于全体会员国更好地作出长期规划，预见并更有效地应对即将发生的翻修／新建供资需求。

例 4. The Breaching Party shall correct such breach within thirty days after receipt of written notice from another Party or the Company specifying the breach and compensate the Company and the other Party for all direct and foreseeable damages caused by the breach. 违约方应当在收到对方当事人或公司指明其违约行为的书面通知以后 30 日内纠正违约行为，并且向公司和对方当事人赔偿由违约行为所造成的所有直接的和可以预见的损害。

例 5. "Bill of Quantities" is the document in which the Contractor indicates the cost of the Works, on the basis of the foreseen quantities of items of work and the fixed unit prices applicable to them. "工程量清单"是承包人根据预测的施工项目的数量及其固定单位价格注明工程造价的文件。

例 6. "Force Majeure" means such unforeseeable events beyond the reasonable control of a Party such as, but not restricted to: Acts of God, war or warlike conditions, riot, sabotage and serious fire, radioactivity, typhoons, flooding, strikes and other internationally recognized events of force majeure, the occurrence or consequences of which are unforeseeable and unavoidable and cannot be overcome. "不可抗力"是指超出当事人合理控制能力的不可预见的事件，例如，但不限于：天灾、战争或类似战争的状态、暴乱、蓄意破坏和严重的火灾、辐射、台风、洪水、罢工及其他国际上承认的不可抗力事件。这些事件的发生或结果无法预见、不能避免，而且无法克服。

例 7. There is no action, arbitration or administrative proceeding of or before any court or agency started or threatened or which is reasonably foreseeable which might, if adversely determined, have a material adverse effect or which purports to affect the legality, validity, binding effect or enforceability of the EPC Contract save as notified to the Security Agent in writing and which is being contested in good faith. 不存在已

经提起或者扬言提起或者按理可以预见的，如果作出不利裁决，可能对 EPC 合同的合法性、有效性、拘束力或者可执行性产生重大不利影响或者表明影响的任何法院或者机构的诉讼、仲裁或者行政听证程序，但已经以书面形式告知担保代理人和被善意地提出异议的除外。

例 8. Notwithstanding any other term or provision of this Agreement to the contrary, the Agent shall not be liable under any circumstances for special, punitive, indirect or consequential loss or damage of any kind whatsoever including but not limited to loss of profits, whether or not foreseeable, even if the Agent is actually aware of or has been advised of the likelihood of such loss or damage and regardless of whether the claim for such loss or damage is made in negligence, for breach of contract, breach of trust, breach of fiduciary obligation or otherwise. The provisions of this Clause 23.17 shall survive the termination or expiry of this Agreement or the resignation or removal of the Agent. 即便本协议其他条款或条文作出相反规定，对于任何特殊的、惩罚性的、间接的或者相应而生的损失或损害，不论其属于何种类型，无论其是否可以预见，即使代理行实际上知道或者已经被告知有可能发生这样的损失或损害，而且无论是以过失、违反契约、违反信托、违反信托义务还是以其他理由提出关于上述损失或损害的赔偿请求，代理行一概不承担责任。即使本协议被终止或期限届满，或者代理行辞职或被解职，第 23.17 条的规定仍然有效。

from time to time & for the time being

from time to time 和 for the time being 在法律文件中做时间状语，使用频率很高。

(1)

from time to time sometimes, but not regularly or very often 不时，适时

例 1. Company shall have the right, in its sole discretion, to change any Annex from time to time during the term of this Agreement without liability to Representative. 在本协议有效期内，公司有权自行决定不时更改任何附件，而无需向代表承担任何责任。

例 2. The rates are determined based on experience and expertise of the lawyers/advisors performing the work. The rates are adjusted from time to time throughout our engagement. In principle, they are reviewed as per 1 January of each year. However, as the hourly rates of our associates depend on their seniority, they may also be subject to change throughout the year. 收费是根据承担工作的律师 / 顾问的经验和知识确定的。在本所受聘期间收费将不时进行调整。原则上，本所在每年一月一日对收费进行审查。然而，由于本所律师的小时收费取决于他们的资历，因此他们的收费在一年内也有可能发生变化。

例 3. "Associated Company", in respect of either Party, means any company which is from time to time a subsidiary or holding company of such Party or a subsidiary of any such holding company (as such terms are defined in the *Companies Act 2006*). "关联公司"，就任何一方而言，是指不时是该方的子公司或控股公司或任何

该控股公司的子公司的任何公司（这些术语在《2006年公司法》中作出界定）。

例 4. Any notice given under this Agreement shall be in writing and served by hand, prepaid first class recorded delivery (including special delivery) or first class registered post or prepaid international recorded airmail to the relevant addressee at the address referred to on Page 1 of this Agreement or such other address as the relevant Party may designate to the other in writing from time to time. Any such notice shall be deemed to have been served at the time of delivery. 根据本协议发出的任何通知均应采用书面形式，并由专人、预付费的头等舱挂号信（包括特快专递）或头等舱挂号信或预付费的国际挂号航空邮件按本协议第一页所述地址送达相关收件人或者相关方不时以书面形式指定给另一方的其他地址。任何此类通知应视为已在交付时送达。

例 5. The government procurement process is governed by the *Stores and Procurement Regulations* issued by the Financial Secretary under the *Public Finance Ordinance.* These Regulations are supplemented by *Financial Circulars* issued by the Secretary for Financial Services and the Treasury from time to time. 政府采购程序受财政大臣根据《公共财政条例》签发的《物料及采购规章》规限。财经事务及库务局局长不时发布的《财务通告》对该规章作出补充。

例 6. The Public Accounts Committee examines and reports from time to time on "the accounts showing the appropriation of the sums granted by Parliament to meet the public expenditure and such other accounts laid before Parliament as the Committee may think fit" (House of Commons Standing Order 122). 政府账目委员会不时审查并报告"显示议会为应付公共开支而批给款项拨配情况的账目，以及委员会认为适合提交议会的其他账目"（下院第 122 号常规）。

例 7. Owner desires to retain Contractor from time to time to provide the services, as more particularly described in Attachment F, for Owner at the Premises (defined in Paragraph 1 below). 所有人希望不定时地聘请承包人在场所（见下文第 1 节的定

义）为所有人提供服务，附件 F 对上述服务予以更详尽的说明。

(2)

for the time being: for a short period of time from now, but not permanently 目前，暂且

例 8. "United States Dollars", "US$" and "USD" means the lawful currency for the time being of the United States of America. "美元（US$ 和 USD）"是指美利坚合众国目前的合法货币。

例 9. The Company agrees that the process by which any Proceedings are begun may be served on it by being delivered in connection with any Proceedings in England, to [•] (Attention: [•]) or otherwise its registered office for the time being. 公司同意，据以提起诉讼程序的诉讼书状可以通过在英格兰的诉讼程序送交［•］（收件人：［•］）或者公司目前的注册住所。

例 10. (2) The authority conferred by a contractor licence:
(a) is subject to the conditions applicable to the contractor licence for the time being, and
(b) may, on the application of the holder of the contractor licence, be varied by an order of the Secretary set out in a notice served on the holder of the contractor licence.
（2）承建商牌照所授予的权限：
（a）须遵守当时适用于承建商牌照的条件，而且
（b）可应承建商牌照持有人的申请，借由部长在送达承建商牌照持有人的通知书内所列的命令而予以变更。

例 11. The quorum necessary for the transaction of the business of the Directors may be fixed by the Directors and unless so fixed at any other number shall be two but in the event of there being only one Director, one Director shall be a quorum. A meeting of the Directors at which a quorum is present shall be competent to exercise all the powers and discretions for the time being exercisable by the Directors. 处理董事事务

所需法定人数可由董事确定，除非另有规定，否则法定人数应为两人，但如果只有一名董事，则一名董事即为法定人数。出席人数达到法定人数的董事会议有权行使董事当时可以行使的一切权力和裁量权。

例 12. "The Act" means the *Companies Act*, Cap. 50 or any statutory modification, amendment or re-enactment thereof for the time being in force or any and every other act for the time being in force concerning companies and affecting the Company and any reference to any provision of the *Act* is to that provision as so modified, amended or re-enacted or contained in any such subsequent *Companies Act*. "法律"是指《公司法》（第 50 章）或任何现行的依法对该法所作的修改、修订或重新制定，或任何其他与公司有关并影响本公司的现行法律，凡提述《法律》的任何条款均指经如此修改、修订或重新制定的条款或任何后续的《公司法》所载的条款。

gazump & gazunder

gazump 和 gazunder（包括它们各自的动名词 gazumping 和 gazundering）是英国英语中一对押头韵的口语词汇，它们表示不动产买卖法律关系中两种对立的情况。

gazump [gəˈzʌmp] 是及物动词，意思是 the improper sale of a house, usually by raising the price after accepting an offer。

gazunder [gəˈzʌndə] 也是及物动词，意思是 to reduce the offer price of a property after agreeing to a higher one (normally just before contracts are exchanged)。

gazumping 和 gazundering 在英格兰和威尔士并非违法行为。前者通常表现为卖方在接受买方的要约以后提高屋宇售价。后者通常表现为买方在买卖双方交换合同之前降低屋宇报价。

鉴于它们目前不构成违法行为，译成"毁约抬价 / 毁约压价"似乎不妥，因为"毁约"在法律语境中具有应当承担违约责任的意思，而且这两个词带有口语色彩，我们不妨把 gazump 译成"（卖方）变卦抬价"，把 gazunder 译成"（买方）变卦压价"。

identify & identity

identify [aiˈdɛntifai] *v.t.* 分辨出，认出，识别，确定

identification [aiˌdɛntifiˈkeiʃən] *n.[U]*

identifiable [aiˌdentiˈfaiəbl] *adj.* 能够辨认 / 识别的

identity [aiˈdentəti] *n.[U]* 身份

例 1. UNCTAD could intensify its technical assistance, either from its trust funds on a demand- and needs-based basis or as a result of the beneficiary country having identified such needs as part of its national development plan or PRSP, and where the beneficiary had identified UNCTAD as its preferred implementing agency. 贸发会议可以强化其技术援助，技术援助可在需求或需要基础上从其信托基金中提供，也可以是由于受益国作为其国家发展计划或减贫战略文件的一部分查明了此种需要，并将贸发会议指明为首选执行机构。

例 2. This paper takes stock of recent trends in, and characteristics of, the existing universe of international investment agreements (IIAs), and identifies the most significant development-related challenges associated with the current investment regime. 本文件将评估目前国际投资协定大千世界的最新趋势和特征，并确定现有投资制度带来的与发展有关的最重要挑战。

例 3. Bills normally are submitted quarterly, monthly or at the conclusion of a matter. They identify the period and the matters covered, and may include, if the client desires, a description of the work covered by the fee. 本所通常按季度、按月份或者在完成一项事务时提交账单。账单标明收费所涉及的期间和事务，如果客户愿意，账单还可以对收费涉及的工作作出说明。

例 4. The application shall identify the question of law to be determined and, except where made with the agreement of all Parties to the proceedings, shall state the grounds on which it is said that the question should be decided by the Court. 当事人提出的申请应当认定需要高等法院查明的法律问题，除取得仲裁程序全体当事人同意的申请外，申请还应当说明基于何种理由应当由高等法院查明该法律问题。

例 5. The Hazard and Operability (HAZOP) study is a structured and systematic examination of a planned, modified or existing process intended to identify and evaluate problems that have a reasonable potential to present a risk to personnel, the environment, property or equipment, or prevent efficient operation. 危险与可操作性（HAZOP）研究是对经过规划的、经过修改的或既有的流程进行结构性和系统性检查，其目的是辨别和评估具有给人员、环境、财产或设备带来危险或者妨碍有效率运行的合理可能性的问题。

例 6. XYZ also stated in the 1998 Financial Statements that, during 1998, the sale of logs and lumber to ABC amounted to approximately US$537,000. These sales were identified in the notes to the 1998 Financial Statements as related party transactions. XYZ 还在 1998 年财务报表中表示，在整个 1998 年，XYZ 对 ABC 的原木和木材销售额约为 53.7 万美元。上述销售额在 1998 年财务报表备注中被认定为关联方交易。

例 7. Although the Fund is considered to be similar to an investment company, the Fund does not intend to register as such under the *Investment Company Act of 1940*, in reliance upon an exemption available to privately offered investment funds, and accordingly the provisions of the *Investment Company Act of 1940* (which, among other matters require investment companies to have disinterested directors, require securities held in custody to at all times to be individually segregated from the securities of any other person and marked to clearly identify such securities as the separate property of such investment company, and regulate the relationship between the adviser and the investment company) will not be afforded to the Fund or the Limited Partners of the Fund. 尽管本基金被视为类似于一个投资公司，但是本基金依赖私募投资基金可以享受的豁免，并不打算按照《一九四〇年投资公司法》的规定以投资公司的身份办理登记，因此该法规定的保障措施（除其他事务以外，要求投资公司具有无利害关系的董事；要求被托管的证券始终与其他人的证券各自区分和标识，以便清楚地将托管证券划定为属于该投资公司自有财产的证券；对顾问和投资公司之间的关系进行监管）不适用于本基金或者本基金的有限合伙人。

例 8. In Paragraph 95 of the report, he went one step further by stating that legal empowerment, access to justice and an independent judiciary and universal legal identification could also be critical for gaining access to public services. 在该报告第 95 段中，他进一步表示，法律赋权、司法救助、司法独立和普及合法身份，对获得公共服务而言同样至关重要。

例 9. In the context of Paragraph 2 (a) of this article, each State Party shall implement measures to ensure that its financial institutions maintain adequate records, over an appropriate period of time, of accounts and transactions involving the persons mentioned in Paragraph 1 of this Article, which should, as a minimum, contain information relating to the identity of the customer as well as, as far as possible, of the beneficial owner. 在本条第二款第（一）项情况下，各缔约国均应当实行措施，以确保其金融机构在适当期限内保持涉及本条第一款所提到人员的账户和交易的充分记录，记录中应当至少包括与客户身份有关的资料，并尽可能包括与实际受益人身份有关的资料。

implication

implication [ˌimpliˈkeiʃən] *n.[C,U]* 影响；指证；默示

例 1. A meeting of experts on the development implications of international investment rule—making was convened in Geneva (28—29 June 2007). Three challenges arising from the rapid proliferation, increasing complexity and diversity of IIAs—promoting policy coherence, balancing public and private interests, and enhancing the development dimension of IIAs for developing countries—were discussed at the meeting. 在日内瓦举行了关于国际投资规则制定所具有的发展影响的专家会议 (2007 年 6 月 28 日至 29 日)。会上讨论了国际投资协定的迅速增多、日益复杂以及多样化所产生的三项挑战，即促进政策的协调一致、平衡公共与私人利益、促进国际投资协定对发展中国家的影响。

例 2. The public hearing process is typically lengthy and expensive. This is particularly the case in circumstances where there may be significant environmental implications of the proposed pipeline. 公开听证程序往往时间冗长而且费用高昂。倘若拟铺设管道对环境可能产生重大影响，情况尤其如此。

例 3. The Police has tried to encourage students and parents to report school bullies but in small communities the implication of locals tends to be fairly risky. 警方试图鼓励学生和家长举报校园霸凌者，可是在这些小社区，指证当地人要冒相当大危险。

例 4. Each Finance Party irrevocably authorises the Security Agent to take such action on its behalf and to exercise and enforce such rights, powers and discretions as are expressly or by implication delegated to such Security Agent by the terms of this Agreement and the Security Documents and such rights, powers and discretions as are reasonably incidental thereto. 各位融资当事人不可撤销地授权担保事务代理人代表自己采取根据本协议和担保文件明示或默示委托担保事务代理人采取的行动，行使和执行根据本协议和担保文件明示或默示委托担保事务代理人行使和执行的权利、权力和裁量权以及合理地附带于上述权利、权力和裁量权的权利、权力和裁量权。

impose, imposition, impost & impostor

(1)

impose [im'pəʊz] *v.t.* 强制推行或实施

例 1. A certificate of public convenience and necessity issued by the NEB requires the approval of the Governor in Council (that is, the Canadian federal government cabinet). Generally, the NEB will also impose a series of conditions on issuing a certificate, relating to such matters as obtaining all other required federal and provincial approvals and evidence of binding transportation agreements for the proposed pipeline. 国家能源委员会签发的便利公众且为公共利益所必需的证明须经院督（即，加拿大联邦政府内阁）批准。大体上讲，国家能源委员会还将为签发证明规定一系列条件，这些条件涉及诸如取得联邦和省的所有其他必要的批准文件以及出具为拟铺设管道订立有约束力的运输协议的证据。

例 2. Where the law allows for different kinds of punishments to be imposed for conviction of an offence, the Court may, within the limits set by law, impose one or more of the prescribed punishments and determine the amount of each punishment. 凡法律容许一经定罪可处以不同种类的刑罚，法院可以在法律规定的范围内，判处法律订明的一种或多种刑罚并决定每种刑罚的额度。

例 3. Under the Act No. 94/2000, amending the *Code of Criminal Procedure*, courts may demand that the police impose what is known as a restraining order, involving a prohibition on a person going to a particular place or entering a specific area, or following, visiting or contacting the person protected by the order in any other way. In order for this order to be imposed, there must be reason to believe that the person concerned would commit an offence or in some other way disturb the peace of the other person. 根据第 94/2000 号法对《刑事诉讼法》的修订，法院可要求警方强制执行限制行动令，包括禁止某人前往特定地点或进入特定区域，或者以任何其他方式跟踪、访问或联系受到限制行动令保护的人。为强制执行此限制行动令，必须有理由相信有关人员会实施犯罪或者以其他方式妨碍另一方。

例 4. In addition to the federal income tax consequences described above, prospective investors should consider potential state, local and foreign tax consequences of an investment in the Fund. A Limited Partner may be subject to other taxes, such as estate, inheritance or intangible property taxes that may be imposed by various jurisdictions. Each prospective Limited Partner should consider the potential consequences of such taxes on an investment in the Fund. 除上文描述的在联邦所得税方面的后果外，潜在投资人应当考虑对本基金进行的投资在州、地方以及外国税收方面有可能产生的后果。有限合伙人可能需要缴纳不同法域课征的其他税金，例如遗产税、继承税或无形财产税。每一位潜在的有限合伙人都应当考虑上述税收对于向本基金进行的投资有可能产生哪些后果。

例 5. OLA supports the Secretariat services that are involved in construction operations, and, in particular, the Office of Central Support Services (OCSS) of the Department of Management. OLA advises them what to do contractually from a practical point of view. The offices away from Headquarters (OAH) consult OLA for any major project. However, the headquarters and OAH do not always comply with all of its suggestions. OLA gives guidance, but cannot impose its suggestions: business people in the field examine the options and make their decisions. The record shows that OLA should be consulted as early as possible, as such consultations normally lead to transparent procurement actions. Most claims occur when OLA has not been involved from the beginning. 法律厅支助参与施工运营的秘书处机构；特别是，法律厅支助管理事务部的中央支助事务厅。法律厅从务实的角度建议这些机构怎样按照合同办事。总部外办事处就重大项目向法律厅咨询。不过，总部和总部外办事处并不总是依从法律厅的一切建议。法律厅提出指导意见，但是不能强迫对方接受

意见，外勤业务人员审查这些选择方案然后作出决定。记录显示，应当尽早向法律厅咨询，因为咨询通常会促成透明的采购行动。大部分申索都是在法律厅没有从一开始就参与的情况下发生的。

(2)

imposition [ˌɪmpəˈzɪʃən] *n.[C,U]*

例 6. One of the innovations introduced into the code was a broadening of the definition of rape, with the result that "rape" in Article 194 of the code now includes other forms of sexual coercion and the exploitation of the victim's poor mental condition or inability to resist the action or to realise its significance. As a result of the amendment, offences in this category now carry far heavier punishments than before: imprisonment of 1−16 years, instead of a maximum of six years previously. Furthermore, circumstances leading to the imposition of heavier punishments for rape are defined in the law. Allowance is made for heavier punishments, firstly, if the victim is a child under the age of 18, secondly if the violence committed by the perpetrator is of major proportions and thirdly if the offence is committed in a way that inflicts particularly serious pain or injury. 该法典所作革新之一是扩大了强奸的定义，使法典第194 条的 "强奸" 现在包括了其他形式的性胁迫以及利用受害者较差的精神状态或不能反抗抑或不明白其重要性。由于这项修正案，该类犯罪行为现在接受的惩罚比以前重多了：监禁 1—16 年而非以前的最高 6 年。此外，法律界定了导致对强奸实施更重处罚的情况。第一，如果受害者是未满 18 岁的孩子，第二，如果犯罪人施予的暴力占主要部分，第三，如果以一种造成特别严重的疼痛或损伤的方式实施犯罪，可考虑给予更重的处罚。

(3)

impost [ˈɪmpəʊst] *n.[C]* a tax or duty, esp. a customs duty 税负（尤指进口税）

例 7. All sums payable by the Licensee under this Contract shall be paid in full, free of any restriction or condition, without set-off or counterclaim and free and clear of any deduction of taxes (including but not limited to withholding taxes), levies, imposts, duties, charges, fees deductions or withholdings of whatsoever nature. 被许可人根据本合同应当支付的所有款项应当足额支付，被许可人不得设定任何限制或者条件，不得抵消或者提出反请求，不含而且不得扣减任何税款（包括，但不限于，预扣税款）、捐税、进口税、关税、规费、扣除费用或者无论何种性质的扣缴名目。

(4)

impostor [im'pɒstə] *n.[C]* one who pretends to be someone else to deceive others, esp. to receive
the benefits of a negotiable instrument 冒名顶替者

(5)

imposture [im'pɒstʃə] *n.[C, U]* 冒名行骗

(6)

superimpose [ˌsuːpərim'pəʊz] *v.t.* 使叠加

例 8. All conservation projects should begin with substantial scholarly investigations. The aim of such investigations is to find out as much as possible about the fabric of the structure and its superimposed layers with their historical, aesthetic and technical dimensions. This should encompass all material and incorporeal values of the painting, including historic alterations, additions and restorations. This calls for an interdisciplinary approach. 所有保护项目均应首先进行大规模的学术调查。此类调查的目的是尽可能多地查明建筑物的构造、建筑物的叠加层以及这些叠加层在历史、审美和技术方面的含义。这项工作应当涵盖壁画的所有有形和无形价值，包括历史性改建、添附和修复。这就需要采用跨学科方法。

incorporate & incorporeal

(1)

incorporate [inˈkɔːpəreit] *v.t.* ① to form a legal corporation 成立为法人；② to combine with something else 包含，将……包括在内；③ to make the terms of another (esp. earlier) document part of a document by specific reference 吸纳

关于第一个义项，我们在处理法律文件的时候经常遇到企业名称后面带有 Inc.，我们学过 incorporated body 的意思是"法人"，Inc. 是形容词 incorporated 的缩写，也就是说 这个企业是组成法人的实体。另外，在法律文件中，介绍当事人的时候，经常使用 这样的句型：某公司是根据某法律成立并存续的法人。

例 1. The Mortgagor is a corporation, duly incorporated and validly existing un-der the law of the Cayman Islands. 抵押人是依照开曼群岛的法律正式成立和有效 存在的法人。

关于第一个义项，我们还可以体会下面的例句：

例 2. The Company is not a member of any joint venture, partnership or unincor-porated association (including a recognized trade association); or the holder of shares or other securities in any body corporate (wherever incorporated). 对象公司不是任何 合营、合伙或者非法人组织（包括获得公认的行业协会）的成员；对象公司也 未持有任何法人（不论在何处成立为法人）的股份或者其他证券。

例 3. Any judgment obtained in England in relation to a Finance Document will be recognized and enforced in the Borrower's jurisdiction of incorporation. 在英格兰 获得的任何与某一份融资文件有关的判决在借款人成立为法人的法域内将会得

到承认和执行。

关于第二个义项，incorporate 常常构成这样的句型：incorporate sth. into sth.。

例 4. The thing that chiefly struck visitors is that Le Corbusier, by employing architectural ingenuity, incorporated many environmentally-friendly features into the design of the building. 令游客们印象最深的是柯布西耶在建筑风格上颇花了一番心思，这座楼宇的设计含有许多环保特征。

例 5. Contract Equipment means the equipment, spare parts, part thereof supplied by the Seller including those which shall be incorporated in the Contract Project in order to ensure the designed capabilities, details of which are specified in the respective Sections. 合同设备是指由卖方提供的设备、设备的备件和部件，包括为确保设计性能而成为合同项目组成部分的设备、备件和部件。有关详情载于《技术规格》的各该条款。

例 6. Contractor shall incorporate safety, health, security, environmental and quality concerns, practices and procedures into all work to be performed for Owner. 承包人应当在为所有人履行的所有工作中注重安全、健康、治安、环境和质量问题，执行这些方面的惯例和程序。

例 7. The terms and conditions of this Agreement shall apply and shall be deemed incorporated into all purchase orders (each an "Order") which Owner subsequently may place with Contractor for the furnishing of services at the following location or at any other location specifically set forth in the Order (the "Premises"). 本协议的条款和条件，应当适用于并且应被视为纳入所有人此后可能向承包人签发的所有订单（各份订单下文称为"订单"），根据订单，承包人在下列地点或者在订单中专门规定的其他地点（"场所"）提供服务。

例 8. In case of LICENSOR's Background Works are incorporated into the Deliverable, LICENSOR shall grant to ABC a perpetual, fully paid up, non-exclusive, royalty free, non-transferable license to use any Background Works of LICENSOR in or connected to the Deliverable. 如果许可人的背景作品被纳入可交付作品，则许可人应赋予 ABC 一项有关使用可交付产品中包含的或者与可交付产品有关的许可人背景作品的永久性、完全付讫的、非独占性、免交使用费的、不可转让许可。

例 9. Notwithstanding anything contained to the contrary, Licensor shall be entitled to terminate this Agreement, at any time, by notice in writing to Licensee, in the event of Licensee becoming insolvent or making an assignment for the benefit of creditors, or a voluntary or involuntary petition in bankruptcy or insolvency being filed by or against Licensee or a receiver or trustee of the Business of Licensee being appointed or an attachment being levied against the property of Licensee and such receivership, trusteeship or attachment not being dissolved within forty-five (45) days from the date thereof, or of Licensee being in a similar situation pursuant to the laws of the country of incorporation of Licensee. 尽管存在相反规定，倘若被许可人无偿付能力或者向债权人转让财产、权利，或者被许可人自愿或者非自愿地提出破产申请，他人针对被许可人提出此类申请，或者任命对被许可人企业的破产财产管理人或者受托管理人，或者被许可人的财产被查封，且从实施破产财产管理、托管或者查封之日起四十五（45）日内，上述措施未被解除，或者依照成立被许可人成立为法人的国家法律的规定，被许可人遭遇类似处境，许可人应有权通过给予被许可人书面通知，随时终止本协议。

关于第三个义项，在法律文件中，incorporate 经常构成一个使用频率极高的句型：incorporated by reference into ... 意思是藉提述而被纳入……，其作用是行文简洁，避免冗赘，有些类似于我国法学界所称的"引用性法条"。

比如：《中国人民共和国合同法》第一百二十三条　其他法律对合同另有规定的，依照其规定。

第一百二十四条　本法分则或者其他法律没有明文规定的合同，适用本法总则的规定，并可以参照本法分则或者其他法律最相类似的规定。

第一百八十四条　供用水、供用气、供用热力合同，参照供用电合同的有关规定。

我们可以结合下面的例句体会这个句型的实际用法：

例 10. The following Exhibits attached to this Agreement are considered a part of this Agreement and are incorporated by reference. 附录于本协议的下列附件被视为本协议的组成部分，它们通过引述被纳入本协议。

例 11. "Agreement" means this master purchase agreement including all annexes and any other document specifically incorporated herein by reference. "本协议"是指此份主要买卖协议，包括它的所有附件以及经引述而明确地成为它的组成部分的其他文件。

例 12. Manufacturer certifies that the Equipment shall be designed, manufactured and assembled in compliance with those "Machine Safeguarding Specifications for New Equipment" set forth on Schedule 10(b) attached hereto and incorporated herein by reference, and Manufacturer will provide the documentation listed therein to XYZ upon or before delivery of the Equipment. 制造商现证明，设备的设计、制造和组装遵照本协议附件 10（b）列明的并且通过提述而被纳入本协议的"新设备机械安全防护规格说明"，而且制造商将在交付设备时或交付设备之前向 XYZ 提供该附件中所列的文献资料。

(2)

incorporeal [ˌinkɔːˈpɔːriəl] *adj. (formal)* 非物质的，无形体的

inhabit & inhibit

(1)

inhabit [inˈhæbit] *v.t.* to dwell in; to occupy permanently or habitually as a residence 在……居住

inhabitant [inˈhæbitənt] *n.[C]* 居民

注意区分下面的关联词：

inhabitable [inˈhæbitəbəl] *adj.* 适合居住的

habitable [ˈhæbitəbəl] *adj.* 适合居住的

uninhabitable [ˌʌninˈhæbitəbəl] *adj.* 不适宜居住的

inhabited [inˈhæbitid] *adj.* 有人居住的

uninhabited [ˌʌninˈhæbitid] *adj.* 无人居住的

例 1. The girl should have been alert when the local of whom she inquired this Instagrammable uninhabited island gave her an inscrutable smile. 这位姑娘向一个当地人打听那座网红无人岛，当地人脸上露出捉摸不透的笑容，当时她本该心生警惕。

例 2. The term "Montagnards" is a loose designation of some 30 tribes of "mountain people" in the central highlands of Viet Nam, composed of six distinct ethnic groups, including the Jarai. The area inhabited by the Jarai straddles Cambodia and Viet Nam; the Jarai on the Cambodian side are concentrated in the province of Ratanakkiri. "山民"这个词是对居住在越南中部高原的大约30个"山地人"部落的不严谨称谓，他们由六个明显不同的族群构成，其中就包括嘉莱族。嘉莱族居住的区域横跨柬埔寨和越南；居住在柬埔寨一边的嘉莱族集中在拉达那基里省。

例 3. Austen also wrote explicitly about houses, making the dwellings almost as important as the characters who inhabited them. 奥斯汀也详细描写房子，使住宅和住在里面的人几乎同样重要。

例 4. The Delegation of Austria stated that Austria was a federal republic state in Central Europe, with a parliamentary democracy, a member of the European Union, of the United Nations, as well as of most UN organizations. Of the approximately 8 million inhabitants, 98 per cent spoke German. However, like international applications filed at the Austrian Patent Office, national patent applications could also be filed in English or French. 奥地利代表团发言说，奥地利是中欧的一个实行议会民主制的联邦共和国，也是欧洲联盟、联合国以及大多数联合国组织的成员。在大约 800 万居民中，98% 的居民会说德语。不过，就像在奥地利专利局提交的国际申请，国内专利申请也可以使用英文或法文提交。

例 5. A speaker from Fiji described the myriad of efforts her government has taken on a national level to protect coasts and coastal inhabitants, as well as local government efforts to involve their communities in learning how to mitigate the effects of climate change. 斐济的一位发言人描述了斐济政府为保护沿海地带和沿海居民而在国家层面付出的各种努力，还有地方政府为了让本地社区了解如何减轻气候变化的影响而付出的努力。

例 6. The organization strives to promote a fairer and more inclusive society in which the right to health is applied equally to all inhabitants. 协会努力促进更公平和更包容的社会，让所有的居民平等地享受健康权利。

例 7. The WNBR is a unique forum for the co-production of knowledge for sustainable development between the inhabitants of biosphere reserves, practitioners and researchers. 世界生物圈保留地网络是生物圈保留地居民、从业人士和研究人员之间共同创造可持续发展知识的独一无二的论坛。

例 8. Curaçao is a small island (444 km2), with a small population (around 150,000 inhabitants in 2011), comparable to a small municipality in the Netherlands. News spreads fast, and what the community thinks matters. 库拉索岛是一座小岛（444平方公里），人口不多（在2011年约有15万居民），相当于荷兰的一个小自治市。消息传播速度快，社区的想法不容小视。

例 9. Today, with the climatic changes under way here, combined with high population levels and poor water management, many tribes' ancestral lands in this part of south-eastern Pakistan are becoming almost uninhabitable. 如今，随着此地正在发生气候变化，加上人口众多和水资源管理不善，巴基斯坦东南部这一地区许多部落的祖传土地正变得几乎无法居住。

例 10. With regards to your interest, we recommend that you take out a contents insurance policy, which includes the cost of alternative accommodation or loss of rent while your flat is uninhabitable. 为您的利益起见，我们建议您购买一份财物保险，其中包括您的公寓不适合居住的时候的替代住宿或租金损失的费用。

(2)

inhibit [in'hibit] *v.t.* ① to prevent something from growing or developing well 抑制，约束，妨碍；② to make someone feel embarrassed or nervous so that they cannot do or say what they want to 使……有顾虑：inhibit sb. from doing sth.

inhibited [in'hibitid] *adj.* 拘谨的，有顾虑的：be inhibited about (doing) sth.

inhibition [ˌinhi'biʃən] *n.[C,U]*

例 11. There is a good reason why people feel inhibited about commenting on this case. 人们不愿意就这个案子发表看法是有充分理由的。

例 12. Guarantee of anonymity given by the investigators dispelled this witness' inhibition. 调查人员保证不对外透露姓名，打消了这名证人的顾虑。

例 13. The current practice inhibits UNIDO from replenishing its pool of internal skills and competencies from the external market. This adds to the risk of lowering the level of in-house technical expertise, ultimately preventing the Organization from keeping pace with its external environment. 目前的做法妨碍工发组织从外部市场补充其内部技能和能力。这增加了内部技术专长水平下降的风险，最终使工发组织赶不上外部环境的新发展。

例 14. The Delegation of Namibia mentioned the discovery of penicillin, based on the observation that bacterial growth on dishes was being inhibited by mold containing penicillin. 纳米比亚代表团提到发现青霉素是基于观察到这样的现象：含有青霉素的霉菌抑制餐具上的细菌生长。

例 15. In respect of several UPR recommendations on domestic and gender-based violence, JS1 stated that domestic violence remained an acute problem. Legal loop-holes, inhibiting access of victims to justice, remained. 关于几项涉及家庭暴力和性别暴力的普遍定期审议建议，联署材料 1 指出家庭暴力仍然是一个严重问题。仍然存在妨碍受害人获得司法救助的法律漏洞。

irrevocable & irreparable

irrevocable [iˈrevəkəbəl] *adj.* 不可撤销的

irrevocably *adv.*

例 1. The Option Notice, once given, shall be irrevocable and binding on the Company and XYZ, and XYZ (or its designated Affiliate) shall be bound to purchase the Option Shares for the Purchase Price as set forth in the Option Notice. 行权通知一旦发出，即不可撤销并对公司和 XYZ 具有约束力，XYZ（或其指定的关联人）应当有义务按照行权通知中规定的购买价购买期权股份。

例 2. This letter Agreement is governed by the laws of New South Wales, Australia, and each party irrevocably submits to the non-exclusive jurisdiction of the courts of the state of New South Wales, Australia. 本协议书由澳大利亚新南威尔士州法律管辖，各方不可撤销地接受澳大利亚新南威尔士州相关法院的非专属管辖。

例 3. Each Party hereto irrevocably waives any objection which it might now or hereafter have to the courts referred to in Clause 10.2 (English courts) being nominated as the forum to hear and determine any Proceedings and to settle any Dispute and agrees not to claim that any such court is not a convenient or appropriate forum. 本协议各方当事人不可撤销地放弃自己现在或者今后对于第 10.2 条所称被指定为审理和裁决诉讼以及解决争端的法院（英格兰法院）可能提出的异议，并且同意不提出该法院并非方便或适当法院地的主张。

例 4. "Release Date" means the date on which the Facility Agent has certified that all amounts outstanding from the Company or the Project Company under the Finance

Documents have been irrevocably and unconditionally paid and discharged in full and no commitment to lend money to the Company or the Project Company is in force (such certification not to be unreasonably withheld or delayed); "清偿日期"是指某一特定日期，贷款代理人于此日已经证明公司或者项目公司融资文件项下的所有未偿付金额已不可撤销地和无条件地全额支付和清偿，而且，在该日已不存在向公司或者项目公司贷款的有效承诺（此等证明不得无故拒绝或者拖延）；

例 5. To the fullest extent permitted by law, the Company hereby irrevocably agrees that no immunity (to the extent that it may at any time exist, whether on the grounds of sovereignty or otherwise) from any proceedings, from attachment (whether in aid of execution, before judgment or otherwise) of its assets or from execution of judgment shall be claimed by it or on its behalf or with respect to its assets, any such immunity being irrevocably waived. To the fullest extent permitted by law, the Company hereby irrevocably agrees that it and its assets are, and shall be, subject to such proceedings, attachment or execution in respect of its obligations under the Finance Documents. 在法律允许的最大范围内，公司特此不可撤销地同意公司不主张亦不由他人代表公司主张，使公司的资产豁免（倘若不论在什么时候可能存在豁免，无论豁免是依据主权还是其他理由）任何诉讼程序、扣押（无论是在判决之前还是其他情况下为协助执行）或者豁免执行判决，或者对于公司的资产，不可撤销地放弃上述豁免。在法律允许的最大范围内，公司特此不可撤销地同意公司和公司的资产接受，而且应当接受与公司根据融资文件承担的义务有关的诉讼程序、扣押或执行。

(2)

irreparable [iˈrepərəbl] *adj.* 无法弥补的（是指难以用金钱补救）

例 6. The award of the arbitration tribunal shall be final and binding upon the disputing parties, and any Party to the Dispute may apply to a court of competent jurisdiction for enforcement of such award. Any Party to the Dispute shall, prior to the appointment of the arbitral tribunal, be entitled to seek preliminary injunctive relief, to prevent irreparable harm from any court of competent jurisdiction pending the constitution of the arbitral tribunal. Without prejudice to such provisional remedies that may be granted by a national court, the arbitral tribunal shall have full authority to grant provisional remedies, to order a party to seek modification or vacation of an injunction issued by a national court, and to award damages for the failure of any party to respect the arbitral tribunal's orders to that effect. 仲裁庭作出的仲裁裁决应当是终局裁决，对纠纷的各方当事人具有约束力，纠纷的任何一方当事人均可以向具有管辖权的法院申请执行该仲裁裁决。在指定仲裁庭的组成人员之前，纠纷的任何一方当事人有权提请任何具有管辖权的法院给予临时性禁制救济，以防止在仲裁庭组成期间遭受无法用金钱弥补的损害。仲裁庭应当具有给予临时性救济的充分权力，有权责令一方当事人设法修改或撤销由本国法院签发的禁制令，倘若当事人不遵守仲裁庭的上述命令，仲裁庭有权裁决其赔偿损失，但是仲裁庭不得损害可以由本国法院给予的上述临时性救济。

例 7. Manufacturer understands and agrees that any breach of the terms of this Section would result in irreparable injury and damage to ABC for which ABC would have no adequate remedy at law; Manufacturer therefore also agrees that, in the event of said breach or any threat of such breach, ABC shall be entitled, in addition to any other remedies to which ABC may be entitled at law or in equity, to an immediate injunction and restraining order to prevent such breach and/or threatened breach and/or continued breach by Manufacturer and/or any and all persons and/or entities acting for and/or with and/or on behalf of Manufacturer, without the necessity of proving its damages. Manufacturer agrees that it will not use ABC's name whether by including reference to ABC in any list of customers advertising that its services or products are used by ABC or otherwise, without written authorization by ABC. 制造商理解并且同意违反本条的规定将给 ABC 造成难以用金钱弥补的伤害和损害，对此 ABC 无法获得法律上的充分补救；因此，制造商还同意，如果发生违反本条的情形或有这样的危险，ABC 除可以在普通法或衡平法上享有的任何其他补救外，ABC 还应当有权获得即时禁制令和限制令，以阻止制造商和 / 或为制造商执行事务和 / 或与制造商一起执行事务和 / 或代表制造商执行事务的所有人和 / 或实体违反

本条和 / 或威胁违反本条和 / 或继续违反本条，ABC 无须证明自己所受损害。制造商同意，在未征得 ABC 书面授权的情况下，制造商不会采取在任何客户名单中提及 ABC 名称的办法或是使用 ABC 名称的其他办法，借此宣传 ABC 使用其服务或产品。

judicial, judicious, judiciary & judicature

注意：不要混淆形容词 judicial 和 judicious 的意思，judiciary 和 judicature 是集合名词。

(1)

judicial [dʒuːˈdiʃəl] *adj.* relating to the law, judges, or their decisions 司法的

例如：the judicial system 司法系统；the judicial review 司法审查。

(2)

judicious [dʒuːˈdiʃəs] *adj. (formal)* done in a sensible and careful way: 审慎的

例 1. Negative media coverage has not been provoked due to the court's judicious application of the rule of evidence. 法庭慎重运用了这项证据规则，所以没有招致媒体的负面报道。

例 2. The defense attorney gave a judiciously worded statement yesterday. 辩护律师昨天发表了一份措词审慎的声明。

(3)

the judiciary [dʒuːˈdiʃəri] 司法机构；司法系统；司法部门

(4)

the judicature [ˈdʒuːdəkətʃə] 司法机构；司法系统；司法部门

justify

justify [ˈdʒʌstifai] *v.t.* 列出理由证明；有充分理由支持；具有正当理由；提出……的理由

例 1. The directors may from time to time pay to the members such interim dividends as appear to the directors to be justified by the profits of the Company. 董事可以不时向成员支付在董事看来根据公司利润正当合理的期中股息。

例 2. No order has been made, or application filed, or resolution passed or a notice of intention given to pass a resolution for the winding up or bankruptcy of the Company and, to the best of the Vendors' knowledge, information and belief, there are no circumstances justifying commencement of any such action. 对于 XX 公司，没有作出责令其停业清理或者破产的命令，或者提交这样的申请，或者通过这样的决议，或者发出意图作出此类决议的通知，而且就卖方所确知及确信，不存在开始上述任何行动的正当情势。

例 3. The projected creation of 267 jobs is more than sufficient to justify raising $16 to $18 million from 16 to 18 qualified foreign investors at $1,000,000 each. 预计创造的 267 个工作岗位可以绰绰有余地证明向 16 到 18 位合格外国投资人筹集（每人 100 万美元）1600 万到 1800 万美元是合情合理的举措。

例 4. Thus understood, on the findings of the judge in the petition and the cross-petition, I am unable to see any justification for allowing an interest factor on the purchase price in the present case to give compensation to XYZ for any injury done to it for not participating in the benefits of the Company when it was excluded after the presentation of its petition, which was dismissed. 按照这样的理解，根据 XXX 法官

对呈请和交叉呈请得出的调查结论，我无法看出在本案中有何正当理由容许购买价款的利息因素，以便就 XYZ 遭受的损害——因为 XYZ 在提出它的呈请（该呈请被驳回）之后遭到排斥，无法参与分享 XX 公司的权益——给予其补偿。

例 5. Where any person is approached in connection with his possible appointment as an arbitrator, he shall disclose any circumstance likely to give rise to justifiable doubts as to his impartiality or independence. 凡有可能被委任为仲裁员的人均应披露任何有可能导致对其是否具备公正或独立品性产生正当疑虑的情况。

例 6. Notwithstanding any delay in raising a plea referred to in Subsection (4) or (6), the arbitral tribunal may admit such plea if it considers the delay to be justified in the circumstances. 即便当事人提出本条第（4）款或第（6）款中提到的抗辩时发生延误，但是如果仲裁庭根据具体情况认为所发生的延误具有正当理由，则仲裁庭可以受理上述抗辩。

例 7. Moreover, the right to equality before the courts prohibits any distinction regarding access to courts and tribunals that are not based on law and cannot be justified on objective and reasonable grounds. 另外，在法院面前平等的权利禁止在未依法以及不能依据客观合理的理由认定合理的情况下诉诸法院和法庭方面进行任何区别待遇。

levy

在法律文件中经常用到 levy 这个词，它既可以用作及物动词，也可以用作名词。《布莱克法律词典》对这个词给出了如下释义：

levy [ˈlɛvi] *n.[C]* the imposition of a fine or tax; the fine or tax so imposed

v.t. to impose or assess (a fine or a tax) by legal authority

作为动词，levy 常构成这样的短语：levy a tax on sth.。

根据上述释义，我们可以看出动词 levy 的意思是征收（罚款或税款），名词 levy 的意思是（征收的）罚款或税款。

例 1. Tax means a tax, levy, duty, charge, deduction or withholding, however it is described, that is imposed by law or by a Government Agency, together with any related interest, penalty, fine or other charge. 赋税是指由法律或由政府机构征收的各类税捐、费用、扣减或预提（不论其名称为何），包括任何相关利息、罚款、罚金或其他收费。

备注：句中 tax、levy、duty 三个词均有税款的意思，中文译文不易体现，且句中 however it is described，所以处理成"各类税捐"。

例 2. In the Province of Alberta, the *Mines and Minerals Act* (Alberta) governs the management and disposition of rights in Crown-owned mines and minerals, including the levying and collecting of bonuses, rentals and royalties. 在阿尔伯塔省，对王室所有的矿藏和矿物权利进行管理和处分，包括课征和收取红利、租金和使用费，应当遵守《矿藏和矿物法》（阿尔伯塔省）的规定。

例 3. The Board of Trustees shall determine whether or not any charge for tuition, or registration fee, shall be levied in any department of the University, and the amount of such charge or fee; and it may exempt residents of California from the payment of any such charge or fee. 受托人董事会应当决定斯坦福大学的院系是否收取学费或注册费以及学费或注册费的金额；受托人董事会可以免除加利福尼亚居民交纳学费或注册费的义务。

例 4. The Parent shall pay to the Contractor the amount calculated under Clause 2.2 (the "Incentive") as incentive for an early completion of the Project and as compensation for any and all cost increases which is and/or will be suffered by the Contractor due to the late effectiveness of the EPC Contract, all fees and charges which will be levied in connection with the Governmental Approvals and the termination of the *Consultancy Agreement.* 母公司应向承包商支付根据第 2.2 条计算出来的金额（"奖励金"），用以奖励项目尽早完工，并补偿承包商因工程总承包合同延迟生效而增加和 / 或将要增加的一切开支，以及补偿与政府批准和终止《顾问协议》有关的全部费用。

例 5. All payments of principal and interest by the Borrower shall be made without set-off or counterclaim and free and clear of and without deduction for or on account of any and all taxes, levies, imposts, deductions or withholdings of whatever nature now or hereafter imposed. In the event that the Borrower is required by law or regulation to make a payment subject to any tax or other deductions, then the Borrower shall pay such additional amounts as will ensure that the Lender receives the amount that it would have been entitled to receive if no such deduction or withholding were required or made. 借款人不得对其偿付的所有本金和利息进行抵消或者提出反请求，借款人偿付的所有本金和利息不含而且未扣除目前或者今后课征的任何和所有税金、捐税、进口税、扣除费用或者扣缴费用。如果有关法律或者规定要求借款人缴纳任何税款或者扣除其他费用，那么借款人应当支付额外的款项，以便确保贷款人收到的款额等于假若没有要求或者进行扣除或者扣缴，贷款人原本有权收到的款额。

例 6. All payments to be made by the Company to any person under any Finance Document shall be made free and clear of and without deduction or withholding for or on account of Tax imposed or levied by or on behalf of any taxing authority in the PRC and/or any jurisdiction from or through which any payment is made or caused to be made by or on behalf of the Company unless the Company or any person on its behalf is required to make such a payment subject to the deduction or withholding of such Tax, in which case the sum payable by the Company in respect of which such deduction or withholding is required to be made shall be increased to the extent necessary to ensure that, after the making of the required deduction or withholding, such person receives and retains (free from any liability in respect of any such deduction or withholding) a net sum equal to the sum which it would have received and so retained had no such deduction or withholding been made or required to be made. 公司根据融资文件应当向任何人支付的款项，应当免除而且不得扣除或扣缴中国和 / 或公司支付或代表公司支付或者促使公司支付或促使代表公司支付该款项所在或所经过的司法管辖区的税务机关规定或征收或者代表上述税务机关规定或征收的税款，除非公司或代表公司的任何人支付该款项必须扣除或扣缴上述税款，在此情形下，应当提高必须扣除或扣缴税款的公司应付款项的金额，以便确保在扣除或扣缴必要税款之后，收款人收到和保有（不承担扣除或扣缴税款的义务）的净金额等于假若没有扣除或扣缴税款或者没有被要求扣除或扣缴税款，收款人原本应当收到的款额。

mediate & meditate

(1)

mediate ['miːdieit] *v.t.* & *v.i.* 调解，调停

mediation [ˌmiːdi'eiʃən] *n.[U]* 调解，调停

mediator ['miːdieitə] 调解人；通过调解程序帮助争议双方达成和解的中立的第三方

例 1. It is reported that Switzerland has agreed to mediate talks between Cameroonian authorities and separatists in a bid to end escalating violence in the country's Anglophone regions. 据报道，瑞士已经同意调停喀麦隆政府与分离主义分子之间的会谈，试图结束喀麦隆英语区不断升级的暴力冲突。

例 2. ALTERNATIVE MEANS OF DISPUTE RESOLUTION

SEC. 118 (42 *U.S.C.* 1981 note)

Where appropriate and to the extent authorized by law, the use of alternative means of dispute resolution, including settlement negotiations, conciliation, facilitation, mediation, factfinding, minitrials, and arbitration, is encouraged to resolve disputes arising under the Acts or provisions of Federal law amended by this title.

解决争端的替代性方法

第 118 条（《美国法典》第 42 编第 1981 条注释）

在适当的情况下和在法律准许的范围内，鼓励使用包括和解谈判、和解、斡旋、调解、事实调查、非讼公断和仲裁在内的解决争端的替代性方法，以便解决在经过本编修订的各该法律或者联邦法律规定之下产生的争端。

例 3. In any case where an agreement provides for the appointment of a mediator by a person who is not one of the parties and that person refuses to make the appointment or does not make the appointment within the time specified in the agreement or, if no time is so specified, within a reasonable time of being requested by any party to the agreement to make the appointment, the Chairman of the Singapore Mediation Centre may, on the application of any party to the agreement, appoint a mediator who shall have the like powers to act in the mediation proceedings as if he had been appointed in accordance with the terms of the agreement. 凡有协议规定由不属于双方当事人中任何一方的人委任调解人，此人拒绝委任调解人或者在协议指定的时间内没有委任，或者如果协议没有规定作出委任的时间，此人在协议任何一方当事人要求其委任调解人的合理时间内没有委任，则新加坡调解中心主席可以按照协议任何一方当事人的申请委任一位调解人，该调解人应当享有假如他或她是依照协议的条件被委任，他或她在调解程序中所享有的类似权力。

例 4. Unless a contrary intention appears therein, an agreement which provides for the appointment of a mediator shall be deemed to contain a provision that in the event of the mediation proceedings failing to produce a settlement acceptable to the parties within 4 months, or such longer period as the parties may agree to, of the date of the appointment of the mediator or, where he is appointed by name in the agreement, of the receipt by him of written notification of the existence of a dispute, the mediation proceedings shall thereupon terminate. 凡协议规定委任调解人，除非该协议表明相反的意图，该协议应被视为含有这样一个条文，即，如果自委任调解人之日起，或者凡在协议中指定调解人的姓名，则自调解人收到关于存在纠纷的书面通知之时起，调解程序在四个月内，或者在双方当事人认可的更长期限内，没有达成可以让双方当事人接受的和解结果，则调解程序届时应当终止。

(2)

meditate ['mɛditeit] ① v.i. 默想，冥想；② v.i. 沉思，思索 meditate on/upon sth.; ③ v.t. (formal) 筹划，策划

注意：meditate 的前两个义项是不及物动词，第三个义项是及物动词。第二个义项"思索"后面搭配的介词是 on 或 upon。

meditation [ˌmɛdiˈteiʃən] ① n.[U] 默想，冥想；② n.[C usually plural, U] 沉思，思索，思考

meditative ['mɛditeitiv] *adj.* 思索的；冥想的

例 5. They have been meditating on the very great pleasure which a feast in this fancy restaurant in the Upper East Side can bestow. 他们在回味上东区的这家豪华餐馆的一场盛宴所能赐予的莫大快乐。

例 6. The air blew cold on our foreheads, and the coarse African wine still tasted good: we were still happy, but meditatively, with the shouting and hilarious mood finished. 冷风吹上了我们的额头，低劣的非洲葡萄酒味道仍是不错，我们仍然开心，然而有了心事，没心情喊叫和欢闹。（选自《巴黎伦敦落魄记》孙仲旭译文）

还要注意 meditate 的一个派生词：premeditated [ˌpriːˈmediteitid] *adj.* done with willful deliberation and planning; considered beforehand 预先考虑的，预先谋划的；有预谋的。
premeditated murder 预谋杀人；蓄意杀人
premeditation [priːˌmediˈteiʃən] *n.[U]* 预谋，预先策划

例 7. The defense attorney has employed every trial tactic to inculcate into the jury such an idea that it is a case of diminished responsibility rather than a case of premeditated murder. 辩护律师用了各种庭审策略灌输给陪审团这样的想法：被告人并非预谋杀人，而是精神失常，需要减轻刑事责任。

negligent & negligible

negligent ['neglidʒənt] *adj.* 过失的；疏忽的

例 1. This Agreement constitutes the entire agreement and understanding of the Parties relating to the subject matter of this Agreement and supersedes any previous agreement or understanding between the Parties in relation to such subject matter. In entering into this Agreement, the Parties have not relied on any statement, representation, warranty, understanding, undertaking, promise or assurance (whether negligently or innocently made) of any person (whether Party to this Agreement or not) other than as expressly set out in this Agreement. Each Party irrevocably and unconditionally waives all claims, rights and remedies which but for this Clause it might otherwise have had in relation to any of the foregoing. Nothing in this Clause shall limit or exclude either Party's liability for fraud. 本协议构成双方关于本协议标的的完整协议和谅解，并取代双方以前关于该标的达成的任何协议或谅解。双方在订立本协议时，除本协议明确规定外，不依赖任何人（无论是否为本协议的当事方）的任何说明、陈述、担保、谅解、承诺、允诺或保证（无论是出于疏忽为之还是无心为之）。各方不可撤销且无条件地放弃若无本条之规定该方原本可就前述任何一项享有的一切申索、权利和补救措施。本条款的任何内容不得限制或排除任何一方应承担的欺诈责任。

例 2. Art. 15 Definition of Criminal Negligence.

(1) In this Code and in the provisions of any law that defines offences:

(a) a person negligently engages in conduct where the conduct is a marked departure from the ordinary standard of reasonable care; and

(b) conduct is engaged in negligently in respect of a result or circumstance where it is a marked departure from the ordinary standard of reasonable care to take the risk that the result will come about or that the circumstance exists.

(2) The standard of reasonable care shall be interpreted with regard to all the circumstances of the case, including the age, experience, education, occupation, rank and any other relevant characteristics of the accused.

第 15 条　刑事疏忽的定义

(1) 在本法典以及任何界定罪行的法律条文中：

(a) 凡一个人的行为明显违反通常的合理谨慎标准，此人即因疏忽而作出该行为；及

(b) 如冒将会发生某种结果或存在相关情况的风险而行动是明显违反通常的合理谨慎标准，那么就这种结果或情况而言，该行动是因疏忽而作出的。

(2) 对合理谨慎标准进行解释须考虑案件的所有情况，包括被控告人的年龄、经历、教育、职业、地位以及任何其他相关的特征。

例 3. Limitation of liability: Seller shall not be liable to buyer in any action or claim for incidental, special, consequential, indirect, punitive, exemplary or statutory damages arising out of or related to this contract, whether the action in which recovery of damages is sought is based upon contract, tort (including, to the greatest extent permitted by law, the sole, concurrent or other negligence, whether active or passive, and strict liability of seller), statute or otherwise even if seller has been advised of such possibility of such damages. Seller's liability for any claim of any kind, for any loss or damage arising out of, connected with or resulting from this agreement, or from the performance or breach thereof, shall in no case exceed (at seller's sole discretion) the purchase price allocable to the goods or unit thereof which gives rise to the claim or the replacement of such defective goods or such unit thereof by seller. For undelivered goods, seller's liability is limited to the difference between the market price and seller's price. Seller shall not be liable for penalty clauses of any description. Any action resulting from any claim arising under this agreement which is brought by buyer against seller must be commenced within one (1) year after the cause of action has accrued. 责任限制：卖方无须就任何寻求本合约引起的或与本合约有关的附带、特

214

别、相应而生、间接、惩罚性、惩戒性或法定损害赔偿的诉讼或申索向买方承担责任，无论寻求追讨损害赔偿的诉讼所依据的是合约、侵权（在法律允许的最大范围内，包括卖方的单一、并存或其他疏忽，不论其为积极疏忽还是消极疏忽，还包括卖方的严格责任）、成文法抑或其他情况，即使已经告知卖方可能发生该损害赔偿。对于本协议产生的、与本协议有关的或本协议引致的或者由于履行或违反本协议引起的不论何种申索、损失或损害，卖方承担的责任在任何情况下不得超过（由卖方全权酌情决定）引起上述申索的货品或货品单元的购买价款或者由卖方更换该有缺陷的货品或货品单元。对于尚未交付的货品，卖方的责任限于市场价格与卖方的价格之间的差额。卖方无须就任何类型的处罚条款承担责任。凡买方针对卖方提起诉讼，而引起该诉讼的是根据本协议产生的任何申索，该诉讼必须在产生诉因之后一（1）年内开始。

注意 negligent 与 negligible 的区别：

negligible [ˈneɡlidʒəbl] *adj.* 微不足道的；微乎其微的

例 4. Economists say raising the minimum wage would have a negligible effect on employment rates. 经济学家们说提高最低工资对提高就业率所起的作用微不足道。

nominate & denominate

(1)

nominate ['nɒmineit] *v.t.* ① 提名，推荐；② 任命，指定

nomination [ˌnɒmi'neiʃən] *n.[C,U]*

nominee [ˌnɒmi'ni:] *n[C]* 被提名者；被任命或指定者

例 1. The Company irrevocably waives any objection which it might now or here-after have to the courts referred to in Clause 26.1 (English Courts) being nominated as the forum to hear and determine any Proceedings and to settle any Disputes and agrees not to claim that any such court is not a convenient or appropriate forum. 对于第 26.1 条（英格兰法院）提到的被指定为审理和裁决任何法律程序以及解决争端的法院，公司不可撤销地放弃自己现在或者今后可能提出的异议，并且同意不会主张该法院并非方便或适当法院。

例 2. The appointing authority, or an arbitral or other institution or person by whom an arbitrator is appointed or nominated, shall not be liable, by reason only of having appointed or nominated him, for anything done or omitted by the arbitrator, his employees or agents in the discharge or purported discharge of his functions as arbitrator. 委任机关或者委任或指定仲裁员的仲裁机构或其他机构或个人，不得仅仅由于其委任或指定仲裁员，而对该仲裁员、该仲裁员的雇员或代理人在履行或据称是履行其作为仲裁员的职责过程中所完成或未完成的事情承担责任。

例 3. Directors shall serve for a period of three (3) years and shall be eligible for re-election. If a Shareholder ceases to hold Shares, it will procure the resignation of all the Director(s) nominated by it. 董事的任期为三（3）年，而且可以连选连任。如

果某位股东不再持有股份，该股东应当保证其任命的所有董事辞去董事职务。

例 4. The reserve director shall be deemed to be a director of the Company in the event of the death of the director in respect of whom the reserve director is nominated until such time when another person is appointed as a director of the Company or the reserve director resigns from his office of director, whichever is the earlier. 如果提名候补董事的董事死亡，候补董事应当被视为公司的董事，候补董事任期截止于另外一人被任命为公司董事或者候补董事辞去董事职务之时，以最先发生的时间为截止时间。

(2)

denominate [diˈnɒmineit] *v.t.* 以（……货币）计值单位

denomination [diˌnɒmiˈneiʃən] ① *n.[C]* an act of naming. 命名；② *n.[C]* a collective designation, esp. of a religious sect 宗教派别；③ *n.[C]* 面值，面额

denominator [diˈnɒmiˌneitə] *n.[C]* 分数的分母

例 5. "Currency of Account" means the currency in which the relevant is denominated or, if different, is payable. "记账货币" 是指用于相关债务标价的货币；如果相关债务采用其他货币标价，则指用以偿还相关债务的货币。

例 6. Subject to availability, the currency of disbursement of XYZ shall be euro or USD. Disbursement may also be made in RMB, provided THE BANK has been granted all the necessary approvals by the Chinese authorities to issue RMB-denominated bonds and that THE BANK has actually raised suitable funds in RMB. 根据货币供给是否充足，XYZ 的拨付货币应当是欧元或者美元。如果银行已经取得中国当局对于发行人民币标价的债券的所有必要批准，而且银行已经实际筹集到适当的人民币资金，也可以采用人民币拨付贷款。

例 7. We write further to our letter dated November 20, 2019 under which we reminded the Borrower of its obligations under clause 19.14 of the Facility Agreement to deposit or procure all of its operation revenue to be deposited into the US Dollar de-nominated deposit account in the name of the Borrower with the Lender with account number … (the "Account"). 我们寄发本函是为了对 2019 年 11 月 20 日去函作进一步说明。在 11 月 20 日去函中，我们就借款人在贷款协议第 19.14 款下的义务提醒借款人将其所有营业收入存入或确保该等收入存入以借款人名义在放款人处开设的美元存款账户，账号：XXX（下称"账户"）。

例 8. The Company may by ordinary resolution convert any paid-up shares into stock, and reconvert any stock into paid-up shares of any denomination. 公司可以通过普通决议将已经缴足股款的股份转化成股票，将股票转换成已经缴足股款的任何面值的股份。

other than

other than 是介词，与 except 是同义词，意思是"除……以外"。

例 1. Business Day means any day other than a Saturday, Sunday or statutory holiday on which banks in Luxembourg, Grand Duchy of Luxembourg, are open for business. 营业日是指在卢森堡大公国卢森堡市，除星期六、星期日或者法定节假日以外，银行对外营业之日。

例 2. Other than in relation to Extraordinary Management Matters and an increase in the authorised capital a General Meeting shall deliberate in accordance with the quorum and majority requirements provided for in New Jersey law. Fractions of Shares are not entitled to a vote. 股东大会应当依照新泽西州法律规定的法定人数和半数以上要求审议事务，但涉及特别管理事项和增加核定资本的事务除外。不足一股的股份不享有表决权。

例 3. Each Shareholder undertakes that it shall, to the extent reasonably possible and within its powers, procure that the MANAGEMENT COMPANY shall remain an entity fully liable to tax in the Isle of Man under the taxation laws of the Isle of Man by reason of its domicile, residence and place of incorporation and that the MANAGE-MENT COMPANY shall not become tax resident in any jurisdiction other than the Isle of Man. 每一位股东承诺将在合理可能的范围内和在其权限内，保证管理公司始终是由于其住所、居所和法人成立地，根据马恩岛税收征管法律，在该岛完全承担纳税义务的实体，而且管理公司不得在马恩岛以外的任何司法管辖区域内成为纳税居民。

例 4. "Class" and "Class Members" means all persons and entities wherever they may reside who acquired securities of the Defendant during the Class Period either by primary distribution in Canada or an acquisition on the TSX or other secondary market in Canada, other than the Defendants, their past and present subsidiaries, affiliates, officers, directors, senior employees, partners, legal representatives, heirs, predecessors, successors and assigns, and any individual who is an immediate member of the family of an Individual Defendant; "诉讼集团"和"诉讼集团成员"是指在诉因形成期间，所有通过在加拿大境内的初次销售或者通过在多伦多证交所或加拿大境内的其他二级市场进行收购，取得被告人证券的人和实体（不论其住所在何处），但是不包括被告人、被告人过去的和现在的子公司、关联人、高级管理人员、董事、资深雇员、合伙人、遗嘱执行人、继承人、前任、继任者和受让人以及自然人被告人的近亲属。

例 5. Where the Company has only one member and that member is the sole director of the Company, the Company may, but is not obliged to, in general meeting nominate a person (other than a body corporate) as a reserve director of the Company to act in the place of the sole director in the event of his death. 如果本公司仅有一名成员，这名成员是本公司唯一的董事，本公司可以，但是没有义务，在全体会议上指定一人（法人除外）担任本公司的候补董事，如果本公司唯一的董事死亡，候补董事将接替他的职务。

例 6. Other than a veto over other investments proposed by the General Partners (which would only occur in limited circumstances), the Limited Partners will not participate in the management of the Fund, and will have no right to influence the management of the Fund by removing or replacing the General Partners. 除否决普通合伙人提议的其他投资外（有限合伙人只能在有限的情形下行使否决权），有限合伙人不参与本基金的管理工作，因此无权通过解雇或者替换普通合伙人对本基金的管理施加影响。

overtake & takeover

(1)

overtake [ˌəʊvəˈteik] *v.t.* ① to come from behind another vehicle or person and move in front of

them 追上，超过；② to go beyond something by being a greater amount or degree（在

数量或程度上）超过；③ to occur unexpectedly 意外地发生在……

overtake 是不规则动词，它的过去式和过去分词是 overtook 和 overtaken。

例 1. For want of witness or survivor, the detective ruled out foul play and theorized that the car careened down the cliff when the driver, rushing to overtake another vehicle, took no notice of the traffic sign of steep hill. 由于缺少目击者和幸存者，侦探排除了谋杀的可能性，推测驾车人急着超车，没看到陡坡标志，结果车辆冲下山崖。

例 2. By 2050, both China and the India will overtake the U.S. in terms of GDP, according to new research. 根据新的研究，到 2050 年，中国和印度的国内生产总值都会超过美国。

例 3. Although reliable architects and builders had been employed, both schedule and budget were overrun, because landscaping efforts were overtaken by downpours which washed away the topsoil and flower seeds in the garden. 虽然聘请了可靠的建筑师和施工方，几场不期而至的暴雨冲走了花园里的表土和花种，打乱了景观设计工作，结果超出了施工进度和预算。

(2)

takeover [ˈteikəʊvə] *n.[C]* the acquisition of ownership or control of a corporation. A takeover is typically accomplished by a purchase of shares or assets, a tender offer, or a merger. 收购

例 4. AAA's entrance into Canada's capital markets was effected by means of a "reverse takeover". In a reverse takeover, a public shell company acquires a private company that is seeking to become public. The private company (Sino, in this case) becomes public without the scrutiny of an IPO. AAA 进入加拿大资本市场是采用"反向收购"的手段实现的。在反向收购交易中，一个上市空壳公司收购一个谋求上市的私营公司。这个私营公司（在本案中就是 AAA）无须接受首次公开募股审查即可上市。

例 5. In a takeover situation, the directors are in a strategic position, and it is natural that individual shareholders should look to them for advice. However, it is no part of the duty of directors to the company to give advice to individual shareholders regarding the purchase of their shares. 在收购的情况下，董事处于战略性地位，个人股东自然会向董事征询意见。不过，就个人股东所持股份购买事宜向个人股东出具意见并非董事对公司承担的义务。

例 6. In practice, the concept of a dominant purpose is not easy to apply. Therefore, acting bona fide in the interests of the company is not an excuse for acting for a dominant improper purpose, especially where the directors are acting in their own self-interest, such as when they issue shares to defeat a takeover bid and maintain their own positions as directors. 在实践中，主要目的这个概念并不容易适用。因此，为公司着想真诚行事不能当作为某种主要的不正当目的行事的理由，特别是在董事为自身利益行事的情况下，例如他们发行股票以求挫败某一收购要约并维持自己的董事地位。

例 7. The directors issued shares with special voting rights to trustees of an employee share scheme, and made a loan to enable the trustee to purchase more shares. This was part of an attempt to forestall a takeover bid. 董事向雇员股份计划的受托人发行有特别表决权的股份，并提供贷款，使受托人能够购买更多股份。这是为

阻止收购出价而采取的部分对策。

(3)

take sth. over 接管，接手；收购

例 8. Distributor shall cooperate with BBB to allow BBB, to take over all Distributor accounts that may wish to continue to obtain BBB Products. 经销商应当配合 BBB，使 BBB 可以接管经销商的所有账目，掌握可能希望继续获得 BBB 产品的用户。

例 9. If the Purchaser gives the Vendor Representative notice of a Third Party Claim and the Vendors fail, within the specified time, to take over the control of such Third Party Claim, the Purchaser may, at its own cost, take such actions as the Purchaser deems fit in connection with such Third Party Claim, including negotiating, defending and/or settling such Third Party Claim. 如果买方将第三方权利请求通知卖方代表，但是卖方未在规定时间内接手处理第三方权利请求，买方可以自行承担费用采取它认为适合的行为处理第三方权利请求，包括就第三方权利请求进行谈判、抗辩及 / 或和解。

例 10. Upon transfer of a given use contract due to change of the contracting party, AAA shall take over the collection of maintenance service fees agreed between the Company and the Customer and owed to the Company by the Customer. 在因缔约人发生变化而转让特定用益合同时，AAA 应当接收公司与客户约定的和客户应当向公司支付的维护服务费用。

pawn & prawn

pawn 和 prawn 拼写相近，意思却迥然不同，要注意区分。

(1)

pawn [pɔ:n] *n.[C]* （国际象棋的）兵；（受人摆布的）棋子，爪牙；*v.t.* 当押，典当

pawned goods/items 当押物品，当物

pawnshop *n.[C]* 当铺

pawnbroker *n.[C]* 当铺经营人；当铺老板；当押商

pawnee ['pɔ:ni:] *n.[C]* 承典人

pawner ['pɔ:nə] *n.[C]* 出典人（当户）

下面两个词组需要注意：

pawn off sth. on sb.

pawn sb./sth. off as sth.

例 1. Don't let him pawn off a jalopy on you—get a new one. 别让他拿辆老破车打发你——自己买辆新的吧。

例 2. The tabloids often pawn off gossip and trivia as breaking news. 通俗小报常拿流言蜚语和鸡零狗碎的事充当重磅新闻。

(2)

prawn [prɔ:n] (especially BrE) *n.[C]* 海虾

prawn cocktail *n.[C]* 鲜虾冷盘

美式英语使用 shrimp，所以美式英语中"鲜虾冷盘"是 shrimp cocktail。

几个与 pawn 和 prawn 押韵的有趣且实用的词汇：

(3)

dawn [dɔːn] *n.[C,U]* 拂晓，黎明

例 3. The first ferry sets off at dawn. 头班渡轮天一亮就开船。

例 4. He worked from dawn to dusk to meet the deadline. 他从早到晚赶工，好在最后期限之前交工。

例 5. The invention of writing marked the dawn of civilization. 文字的发明标志着文明的开端。

dawn 还是不及物动词，有下面几个义项：①天亮，破晓；②事情见分晓，变明朗；③到来，开始。

例 6. The morning dawned fresh and clear after the storm. 风暴过后，黎明时分天清气朗。

例 7. It eventually dawned that the press conference was cleverly stage-managed. 人们终于明白这场新闻发布会是精心策划好的。

例 8. As the 17th day of October AD 79 dawned, few people could have predicted that an eruption of Mount Vesuvius would wipe off Pompeii together with more than 30,000 residents. 公元 79 年 10 月 17 日这一天到来的时候，没有几个人能预见到维苏威火山爆发将把庞贝城彻底摧毁，使三万多居民罹难。

还应当注意 sth. dawn on sb. 这个词组，或形式主语 it + dawn on sb. + 连接代词 that + 主语从句，意思是某人明白，某人意识到。

例 9. The ghastly truth dawned on me. 我想明白了令人毛骨悚然的真相。

例 10. It dawned on her that the defense attorney tried to distract her attention from the defendant's depraved character. 她意识到辩护律师试图让她分心，免得她注意到被告人品性败坏。

(4)

drawn [drɔːn] 是动词 draw（draw 的义项非常丰富，我们在学习英文合同的时候，会结合具体语句学习）的过去分词。drawn 用作形容词，意思是"面色憔悴的"。另外，形容词 drawn-out 的意思是"耗费时间的"，例如：The company wants to avoid long drawn-out legal proceedings. 公司想要避免漫长的法律程序。

(5)

lawn [lɔːn] *n.[C,U]* 草坪
mow the lawn 修剪草坪
lawn mower 割草机

(6)

overdrawn 是动词 overdraw（透支）的过去分词，也是形容词，be overdrawn by + 钱数，表示透支了多少钱。

例 11. After a five-day shopping binge, her account is overdrawn by $50,000. 连续五天疯狂购物之后，她的账户透支了五万块钱。

(7)

sawn 是动词 saw（用锯锯东西）的过去分词。例如：sawn-off shotgun 锯短枪管的霰弹枪。

(8)

spawn [spɔːn] *n.[U]* 鱼类或蛙类的卵；*v.t.& v.i.* （鱼类或蛙类）产卵；*v.t.* 催生，产生

例 12. New technology has spawned new business opportunities. 新技术催生了新的生意机会。

spawning ground *n.[C]* 鱼类产卵场

(9)

yawn [jɔ:n] *v.i. & n.[C]* 打哈欠

yawning gap between 巨大的差异

例 13. The yawning gap between the rich and the poor cannot be ignored. 不能对贫富悬殊的现象熟视无睹。

在口语中，a yawn 指乏味的人或事物。

例 14. Despite publicity stunts, the film was a big yawn. 就算用了不少宣传噱头，这部电影还是很乏味。

penalty

(1)

penalty [ˈpɛnəltɪ] *n.[C]* 惩罚，处罚；刑罚；罚金；（体育比赛的）违规处罚

(2)

penal [ˈpiːnl] *adj.* 刑罚的；应受刑罚的；应作刑罚的；作为刑罚的

(3)

penalize [ˈpiːnəlaɪz] *v.t.* ① 处罚；② 使……处于不利地位

例 1. No one shall be held guilty of any penal offence on account of any act or omission which did not constitute a penal offence, under national or international law, at the time when it was committed. Nor shall a heavier penalty be imposed than the one that was applicable at the time the penal offence was committed. 任何人的任何行为或不行为，在其发生时依国家法或国际法均不构成刑事罪者，不得被判为犯有刑事罪。刑罚不得重于犯罪时适用的法律规定。

例 2. Section 304B of the *Indian Penal Code* specifies that "where the death of a woman is caused by any burns or bodily injury or occurs otherwise than under normal circumstances within seven years of her marriage and it is shown that soon before her death she was subjected to cruelty or harassment by her husband or any relative of her husband for, or in connection with, any demand for dowry, such death shall be called 'dowry death' and such husband or relative shall be deemed to have caused her death". 《印度刑法典》第 304B 条规定："凡妇女在婚后七年内死于火烧或肉体伤害或者在其他非正常情况下身亡，并且证明在其身亡之前不久，该妇女由于其夫或其夫之亲属索要嫁妆或与索要嫁妆有关事由而遭受虐待或骚扰，该妇女之死应

当称为'嫁妆致死',应当视为其夫或其夫之亲属导致该妇女死亡。"

例 3. XYZ shall defend, indemnify and hold harmless ABC, Subsidiaries of ABC and Customers from and against any claim, dispute, proceeding, action, fine, penalty, suit, loss, expense, damages including punitive damages, and cost (including reasonable attorney fees) arising out of or relating to any infringement or alleged infringement of any Intellectual Property Right of any third party by the Products and/or use or marketing thereof. XYZ 应当对 ABC、ABC 的子公司以及客户予以保障、给予赔偿、使之免于承受由于产品及 / 或产品的使用或营销侵犯或被控侵犯任何第三方知识产权而产生的或者与之有关的任何请求权、纠纷、程序、诉讼、罚款、处罚、损失、费用、损害赔偿（包括惩罚性损害赔偿）以及支出（包括合理的律师费）。

例 4. A withdrawing Investor shall promptly join in such actions as may be necessary or desirable to obtain any Governmental Authorisations required in connection with the withdrawal and assignments. The non-withdrawing Investors shall use reasonable efforts to assist the withdrawing Investor in obtaining such approvals. Any penalties or expenses incurred by the Investors in connection with such withdrawal shall be borne by the withdrawing Investor. 撤出投资人应当立即参加使撤出和转让行为获得政府批准所必需或适宜的行动。未撤出投资人应当采取合理措施协助撤出投资人获得上述批准。投资人招致的与上述撤出行为有关的罚金或费用应当由撤出投资人承担。

例 5. The review mechanism should promote adherence to the *Convention* and measure progress regarding implementation of the *Convention* in a manner that does not penalize non-compliance and application. 审查机制应当按照对于不履约行为和申请行为不施加处罚的方式，促进各国 / 地区加入《公约》和衡量它们实施《公约》方面的进展。

例 6. No person shall be found guilty for an act penalized by law where it was performed or occurred without there being any criminal guilt on his part and was caused by force majeure, or occurred by accident. 凡某人对于一种受法律处罚的行为的作出或发生没有任何刑事意义上的罪过，而且该行为是不可抗力造成的，或者是意外发生的，不得就该行为裁定此人有罪。

例 7. The Contractor shall conform in all respects with any such Statutes, Ordinances, Laws, Regulations, By-laws or requirements of any such local or other authority which may be applicable to the Works and shall keep the Employer indemnified against all penalties and liabilities of every kind for breach of any such Statutes, Ordinances, Laws, Regulations, By-laws or requirements. 承包人应完全遵守上述制定法、法令、法律、法规、规章或任何上述地方或其他机关可能适用于工程的要求，并且应赔偿雇主使之免于承担由于违反上述制定法、法令、法律、法规、规章或要求而应承担的所有罚金和各类债务。

注意：下面的例句中，"under penalty of perjury" 是宣誓的常用短语。

例 8. IN WITNESS WHEREOF, the undersigned, for the purpose of effectuating the Merger of the constituent corporations, pursuant to the *General Corporation Law of the State of Delaware*, under penalty of perjury does hereby declares and certify that this is the act and deed of the Corporation and the facts stated herein are true and accordingly have hereunto signed this *Certificate of Ownership and Merger* as of the 25th day of April, 1996. 以资证明：为完成对于成员公司的合并，下文签字人，依照《特拉华州普通公司法》，特此宣布和证明，此份证明系公司之行为，此份证明中所阐述之情况符合事实，如作伪证，甘受责罚，因此，下文签字人已于1996 年 4 月 25 日签署此份《所有权与合并证明》。

pending & impending

(1)

pending ['pendiŋ] *prep.* while waiting for something, or until something happens 等到……之

后，直到……为止

pending *adj.* 将要发生的；待定的

作为介词的 pending 用例：

例 1. "Trademarks" shall mean the trademarks whether registered or pending registration in the Peoples' Republic of China ("PRC"); particulars of which are set out in the Schedule attached to this Agreement. "商标"指不论已在中华人民共和国（"中国"）境内注册的各种商标还是正在中国申请注册的各种商标；其细节均在本协议的附件中载明。

例 2. In the case of offences established in accordance with this Convention, each State Party shall take appropriate measures, in accordance with its domestic law and with due regard to the rights of the defence, to seek to ensure that conditions imposed in connection with decisions on release pending trial or appeal take into consideration the need to ensure the presence of the defendant at subsequent criminal proceedings. 就根据本公约确立的犯罪而言，各缔约国均应当根据本国法律并在适当尊重被告人权利的情况下采取适当措施，力求确保就判决前或者上诉期间释放的裁决所规定的条件已经考虑到确保被告人在其后的刑事诉讼中出庭的需要。

例 3. AAA and BBB agree to enter into any further documentation which may be necessary to give full effect to the matters agreed in this letter Agreement. Pending the execution of further documentation, this letter Agreement constitutes a binding agreement. AAA 和 BBB 同意进一步签立必要的文件，使本协议书中约定的事项充分生效。在签立进一步的文件之前，本协议书构成具有约束力的协议。

例 4. The Court may order that any money payable under the award shall be brought into Court or otherwise secured pending the determination of the application or appeal, and may direct that the application or appeal be dismissed if the order is not complied with. 高等法院可以饬令在尚未审结申请或上诉期间将根据仲裁裁决应当支付的钱款上交高等法院提存或以其他方式为该款提供担保，如果申请人或上诉人不遵守该命令，则高等法院可以指示驳回申请或上诉。

例 5. Since the issues and the Parties in the two sets of proceedings are not the same, there is no reason to stop the plaintiff from pursuing the claim in Hong Kong pending the wide-ranging disputes between multiple non-parties in the Mainland proceedings, which will inevitably be time-consuming and governed by Mainland law. 由于以上两宗诉讼程序的争点和当事人并不相同，而诸多非本案当事人借助内地诉讼程序解决它们之间的庞杂纠纷，难免迁延时日，又要受到内地法律约束，所以在上述纠纷审结之前，没有理由阻止本案原告人在香港提出诉讼请求。

例 6. This Agreement and the rights and obligations of the Parties hereof under this Agreement shall remain in full force and effect during any arbitration proceedings, pending an award which shall determine whether and when termination of this Agreement may become effective. 本协议和双方当事人在本协议之下的权利义务在仲裁程序正在进行、尚未作出裁决期间应当保持充分的效力，仲裁裁决应当判定终止本协议的行为是否生效以及这种行为何时生效。

作为形容词的 pending 用例：

例 7. Unless otherwise agreed by the parties, the arbitral tribunal may continue the arbitral proceedings and make an award while an application to the Court under this section is pending. 除非双方当事人另有约定，在当事人根据本条向高等法院

提出的申请审结以前，仲裁庭可以继续仲裁程序并作出仲裁裁决。

例 8. In the absence of a marketing authorization or of a pending application for a medicinal product authorised in another Member State in accordance with this Directive, a Member State may for justified public health reasons authorize the placing on the market of the said medicinal product. 对某一成员国而言，即使某种药品在该国尚未取得销售许可或尚未提出申请，但只要该药品已经依照本指令在另一个成员国取得许可，它仍然可以基于正当的公共卫生理由许可将这种药品投放本国市场。

例 9. Party C represents and warrants to Party A that there is no existing, pending or threatened litigation, arbitration, or administrative proceedings relating to its share of the Equity Interest, its assets, or itself. 丙方向甲方声明并保证：不存在任何正在进行、尚未终结或者表示将要提起的涉及丙方在股本权益之中的股份、丙方的资产或者丙方本人的诉讼、仲裁或者行政听证程序。

例 10. The Corporation shall indemnify to the fullest extent permitted by the *Oregon Business Corporation Act* any person (and his successor in interest) who is made or threatened to be made a party to any threatened, pending or completed action, suit or proceeding, whether civil, criminal, administrative investigative or otherwise (including an action by or in the right of the Corporation) by reason of the fact that he or the person through whom his interest was derived is or was a director, officer, employee or agent of the Corporation or serves or served at the request of the Corporation as a director, officer, employee or agent of another corporation, partnership, joint venture, trust, association or other enterprise. 不论何人，凡因他或他的利益来源人现任或曾任本公司的董事、高级职员、雇员或代理人，或者应本公司的要求担任或曾经担任另一家公司、合伙企业、合营企业、信托、社团或其他企业的董事、高级职员、雇员或代理人，而被当作或被威胁当作任何可能发生的、尚未了结的或已经完成的民事、刑事、行政调查或其他性质的诉讼或法律程序（包括本公司提起的诉讼或符合本公司权益的诉讼）的当事方，本公司应在《俄勒冈州商业

公司法》所允许的范围内尽量对其给予弥偿。

例 11. Final completion is the end of the Contractor's obligation or responsibility. At this point, the constructor prepares to make the final handover to the end user or client. According to the findings of the present review, this is a critical stage where the United Nations system organizations should take the necessary steps to ensure better coordination, before returning the bank guarantee and making the final payment. In accordance with the UNOPS Procurement Manual, a supplier performance evaluation is mandatory for all procurement activities valued at a certain amount and above. When the last payment under a contract has been made and no pending claim is left, the supplier performance evaluation form must be completed. Only once the project is complete should the final balance of the retention be returned by the United Nations system organizations to the Contractors. 项目最终完工，承包商的义务或职责亦告终止。这时，建筑商准备向最终用户或委托人最终移交。根据本次审查报告得出的结论，这是一个至关重要的阶段，联合国系统组织应当采取必要的措施确保在返还银行担保和支付最终款项之前更好地协调。依照联合国项目事务厅采购手册的规定，凡估价为一定金额或该金额以上的采购活动，必须进行供应商履约评估。当合同约定的最后一笔款项已经支付，没有遗留仍未了结的权利请求时，必须填写供应商履约评估表。只有当项目完工，联合国系统组织才应当向承包商退还保留款项的最后余额。

(2)

impending [im'pɛndiŋ] *adj.* 即将发生的（通常指不愉快的局面迫近）

例 12. In addition to helping countries develop effective tools to alert and warn of impending disasters, it is equally important to strengthen the preparedness of every community in its ability to respond to dangers. 除了帮助各国开发出有效的工具，对迫近的灾难发出警报和提醒，同样重要的是，要增强每个社区防备危险的能力。

例 13. Save the Children Vietnam presented an initiative to teach children and adults how to spot the threats that disasters pose to young people and how to reduce the impending risks. 救助越南儿童组织发起了一项倡议，教导儿童和成人如何发现灾难对年轻人造成的威胁以及如何减少迫在眉睫的风险。

perpetrate & perpetuate

(1)

perpetrate [ˈpɜːpətreit] *v.t.* to do something that is morally wrong or illegal = commit 犯罪，作
　　恶，施暴，行凶

perpetration [ˌpɜːpəˈtreiʃən] *n.[U]*

perpetrator [ˈpɜːpətreitə] *n.[C] (formal)* a person who commits a crime or offence 为非作歹者

　　例 1. In order to combat impunity and secure convictions of rapists and those who
perpetrate sexual violence, it is clear that national criminal justice systems must cease
to follow such gender-biased rules of evidence. 为了抵制有罪不受处罚现象并将犯
有强奸和性暴力罪行的歹徒定罪，国家刑事司法系统显然必须停止沿用有性别
偏见的证据规则。

　　例 2. In 2009, the *Temporary Domestic Exclusion Order Act* entered into force.
Under this act, perpetrators of domestic violence may be excluded temporarily from
their homes, so that the victims may continue to live there. 《临时家庭驱逐令法》于
2009 年生效。根据这部法律，可以将实施家庭暴力者暂时从住宅中驱逐出去，
受害人就可以继续在家宅中居住。

　　例 3. The Committee is further concerned that the sanctions for sexual harassment
and abuse in schools are lenient and that teachers working in the education system who
are perpetrators of sexual violence are merely transferred to other schools. 委员会进
而关切的是：对校内性骚扰和性虐待行为的处罚轻，教育系统内任职的教师如
果实施性暴力，只会被调到其他学校。

例 4. Thus, El Salvador said that the death penalty was mandatory under its *Code of Military Justice* for treason, espionage and rebellion perpetrated in an international war. 因此，萨尔瓦多称，根据本国《军事司法法典》，对于在国际战争中犯下叛国罪、间谍罪和叛乱罪的人，必须判处死刑。

例 5. Somalia said that "As the Government extends its authority in those areas, it is committed to eradicating the practice of death by stoning while working towards declaring a moratorium on the death penalty. The perpetrators of such crimes will be held accountable for their actions." 索马里表示"随着政府扩大在这些地区的威信，政府致力于取缔以石刑处决犯人的做法，同时谋求宣告暂缓执行死刑。犯有此类罪行者其行为将被追究责任"。

例 6. Their work helps to deter violence, provide remedies to victims, hold perpetrators criminally accountable through fair trials and ensure safe, secure and humane imprisonment, thereby instilling public trust and confidence in rule of law mechanisms. 他们的工作有助于震慑暴力，为受害人提供救济，通过公正审判追究犯罪分子的刑事责任，确保安全、可靠及人道的监禁刑罚，由此逐步培养公众对法治机制的信任和信心。

例 7. In addition, whereas in the past domestic abuse of a child could only legally occur between a child and its parent, the legal definition of child abuse has now been extended to include abuse perpetrated by a guardian against a child for whom he/she is legally responsible. 另外，鉴于以往依照法律对儿童的家庭虐待只能发生在儿童及其父/母亲之间，现在虐待儿童的法律定义已经引申而包括对儿童负有法定监护义务的监护人对儿童实施的虐待。

例 8. Strong justice and corrections institutions, together with accountable police and law enforcement agencies, which fully respect human rights, are critical for restoring peace and security in the immediate post-conflict period. They allow for perpetrators of crimes to be brought to justice, encourage the peaceful resolution of disputes and restore trust and social cohesion based on equal rights. 充分尊重人权的强大的司法和惩戒机构，连同须负责任的警察和执法机构，对于在当前的冲突后时期恢复和平及安全至关重要。这些机构使犯罪分子被绳之以法，鼓励和平解决争端，恢复以平等权利为基础的信任和社会融合。

例 9. The Committee urges Aruba to promptly enact legislation providing for temporary restraining orders to be imposed on perpetrators of domestic violence (Recommendation 27). 委员会敦促阿鲁巴及时制订法律，规定对实施家庭暴力的人适用临时限制令（第 27 项建议）。

例 10. In the *Declaration of the High-level Meeting on the Rule of Law*, Member States stated their commitment to ensuring that impunity is not tolerated for genocide, war crimes and crimes against humanity or for violations of international humanitarian law and gross violations of human rights law. They also committed to ensuring that such violations are properly investigated and appropriately sanctioned, including by bringing the perpetrators of any crimes to justice, through national mechanisms or, where appropriate, regional or international mechanisms, in accordance with international law. 在《法治问题高级别会议宣言》中，会员国承诺，对于灭绝种族罪、战争罪和危害人类罪，对于违反国际人道主义法行为和严重违反人权法行为，确保绝不容许存在有罪不罚的现象。会员国还承诺，确保对于此类违法行为要进行适当调查，给予适当制裁，包括通过国家机制，或根据国际法酌情通过区域或国际机制，将任何罪行的实施者绳之以法。

(2)

perpetuate [pə'pɛtʃueit] *v.t.* to make something to continue to exist for a long time

注意：perpetuate 的字面意思是"使某种东西长期存在"，在具体语境中要结合上下文灵活传达出它（及同源词）的意思。

perpetuation [pə,pɛtʃu'eiʃən] *n.[U]*

perpetual [pə'pɛtʃuəl] *adj.* ① continuing all the time without changing or stopping = continuous 永久的，长期的；② repeated many times in a way that annoys you = continual 频频，再

三，时常，一再

perpetually [pə'pɛtʃuəli] *adv.*

perpetuity [ˌpɜːpə'tjuːəti] *n[U]*

in perpetuity = forever 永久

例 11. Perpetual motion is the ability of a machine to always continue moving without getting energy from anywhere else, which is not considered possible, as it would violate the first or second law of thermodynamics. 永久运动是指机械能够不从外界获取能量的情况下始终继续运动。人们认为这是不可能做到的，因为这违反热力学的第一或第二定律。

例 12. The aim of the Association is to perpetuate the pottery craftsmanship in this Navajo Community. 协会致力于传承这个纳瓦霍社区的制陶手艺。

例 13. Witnesses shall not be examined to perpetuate testimony unless an action has been begun for the purpose. 除非已有诉讼开展以使证供得以保全，否则不得为此对证人进行讯问。

例 14. The Committee is nevertheless concerned about the fact that women large-ly continue to use the traditional rather than the formal justice system, which limits the enjoyment of their rights by perpetuating and reinforcing discriminatory social norms. 但委员会仍然关切的是：事实上妇女在很大程度上仍然利用传统的而非正规的司法体系，这种局面使歧视性的社会准则得以长期流传和强化，限制了妇女享受她们的权利。

例 15. The civil law system has its origins in Roman law and operates in Europe, South America and Japan. Under a civil law system, law is enacted and codified by parliament. Companies are recognized under both systems as artificial legal persons with perpetual life and limited liability. 民法法系起源于罗马法，施行于欧洲、南美洲和日本。在民法法系的类别中，议会制订法律并将法律编纂为成文法则。这

两大法系都承认公司是拟制法人，具有永久延续性和承担有限责任。

例 17. There is also the possible risk that safe harbour rules are too generous; this, can possibly result in revenue unnecessarily foregone. Or there may be a distortionary impact in that such a regime may encourage and perpetuate an economy based on small-scale or low profit transactions rather than higher risk/higher reward transactions to which the safe harbours will not apply. 还有可能发生这样的危险，即安全港规则过于慷慨；这会导致不必要地放弃财政收入。或者说，安全港可能产生具有扭曲性的影响，因为这样的制度可能鼓励以小规模或低利润的交易——而不是不适用安全港的高风险 / 高报酬交易——为基础的经济并且使这种经济长期存在。

例 18. Furthermore, because it is immutable, if false information is put on to a blockchain, it will remain there in perpetuity. In other words, the technology has a "garbage in, garbage out" dilemma. 此外，由于信息不可更改，如果把虚假信息放到区块链上，该信息就会永久留在那里。换句话说，这项技术存在"入垃圾，出垃圾"的两难境地。

petrol, patrol & parole

(1)

petrol [ˈpɛtrəl] *n.[U]* 汽油

gasoline [ˈɡæsəlin] *n.[U]* 汽油

gas [ˈɡæs] *n.[U]* 汽油

注意：petrol 是英国、澳大利亚、新西兰等英联邦国家的用法。美国和加拿大使用 gaso-
line（gas 是口语）。

能源类词汇：

petroleum [pəˈtrəʊliəm] *n.[U]* 石油

petrochemical [ˌpɛtrəʊˈkɛmikl] *n.[C]* 石油化学产品；*adj.* 石油化学的

petrochemical industry 石化行业

paraffin (UK) [ˈpærəfin] *n.[U]* 煤油

paraffin wax *n.[U]* 石蜡

kerosene [ˈkɛrəsiːn] *n.[U]* 煤油，火油

natural gas *n.[U]* 天然气

liquefied natural gas (LNG) *n.[U]* 液化天然气

coal gas *n.[U]* 煤气

methane [ˈmiːθein] *n.[U]* 甲烷

methanol [ˈmɛθənɔl] *n.[U]* 甲醇

ethane [ˈɛθein] *n.[U]* 乙烷

ethanol [ˈɛθənɒl] *n.[U]* 乙醇

propane [ˈprəʊpein] *n.[U]* 丙烷

butane [ˈbjuːtein] *n.[U]* 丁烷

carbon monoxide [ˈkɑːbən məˈnɒkˌsaid] *n.[U]* 一氧化碳

carbon dioxide [ˌkɑːbən daiˈɒksaid] *n.[U]* 二氧化碳

hydrocarbon [ˌhaidrəʊˈkɑːbən] *n.[C]* 烃；碳氢化合物

(2)

patrol [pəˈtrəʊl] ① *v.t.* (patrolling, patrolled) 巡逻

例 1. A security guard, equipped with a pistol and a German shepherd, patrols this upscale community at night. 夜间，有一名配了手枪，牵着一条德国牧羊犬的保安在这个高档小区巡逻。

例 2. The area should be patrolled by gendarmes in order to give adequate protection to law-abiding local residents. 应当让宪兵在这个地方巡逻，以便为遵纪守法的当地居民提供妥善的保护。

② *n.[C,U]* 巡逻；巡逻的人，飞机、车辆等
例如：patrol officer 巡警；patrol car 巡逻警车。

例 3. A contingent of armored personnel carriers are on patrol day and night in this most dangerous suburb. 一支装甲车队昼夜在这个最危险的城郊巡逻。

(3)

parole [pəˈrəul] *n.[U]* & *v.t.* 假释

例 4. Thanks to clever maneuver by his defense attorney, this convicted felon will be released on parole in October 2020. 多亏辩护律师的巧妙运作，这名重罪犯将在 2020 年 10 月获得假释。

例 5. The man shall be eligible for parole in fifteen years. 这名男子服刑 15 年后有资格获得假释。

例 6. The defendant was sentenced to life imprisonment without the possibility of parole. 被告人被判处终身监禁，不得假释。

parolee [pəˌrəʊˈliː] *n.[C]* 获得假释者

prescribe & proscribe

(1)

prescribe [pri'skraib] *v.t.* ① to say what medicine or treatment a sick person should have 为……
开药或开处方：prescribe sb. sth., prescribe sth. for sth.；② to dictate, ordain, or direct;
to establish authoritatively (as a rule or guideline) 规定，制定；③ to claim ownership
through prescription 因时效经过而取得所有权；④ to invalidate or otherwise make unenforceable through prescription 因时效经过而使权利失效或无法强制执行

prescription [pri'skripʃən] ① *n.[C]* 药方，处方；② *n.[C]* 处方上开的药；③ *n.[C]* 秘诀，诀
窍；④ *n.[C,U]* 制定，规定；制定或规定的规则；⑤ *n.[C,U]* 因时效经过而取得或消
灭（的权利）

例 1. The doctor gave him a prescription for antihypertensive drugs. 大夫给他开
过降压药。

例 2. The controlled substance may be available on prescription subject to prior
approval by relevant authorities. 这种管制物质须事先经相关部门批准后方可凭处
方购买。

例 3. To accuse the president of racial discrimination has been her sole prescription for social diseases of today. 她解决当今社会弊病只有一招，就是指责总统种
族歧视。

prescriptive [pri'skriptiv] *adj.* ① saying how something should or must be done, or what should
be done 指定的，规定的；② 因时效经过而取得或消灭的

例 4. Prescriptive right is a right obtained by prescription. For example, after a nuisance has been continuously in existence for 20 years, a prescriptive right to continue it is acquired as an easement appurtenant to the land on which it exists. 时效权利是指根据时效获得的权利。例如，一种妨害行为在一块土地上连续不断地存在了20年以后，就取得了以从属于这块土地的地役权形式继续这种妨害行为的时效权利。

例 5. Normally, the lease will be fairly prescriptive in this regard, with the insurance proceeds paid into a trust to ensure they are used for their intended purpose. 租约在这方面通常会相当规范，规定将保险收益付给信托，以确保将其用于原定用途。

prescribed [pri'skraibd] *adj.* ① 处方上写明的； ② 规定的

例 6. One of the inconvenience of travelling with a tour group is following a prescribed itinerary. 跟团旅行的一个不便之处是按规定行程作息。

例 7. Several prescribed drugs for depression have been abused beyond a certain level. 滥用几种治疗抑郁症的处方药的现象已经比较严重了。

prescription drug *n.[C]* 处方药
over-the-counter drug *n.[C]* 非处方药

例 8. The healthcare specialist prescribed him wildly overpriced medicines which proved to be ineffective. 保健专家给他开了贵得离谱的药物，结果没什么疗效。

例 9. The drugs prescribed for his osteoporosis have adverse effects on his stomach. 为治疗他的骨质疏松症开的药物对他的胃有副作用。

例 10. Paragraph (1) shall not apply with respect to any employee who is a highly compensated employee (within the meaning of Section 414(q) of Title 26 [the *Internal*

Revenue Code of 1986]) to the extent provided in regulations prescribed by the Secretary of the Treasury for purposes of precluding discrimination in favor of highly compensated employees within the meaning of Subchapter D of Chapter 1 of Title 26 [the *Internal Revenue Code of 1986*]. 如果某位雇员属于（第 26 编第 414（q）条 [《1986 年国内税收法典》] 所指的）报酬丰厚的雇员，对于 [《1986 年国内税收法典》] 第 26 编第 1 章 D 节所指的报酬丰厚的雇员，存在有利于该雇员的差别待遇，在财政部长为了排除这种差别待遇而制定的条例所规定的范围内，对该雇员不适用第（1）段的规定。

例 11. Any regulations prescribed by the Secretary of the Treasury pursuant to Clause (v) of Section 411(b)(1)(H) of Title 26 [the *Internal Revenue Code of 1986*] and Subparagraphs (C) and (D) of Section 411(b)(2) of Title 26 [the *Internal Revenue Code of 1986*] shall apply with respect to the requirements of this Subsection in the same manner and to the same extent as such regulations apply with respect to the requirements of such Section 411(b)(1)(H) and Section 411(b)(2). 财政部长依照第 26 编第 411（b）（1）（H）条（v）目 [《1986 年国内税收法典》] 和第 26 编第 411（b）（2）条（C）项及（D）项 [《1986 年国内税收法典》] 制定的任何条例，以何种方式，在何种范围内，适用于以上第 411（b）（1）（H）条和第 411（b）（2）条的要求，这些条例就应当以相同的方式，在相同的范围内，适用于本款的要求。

例 12. In applying the retirement benefit test of Paragraph (1) of this subsection, if any such retirement benefit is in a form other than a straight life annuity (with no ancillary benefits), or if employees contribute to any such plan or make rollover contributions, such benefit shall be adjusted in accordance with regulations prescribed by the Equal Employment Opportunity Commission, after consultation with the Secretary of the Treasury, so that the benefit is the equivalent of a straight life annuity (with no ancillary benefits) under a plan to which employees do not contribute and under which no rollover contributions are made. 在应用本款第（1）段的退休福利测试时，如果此类退休福利采用除终身定额年金（没有附带福利）以外的其他形式，或者如果雇员为此类计划缴纳款项或者进行滚动式缴纳，此类福利应当依照平等就业机会委员会与财政部部长协商之后规定的条例进行调整，以便使此类福利等于

雇员无须缴纳款项而且不进行滚动式缴纳的计划之下的终身定额年金（没有附带福利）。

例 13. Attorney's fees. —If the presidential appointee is the prevailing party in a proceeding under this section, attorney's fees may be allowed by the court in accordance with the standards prescribed under Section 706(k) of the *Civil Rights Act of 1964* [42 *U.S.C.* 2000e-5(k)]. 律师费。如果总统任命的人是根据本条启动的诉讼程序中的胜诉方，法院可以依照《1964 年民权法》第 706（k）条［《美国法典》第 42 编第 2000e—5（k）条］规定的标准判决律师费的负担。

(2)

proscribe [prəʊ'skraib] *v.t.* to outlaw or prohibit; to forbid 禁止

proscription [prəʊ'skripʃən] *n.[C,U]* ① the act of prohibiting; the state of being prohibited; ② a prohibition or restriction

proscriptive [prəʊ'skriptiv] *adj.* 起禁止或取缔作用的

例 14. The ban follows a crucial ruling in February by Germany's top administrative court that cities had the right to proscribe diesel cars as a last resort to prevent air pollution, in a victory for environmental groups. 颁布此项禁令之前，德国最高行政法院在二月份作出一项重要裁决，裁定城市有权将禁止柴油车作为防止空气污染的最后手段，这是环保组织的一场胜利。

例 15. While there is an argument for allowing contract law to operate freely, it is difficult to object to the government's plans to proscribe the sale of leasehold interests in new individual houses. 尽管有人主张允许不加限制地施用合同法，但是要抵制政府禁止出售新建个人房屋的租赁权益的计划却非易事。

例 16. Under English insolvency law, which is less proscriptive than Ireland's new guidelines, "reasonable" day-to-day expenses for bankrupts include holidays, mobile phones and video rentals. 英国破产法不如爱尔兰的新指导原则严厉，根据该法，破产人的"合理"日常开销包括度假、移动电话和视频租金在内。

preview & purview

(1)

preview ['priːvjuː] *n.[C] & v.t. & v.i.* 预演，预展

例 1. A sneak preview of the new film will be held in the auditorium. 新片的预映将在大礼堂举行。

例 2. Journalists will be able to preview the exhibition tomorrow. 新闻记者明天可以预先观摩展览。

(2)

purview ['pɜːvjuː] *n.[C] (formal)* area of application = scope 范围，领域，范畴

在法律文件中，经常用到 within / outside the purview of sb./sth. 这个词组，意思是属于或超出……的权限范围。

例 3. This case falls within the purview of this court. 这个案子属于本庭的权限范围。

例 4. Will it be said that the fundamental principles of the Confederation were not within the purview of the convention, and ought not to have been varied? 可否说邦联的根本原则不属于公约的范畴，而且原本不应当改变？

principal & principle

　　这两个词发音相同，拼写非常相似，但词性、含义不同，它们在法律文件中出现的频率都很高，学习的时候应当格外注意。

(1)

principal [ˈprinsəpəl] *adj.* = main 主要的，最重要的；*n.[C]* ① 美国中小学校长；② 英国大学校长或学院院长；③ (singular) The amount of a debt, investment, or other fund, not including interest, earnings, or profits 本金；④ one who authorizes another to act on his or her behalf as an agent（代理关系中的）本人 / 委托人 / 被代理人；⑤ 负责人，主管人；⑥ 主债务人

principally [ˈprinsəpli] *adv.* = mainly

形容词 principal 及副词 principally

形容词 principal 用作定语，在表示协议订立方的句式中常构成 principal place of business（主要营业地点）的固定搭配。例如：

　　例 1. "Environmental Laws" means Relevant Laws, being laws of which a principal objective is the preservation, protection or improvement of the Environment, and includes legislative provisions giving effect to international agreements concerning the Environment. "环境法"是指主要目标是保全、保护或者改善环境的相关法律，包括赋予国际环境协定效力的立法条文。

　　例 2. This *Distributor Agreement* (*Agreement*) is made by and between AAA, a company incorporated in Hong Kong, with its principal place of business at ⋯, Hong Kong ("AAA") and the authorized distributor identified below ("Distributor") as of _____, 2019 ("Effective Date"). 本《经销协议》（《协议》）由 AAA——

一家在香港注册成立的公司，其主要营业地在香港……（"AAA"），与下文确定的被授权经销商（"经销商"）于 2019 年 ×× 月 ×× 日订立（"生效日"）。

例 3. The Fund's investments will consist principally of loans to the Developer, and thus its investments will be undiversified and wholly dependent on the performance of the loans. 本基金从事的投资将主要由向开发商提供的贷款构成，因此该投资将会比较单一，完全取决于贷款的绩效。

名词 principal 的第三个义项（本金）出现频率最高：

例 4. The Mortgagor shall duly and punctually repay the Principal Amount and all other moneys constituting each of its Liabilities when due in accordance with the Finance Documents. 抵押人应当严格而且及时地偿还本金金额以及依据融资文件的规定构成抵押人各笔到期债务的所有其他款项。

例 5. The Company shall, before making any repayment of principal or payment of interest under this Agreement, submit details of such repayment or payment to SAFE, Beijing Branch for approval in accordance with the relevant laws and regulations in force for the time being in the PRC. 公司应当在根据本协议偿还本金或支付利息之前，依照中国当时施行的相关法律法规，将偿还本金或支付利息的详情提请国家外汇管理局（SAFE）北京分局批准。

例 6. Each Note shall bear interest at the rate of 5.00% per annum, paid in arrears bi-annually. While the Notes shall bear interest on a bi-annual basis, the principal amount shall not be due until the maturity date, which is expected to be five years from the date of issuance. 每一份票据按照每年 5.00% 的利率计算利息，每年分两次支付利息。虽然所有票据每年分两次计收利息，但是票据本金应当在到期日偿还，前述到期日预计为出票之日起五年。

例 7. The net returns to the Fund are therefore projected to amount to a return of the principal amount of the Loans in full, plus interest, less expenses of the Fund. 因此据估计本基金的净收益等于贷款本金的全部金额外加利息并减去本基金的开销之后的收益。

例 8. The *Facility Agreement* shall contain default clauses customary for a facility of this nature, including (inter alia) failure of the Borrower to pay principal, interest and other sums under the *Facility Agreement* subject to 10 Business Days grace period in respect of interest and other sums. 《贷款协议》包含习惯上适用于此类贷款的违约条款，包括（除其他外）借款人未在给予利息和其他款项的 10 个营业日的宽限期内偿还《贷款协议》项下的本金、利息和其他款项。

名词 principal 的第四、五、六个义项出现频率也很高：

例 9. Nothing contained in this Agreement shall be construed so as to give either party the power to direct or control the daily activities of the other Party or to render the Parties as joint venturers, partners, employer and employee, or principal and agent. 本协议所包含的内容不应被解释为授予任何一方当事人指导或者控制对方当事人的日常活动的权力，也不应被解释成使双方当事人之间形成合资、合伙、雇佣或代理关系。

例 10. It is agreed that Seller, in rendering any services on Buyer's premises, will be an independent contractor and that neither Seller nor any principal, partner, agent or employee of Seller is the legal representative of Buyer for any purpose whatsoever and has no right or authority to assume or create, by action, in writing or otherwise, any obligation of any kind, express or implied, in the name of or on behalf of Buyer and neither Seller nor any principal, agent or employee of Seller shall be entitled to or be eligible to participate in any benefit program extended by Buyer to its employees. 双方当事人约定，在买方的场所提供服务过程中，卖方是独立缔约人，无论卖方抑或卖方的负责人、合伙人、代理人或雇员，均非买方为任何目的的法定代表人，无权通过行为、以书面形式或其他方式，以买方的名义或代表买方，承担或创

设任何种类的明示或默示义务，无论卖方抑或卖方的负责人、合伙人、代理人或雇员，均无权或没有资格参与买方向本单位雇员提供的福利计划。

例 11. "Liabilities" means all present and future moneys, debts and liabilities due, owing or incurred by any Obligor to the Lender under or in connection with any Finance Document (in each case, whether alone or jointly, or jointly and severally, with any other person, whether actually or contingently and whether as principal, surety or otherwise). "债务"是指任何债务人当向贷款人承担的融资文件项下或与融资文件有关的所有当前的和未来的金钱、债务和负债（无论是单独地或者与任何其他人连带地，或者共同连带地，无论是实际地或者或然地，无论作为主债务人、保证人或者以其他身份）。

(2)

principle ['prinsəpəl] ① n.[C,U] a moral rule or belief about what is right and wrong, that influences how you behave 行为准则，处事原则；② n.[C] the basic idea that a plan or system is based on 原则；③ n.[C] a rule which explains the way something such as a machine works, or which explains a natural force in the universe 原理

in principle 基本上，原则上，大体上

principled (more principled, most principled) ['prinsəpəld] adj. ① 品德高尚的；② 依据道德准则的

unprincipled [ʌn'prinsəpəld] adj. = unscrupulous 无耻的，品德败坏的

例 12. The Equipment shall be delivered in principle in complete set for each system element. 设备的交付原则上应当为每个系统元件的整套设备。

例 13. "GAAP" means United States generally accepted accounting principles and practices in effect from time to time applied consistently throughout the periods involved. "通用会计准则"是指在本协议存续期限内始终不时适用的美国现行的公认会计原则和惯例。

例 14. The same principle of local preferences will also govern the procurement of all goods and materials, ranging from that for construction to furnishing of finished townhome units. 从建筑材料到已完工连排别墅的装修材料，所有商品和材料的采购工作也需要遵守优先照顾本地企业的原则。

例 15. XYZ shall comply with the principles and requirements of the *Code of Conduct for SSS' Suppliers* attached hereto as Annex V (hereinafter the *Code of Conduct*). XYZ 应当遵守作为附件五附于本协议的《SSS 供货商行为规范》所规定的各项原则和要求（以下称为《行为规范》）。

例 16. The notice and opportunity to remedy provision shall not apply to violations of requirements and principles regarding of the child labor as set out in the *Code of Conduct* or willful failures to comply with the *Code of Conduct*'s environmental protection requirements. 违反《行为规范》中关于禁止童工的要求和原则或者故意违反《行为规范》中关于环境保护的规定，则不适用上文关于通知和补救机会的规定。

例 17. Special modules are included that are geared toward understanding the medical and psychosocial complications of injection drug users and commercial sex workers, including the principles of harm reduction and the optimal use of methadone and buprenorphine. 收录了几个特别单元，包括降低有害性原则和适度使用美沙酮和丁丙诺啡原则，意在理解注射毒品者和商业性性工作者在医学和社会心理方面的并发症。

例 18. The computation of liabilities and expenses incurred in Exclusive Operations, including the liabilities and expenses of Operator for conducting such operations, shall be made in accordance with the principles set out in the Accounting Procedure attached hereto as Exhibit "A". 应当依照以附件 A 的形式附录于本协议的会计程序中阐述的诸项原则，计算专属作业中产生的债务和费用，包括作业人开展上述作业活动的债务和费用。

例 19. In any event, the transferring Investor shall obtain the prior written approval of the other Investors to the transfer to said Party, after having demonstrated to the reasonable satisfaction of the other Investors, that said third party is a company of an acceptable technical and financial standing according to generally accepted oil and gas industry and financial principles. 在任何情况下,在令其他投资人合理满意地证明,依照公认油气行业和财务准则,第三方当事人是具备可以接受的技术和财务资格的公司之后,转让投资人应当征得其他投资人对于向第三人转让的事先书面同意。

proactive & reactive

(1)

proactive [prəʊˈæktɪv] *adj.* making things happen or change rather than reacting to events 积极主动的

例 1. In a monitoring and intelligence gathering sense, this sort of structural approach can also enable more proactive analysis and action to deal quickly with emerging issues, such as unexpected falls in revenue from key industries or segment. 在监测和情报搜集的意义上，这种结构方法还能够实现更积极主动的分析和行动，从而迅速处理新出现的问题，比如关键行业或部门收入意外下降。

例 2. Internationally focused officers (including those familiar with the languages most used by international business) who meet routine business needs but are proactive, creative and adaptive to new ideas and challenges, seeing change as an opportunity. 关注国际事务的工作人员（包括那些熟悉国际企业最常用语言的工作人员）不仅满足企业例行需求，还积极进取、独具创意，适应新的思想和挑战，将变化视为机遇。

例 3. The Committee recommends proactive strategies and action to raise extrabudgetary funds and resources, and increased coordination between regular and extrabudgetary project activities. 委员会建议采取积极主动的策略和行动筹集预算外资金和资源，增进常规项目活动和预算外项目活动之间的协调。

例 4. The government of Japan would engage proactively to raise awareness of the problem of hate speech and the importance of embracing diversity with a view to establishing a society in which everyone's human rights were respected. 为了建立一个每个人的人权都得到尊重的社会，日本政府将会积极主动地提高人们对于仇恨言论问题和接受多样性的重要意义的认识。

例 5. The Special Representative notes the need to ensure that sufficient resources are provided to the Office and its partners to enable an increased focus on mandated tasks such as awareness-raising, lessons learned, best practices and proactive engagement with regional and subregional organizations. 特别代表注意到必须确保为她的办公室及其伙伴提供充足的资源，这样才能对提高认识、总结经验教训、最佳做法及与区域和次区域组织积极交往等受托任务增进关注。

(2)

reactive [ri'æktiv] *adj.* ① reacting to events or situations rather than starting or doing new things yourself 反应的，回应的；② a reactive substance changes when it is mixed with another substance 有活性的，起反应的

例 6. Unfortunately, the police deal with crimes in a reactive rather than proactive way. 不幸的是，警察应付犯罪的方式只是发生一起调查一起，而不是主动采取对策。

例 7. The agreed historical facts are thus: in the early hours of April 26 1986, a botched safety test at the plant's Reactor Four caused it to become very unstable. Then, a flaw in the reactor's emergency shutdown system not understood by its operators caused an intense and enormous surge in reactivity. That led to an explosion that blew the 2,000-tonne lid off the reactor vessel, smashed through the roof of the plant, showered the surrounding areas with highly reactive debris and exposed the reactor core and its radioactive contents to the night sky. 于是一致认可了这样的历史事实：1986 年 4 月 26 日凌晨，核电站四号反应堆的一次拙劣的安全测试导致反应堆变得非常不稳定。然后，反应堆应急停堆系统的一个缺陷（操作人员对这个缺陷摸不着头脑）导致反应性急剧增高，引起了爆炸，2000 吨重的反应堆槽盖被掀飞，穿

破了核电站的屋顶，向周边区域喷溅了具有高度反应性的碎屑，反应堆核心及其放射性成分也被暴露在夜空中。

例 8. If we want Global Britain to be more than a bumper sticker, we have to match our ambition with action. Ministers need to look decades ahead because that is what other countries are doing. A piecemeal, reactive approach will not do — we need a confident and considered long-term plan. This means a strategy that brings together migration policy with export opportunities, the potential for young Britons to live and study abroad and moves to make it easier for our universities to expand overseas. 如果我们想要全球化英国具有实实在在的意义，我们就得让行动与抱负相称。大臣们必须为今后几十年做好打算，因为这是其他国家正在做的事情。东一榔头西一棒子、头疼医头脚疼医脚的办法帮不上忙——我们需要一个自信和深思熟虑的长期计划。这意味着采取这样一项策略，也就是将移民政策与出口机会、使英国年轻人在国外生活学习的潜力和促进我国大学向海外拓展的举措结合起来。

例 9. The days of the in-house lawyer being a somewhat reactive function have long since passed. We are having ever more complex and external-facing conversations relating to new and emerging technologies. 企业法务的作用有点像来了问题再出手解决，这样的日子早就结束了。我们正在就新技术和新兴技术进行着更加复杂和面向外部的对话。

例 10. The biomedical scientist and entrepreneur Craig Venter recently described today's approach to healthcare as "medieval". This is not entirely fair; we no longer rely on astrologers for diagnosis or vendors of snake oil for drug discovery. Nevertheless, he makes an important point: we could do much better. More specifically, today's medical systems are too reactive, when they could be more proactive. 生物医学科学家和企业家克雷格·文特尔不久前称当今的医疗方法"老掉了牙"。这么说不完全公平；我们既不依赖占星术士做诊断，也不仰仗卖蛇油的商贩发现药物。不过，他提出了一个很重要的观点：我们可以做得更好。更具体地说，当今的医疗系统在可以更积极主动的时候却太被动了。

procure

procure [prəˈkjʊə] *v.t. (formal)* 争取，促致，获得；做淫媒，拉皮条；采购

procurement [prəˈkjʊə.mənt] *n.[U]*

procurable [prəˈkjʊərəbl] *adj.*

例 1. Ensuring universal access to affordable essential medicines is fundamental to fulfilling the "right to health". The establishment of a national drug policy—which includes an essential medicines list and standard treatment guidelines—and establishing the institutional arrangements to implement and enforce it, is the foundation of ensuring access to medicines. It is also important to have a procurement strategy for obtaining the most cost-effective drugs in the right quantities, of sufficient quality, in a timely manner, and at the lowest possible total cost. Safety and quality of medicines and technologies need to be regulated in relation to entry of medicines into the country, manufacturing, importation and distribution, marketing and provision of information. 确保人人都能获得负担得起的基本药物对实现"健康权"至关重要。制定一项国家药品政策（包括一份基本药物清单和标准治疗准则）和确立实施及强制执行该政策的体制安排是确保人们获得药物的基础。制定采购策略，以尽可能最低的总成本，及时获得具有充足质量、合适数量的最合算的药品，这一点也具有重要意义。需要在药物进入国家、制造、进口和经销、营销和提供信息方面对药物和技术的安全性及质量进行监管。

例 2. The legal regime for public procurement is compromised as a result of the conflicting Bidding Law and the Public Procurement Law. The conflicts can only be satisfactorily resolved if both these laws are repealed or amended so that a single legal code applies to the public procurement process. Legislative action is needed by the

National People's Congress to resolve this issue and it is recommended that prompt action be taken to clarify and unify the basic legal provisions as soon as possible. 由于招标法与公共采购法相冲突，公共采购的法律制度受到损害。只有当这两项法律都被废除或修订，使一个单一的法律法规适用于公共采购过程，冲突才能得到满意的解决。全国人民代表大会需要采取立法行动来解决这一问题，建议尽快采取行动澄清和统一法律的基本规定。

例 3. The Borrower shall procure that no substantial change is made to the general nature of the business of Borrower from that carried on at the date of this Agreement. 借款人应当设法保证借款人在本协议订立之日开展的营业的一般性质不会发生重大变化。

例 4. The Pledgor shall on the date of this Agreement and, where Equity Interests are acquired by it after the date of this Agreement, on the date of that acquisition, deliver (or procure to be delivered) to the Lender, or as it directs, the capital contribution certificate issued by the Company representing Equity Interests (together with the copies of approval certificate, shareholders register and business license of the Company that evidence the ownership of the Pledgor in respect of such Equity Interests). 出质人应当在本协议订立之日，若出质人在本协议订立之后获得股权，则在获得股权之日，向贷款人交付（或者敦促他人向贷款人交付），或者按照贷款人的指示交付，公司核发的代表股权的出资证书（连同证明出质人对股权所享有的所有权的批准证书、股东登记簿和公司的营业执照的副本）。

例 5. The Vendor shall procure each of its nominees on the board of directors of the Company to execute the resolution of the board of directors approving the sale and transfer of the Sale Shares and the appointment of [•] new directors to be on the board of directors of the Company on Completion Date. 卖方应当尽力促成公司董事会中卖方提名的董事在完成日期签署董事会决议，批准待售股份的销售和过户，以及任命［•］位公司董事会的新董事。

例 6. Upon request of the Security Agent, the Contractor shall procure all Subcontractors to perform such agreements, contracts or subcontracts which have been entered into between the Contractor and such Subcontractors for carrying out any part of the Works. 根据担保代理人的要求，承包人应当促使全体分包人履行承包人与分包人为开展工程任何部分施工而订立的协议、合同或者分包合同。

例 7. The Company shall, forthwith upon execution hereof, execute and deliver to the Account Banks with which a Charged Account is opened a notice of assignment in the form set out in Schedule 2 (Notice and Acknowledgement of Charge) and shall procure that such Account Banks acknowledge such notice in the form set out in Schedule 2 (Notice and Acknowledgement of Charge). 公司应当在签署本协议后立即采用本协议附件 2（质押通知和确认）规定的格式，签署并且向在其中开立质押账户的四家开户银行交付转让通知，公司应当设法使上述开户银行按照本协议附件 2（质押通知和确认）规定的格式对上述转让通知予以确认。

例 8. Art. 314. —Prostitution.

A person who, for gain, procures, promotes or aids the prostitution of another person, is guilty of an offence, a Class 1 petty offence, punishable with a definite term of imprisonment of not less than 6 months and not more than 12 months, or a fine of 20,001−50,000 Nakfas, to be set in intervals of 2,500 Nakfas.

第 314 条　卖淫罪

行为人为了牟利，促致、筹办或帮助他人卖淫，即构成卖淫罪，本罪属于第一级轻罪，应当对犯罪人处以不少于六个月，不超过十二个月的定期监禁，或处以 20001 至 50000 纳克法罚金，在此量刑幅度内罚金按 2500 纳克法的额度递增。

prosecute & persecute

(1)

persecute ['pɜːsikjuːt] *v.t.* ① 迫害；② = harass 骚扰

例 1. This young woman, who was recently acquitted in a mysterious homicide case, complained of being persecuted by paparazzi. 这名年轻妇女不久以前在一宗离奇的杀人案中被宣告无罪，她投诉说狗仔队对自己纠缠不休。

persecution [ˌpɜːsiˈkjuːʃən] *n.[C,U]* 迫害
persecution complex *n.[C]* 受迫害妄想症
persecutor ['pɜːsikjuːtə] *n.[C]* 迫害者

(2)

prosecute ['prɒsikjuːt] *v.t. & v.i.* ① *v.t. & v.i.* to commence and carry out a legal action 起诉

例 2. If the plaintiff fails to prosecute or to comply with these rules or a court order, a defendant may move to dismiss the action or any claim against it. 如果原告未提起诉讼或不遵守本规则或法庭命令，被告可以向法庭申请驳回针对被告的诉讼或任何申索。

② *v.t. & v.i.* to institute and pursue a criminal action against (a person) 对……提起刑事检控

例 3. Ted Bundy was prosecuted in the 1970s for the rape and murder of more than 36 women in several states. 泰德·邦迪因强奸和杀害超过 36 位女性而于 20 世纪 70 年代在几个州被起诉。

③ *v.t.* *(formal)* to engage in; carry on 从事，进行

例 4. The investigation cannot be prosecuted further owing to undue interference by the Wall Street movers and shakers. 由于华尔街大佬施加了不当干扰，调查工作进行不下去了。

prosecutable [ˈprɒsikjuːtəbl] *adj.* (of a crime or person) subject to prosecution; capable of being prosecuted 可被提起检控的

例 5. According to the criminal law currently in force, the perpetrator, though might be prosecutable, could hardly be convicted, not to mention being condemned to death. 根据现行的刑法，即使能够起诉这名犯罪分子，也几乎定不了罪，更不用说判处死刑了。

prosecution [ˌprɒsiˈkjuːʃən] *n.[C,U]* 检控；起诉；从事，进行

例 6. Any article seized which is required for the criminal prosecution shall be preserved in a safe place until handed over to the Court as an exhibit. 凡因刑事检控需要而扣押的物品应当在安全的地方存放，直至作为呈堂证物移送法院。

例 7. The President may grant an amnesty in respect to certain offences or certain classes of offenders. Such amnesty may cancel the charges and discontinue any prosecution, or may, where conviction has already occurred, extinguish any and all punishments previously imposed. 总统可以对某些罪行或某些类别的犯罪人准予大赦。大赦可以撤销指控和停止任何检控，或者在已经作出定罪的情况下，大赦可以消灭先前判处的一切处罚。

the prosecution 控方

例 8. If the court is to have the power to interfere with the prosecution in the present circumstances it must be because the judiciary accept a responsibility for the maintenance of the rule of law that embraces a willingness to oversee executive action and to refuse to countenance behaviour that threatens either basic human rights or the rule of law. ... 如果法院在这起案件的情形下行使干涉公诉的权力，那一定是由于司法部门肩负起维护法治的义务，愿意监督行政机关的行为，不赞成威胁基本人权或法治的行为。……

witness for the prosecution 控方证人

例 9. *Witness for the Prosecution,* a 1957 American film set in the Old Bailey in London, is based on the play of the same name written by Agatha Christie.《控方证人》是一部 1957 年上映的美国电影，它取材于阿加莎·克里斯蒂编写的同名剧本，将伦敦的中央刑事法院设为背景。

例 10. (2) An adjournment may be granted if the Court is satisfied that: 如果法庭相信有下列情形，法庭可以准予休庭：
    ……

witnesses for the prosecution or the defense are not present 控方证人或辩方证人没有到庭
prosecutor ['prɔsikju:tə] 检察官，检控人
prosecutorial misconduct [prɔsikju:'tɔ:riəl] *n.[U]* 检方渎职

例 11. In criminal law, prosecutorial misconduct means a prosecutor's improper or illegal act (or failure to act), especially involving an attempt to avoid required disclosure or to persuade the jury to wrongly convict a defendant or assess an unjustified punishment. If prosecutorial misconduct results in a mistrial, a later prosecution may be barred under the Double Jeopardy Clause. 在刑法领域，检方渎职是指检察官的不正当或违法行为（或失职行为），尤其是涉及试图规避规定的披露或试图说服陪审团错误地给被告人定罪或评定错误的处罚。如果检方渎职导致审理无效，可以根据双重起诉条款禁止后续的检控。

prospective & retrospective

(1)

prospective [prəˈspɛktiv] *adj.* ① effective or operative in the future 将来生效或施行的；②
anticipated or expected; likely to come about 预期的；可能发生的

例 1. Once a year, with prior written approval, XYZ may support up to 50% of
the booth rental for international exhibitions held in the Distributor's region that attract
customers or prospective buyers from outside his area of responsibility. 每年，在事先
征得 XYZ 书面批准的情况下，对于在经销商所在地区内举办的吸引来自经销商
负责区域之外的客户或潜在买方的国际展览会，XYZ 可以一次性赞助最多 50%
的摊位租金。

例 2. The value of the assets of the Borrower is less than its liabilities (taking into
account contingent and prospective liabilities). 借款人的资产价值少于借款人的负
债（将未定债务和预期债务考虑在内）。

例 3. In addition to the federal income tax consequences described above, prospective investors should consider potential state, local and foreign tax consequences
of an investment in the Fund. 除上文描述的在联邦所得税方面的后果外，潜在投
资人应当考虑对本基金进行的投资在州、地方以及外国税收方面可能产生的
后果。

例 4. The majority notes that this litigation has persisted for many years, that petitioner has already graduated from another college, that UT's policy may have changed
over time, and that this case may offer little prospective guidance. 大多数法官注意到，

这场诉讼已经持续了许多年，呈请人已经从另一所大学毕业，德州大学的政策可能随着时间推移而改变，而且这宗案件不会有多少前瞻性指导意义。

例 5. In the event of termination of this Agreement, neither party will be entitled to any compensation, damages, loss of profits or prospective profits, with respect to investments made or goodwill established during the term of this Agreement. 在终止本协议的情况下，对于本协议存续期间所作投资或者建立的商誉，当事人均无权获得补偿、损害赔偿金、受偿利润损失或者预期利润损失。

例 6. Two form documents have been developed for your use: (a) a form *RFQ* that can be used to send to the prospective equipment manufacturer, and (b) a form *Equipment Purchase Agreement* (EPA) for use in purchasing the equipment. 有两类表格文件可供使用：（a）《询价单》，可寄送给潜在的设备制造商；以及（b）《设备购买协议》，供购买设备时使用。

注意区分与 prospective 词形相近的 perspective：二者词性不同，prospective 是形容词，
　　perspective 是名词，而且二者意思也不相同。
perspective [pəˈspɛktɪv] ① *n.[C]* a way of thinking about something, especially one which is
　　influenced by the type of person you are or by your experiences = viewpoint 视角，看法；
　　② *n.[U]* 透视法
perspective 的第一个义项"视角，看法"后面常搭配介词"on"。另外，perspective 构成的
　　下面两个词组也很重要：
put something into perspective 客观地看待
get/keep sth. in perspective 正确地看待

例 7. This girl's death and the acquittal of the perpetrator gave the law-abiding members of the public a whole new perspective on crime and punishment. 这位姑娘的死和凶手被裁定无罪让守法良民对罪与罚有了全新的认识。

例 8. From a financial perspective, transfer pricing is probably the most important cross-border tax issue globally. 从财务的角度来看，转让定价大概是全世界最重要的跨境税务问题。

例 9. This target could be linked to those regarding social protection systems and could go beyond the indicator of income to provide a broader perspective on inequalities disproportionately affecting persons with albinism. 可以把这项具体目标与关系到社会保障体系的指标联系起来，而且可以不限于收入指标，以便更全面地反映出过大影响白化病患者的各种不平等现象。

例 10. This film seems to glamorize such villains as Professor James Moriarty because its screenplay is written from a criminal's perspective. 这部影片似乎美化詹姆斯·莫里亚蒂教授这样的恶棍，因为剧本是从罪犯的视角创作的。

例 11. From a resource mobilization perspective, timely and active participation by UNESCO in needs assessments and in the early phase of planning for recovery and reconstruction is of critical importance as well as strong coordination between Headquarters and the Field on outreach to potential donors. 从筹措资金的角度来看，联合国教科文组织及时和积极参加需求评估和恢复及重建规划的早期阶段，以及在总部与总部外办事处之间就动员潜在捐助者进行有力协调，具有至关重要的意义。

例 12. From a policy perspective, failure to tackle excessive interest payments to associated enterprises gives MNEs an advantage over purely domestic businesses which are unable to gain such tax advantages. 从政策的角度来看，不解决向关联企业过量支付利息的问题，跨国企业就比那些不能获得此类税收利益的纯粹国内企业具有优势。

(2)

retrospective [ˌretrəʊˈspektɪv] *adj.* （法律、裁判等）溯及既往的，有追溯效力的；回顾的 retrospective 与 prospective 意思相对，也可以拼写成 retroactive [ˌretrəʊˈæktɪv]。

例 13. The Parties mutually agree to terminate the Agreement to which they are a party with retroactive effect. 双方当事人相互同意溯及既往地终止其作为其一方当事人的本协议。

例 14. The Parties agree that with retroactive effect from 22 September 2019 the first paragraph of Clause 9.03 of the Agreement shall be deleted and restated as follows: 双方当事人同意，自 2019 年 9 月 22 日起溯及既往地删除本协议第 9.03 条第一款，并将该款重述如下：

例 15. The Fund will not request any rulings from the IRS or any tax opinion on the tax consequences described below or any issue. No assurances can be given that the positions taken by the Fund on its tax returns will be respected by the IRS or upheld by the courts and there can be no assurance that the applicable tax laws and regulations upon which these positions are based will not be changed in the future, possibly with retroactive effect to the Fund and the Limited Partners. 本基金不要求就下文描述的在税务方面的后果或者任何事务由国内税务署作出裁决或者求得任何税务意见。无法保证本基金就其纳税申报表采取的立场将会得到国内税务署尊重或者法院支持，也无法保证本基金采取上述立场所依据的税务法律法规今后不会发生变化并有可能对本基金和有限合伙人具有追溯效力。

例 16. Each Party to the Contract releases the other Party to that Contract from any and all of its obligations under that Contract with retroactive effect and shall not hold the other Party liable with regard to any and all of its obligations under that Contract. 合同的各方当事人溯及既往地豁免合同对方当事人在合同之下的一切义务，不得要求对方当事人对于其在合同之下的一切义务承担责任。

provided & proviso

(1)

provided (或 provided that) 是从属连词，在法律文件中常常用来引起表示条件的状语从句。

例 1. The Contractor agrees and acknowledges that the Parent shall be entitled at any time to assign, transfer or charge all or any of its rights and/or obligations under this Agreement, provided however that the Contractor shall have not greater liability under this Agreement than it would have had in the absence of such assignment, transfer or charge. 承包商同意并且承认，母公司有权在任何时候转让、转移其在本协议下的全部或任何权利和／或义务或有权在该权利和／或义务上办理押记，但前提是承包商根据本协议承担的责任不超过倘若未办理这种转让、转移或押记承包商本应承担的责任。

例 2. There shall be three (3) arbitrators. Both Parties shall each appoint one (1) arbitrator. The third (3rd) arbitrator shall be appointed by agreement between the Parties or, failing within twenty (20) days of the appointment of the two party-nominated arbitrators, by the Chairman of the CIETAC, provided that the 3rd arbitrator shall not be a national of the country of incorporation or of the countries of residence of either of the Parties to this Agreement. 应有三（3）位仲裁员。双方各自委任一（1）位仲裁员。第三（3）位仲裁员由双方合意委任，或在双方委任两位仲裁员后二十（20）日内如未能委任第三位仲裁员，则由中国国际经济贸易仲裁委员会主任任命，但第三位仲裁员不得为本协议任何一方成立为法人的所在国国民或居住国国民。

(2)

proviso [prəˈvaizəu] (pl. provisos) *n[C]* *(formal)* 但书；附带条件

《布莱克法律词典》对 proviso 是这样解释的：A limitation, condition, or stipulation upon whose compliance a legal or formal document's validity or application may depend. In drafting, a provision that begins with the words provided that and supplies a condition, exception, or addition.

我们可以看出，但书其实就是法律文件中说明例外情形、限制条件的条文，法律文书的适用范围或效力取决于该条文，而以 "provided that" 开头，表示条件的条文就是但书。

例 3. This was a very important proviso because the plaintiff was contractually bound to pay the purchase price to AAA and not to the BBB and CCC. 这是一个非常重要的但书，因为原告人按照契约的规定，有义务向 AAA 支付购买价款，但是原告人没有义务向 BBB 和 CCC 支付购买价款。

例 4. The Defence is granted leave to file a response to the Prosecutor's Response by Wednesday, 10 February 1999, with the proviso that the matters raised are solely by way of reply. 辩方获准在 1999 年 2 月 10 日星期三之前对检方的答复提交答辩，但条件是只能以答辩状的方式提出事项。

注意这个例句中的短语：with the proviso that。

关于 provide 的用法：

provide [prəˈvaid] v.t. ① 提供

这个义项相当于 supply。注意短语中使用的介词：provide sth. for sb./provide sb. with sth.。

provision [prəˈviʒən] n.[C,U] 提供，准备

provider [prəˈvaidə]

例 5. The heading of the *Memorandum* states that the meeting with the XXX representatives was in relation to the provision of management assistance to the JV Company. 《备忘录》的标题指出会见 XXX 代表团是商讨向合资公司提供管理援助事宜。

例 6. The Court may order the applicant or appellant to provide security for the costs of the application or appeal, and may direct that the application or appeal be dismissed if the order is not complied with. 高等法院可以饬令申请人或上诉人为申请或上诉的费用提供担保，如果申请人或上诉人不遵守该命令，高等法院可以指示驳回申请或上诉。

②（法规或契约）规定

provision [prə'viʒən] *n.[C]*（法规或契约的）规定，条款

例 7. The Court shall not have jurisdiction to confirm, vary, set aside or remit an award on an arbitration agreement except where so provided in this Act. 对于涉及仲裁协议的仲裁裁决，高等法院不享有确认、变更、撤销该裁决或将该裁决发回重审的管辖权，但是本法规定可以确认、变更、撤销或发回重审的除外。

例 8. Where any provision in this Act allows the parties to determine any issue, the parties may authorise a third party, including an arbitral institution, to make that determination. 凡本法的条文允许双方当事人就任何争议点作出裁定，则双方当事人可以授权包括仲裁机构在内的第三方就该争议点作出裁定。

例 9. This Agreement shall constitute the only and entire agreement between the Parties, and unless otherwise expressly provided for in this Termination Agreement, all other agreements, oral or written, made and entered into between the Parties prior to the execution of this Termination Agreement shall be null and void. 本协议构成双方当事人之间唯一的和完整的合意，除非本协议中另有明示规定，在签署本协议之前缔结和订立的所有其他口头或者书面协议应当无效。

provide against sth. 防止，防备
provide for sb. 供养，养活
provide for sth. 为……做好准备；（法规或契约）规定
make provision for sth. 为……做好准备，
make provision against sth. 应对，防备

例 10. But if any provide not for his own, and specially for those of his own house, he hath denied the faith, and is worse than an infidel. 人若不看顾亲属、就是背了真道、比不信的人还不好。不看顾自己家里的人、更是如此。（《圣经和合本》）

例 11. Unless the fees of the arbitral tribunal have been fixed by written agreement or such agreement has provided for determination of the fees by a person or institution agreed to by the parties, any party to the arbitration may require that such fees be taxed by the Registrar of the Supreme Court within the meaning of the *Supreme Court of Judicature Act* (Cap. 322). 除非仲裁庭的酬金已经由书面协议予以确定或者书面协议已经规定由双方当事人认可的个人或机构决定仲裁庭的酬金，仲裁的任何一方当事人均可以要求由《司法系统最高法院法》（第322章）所规定的最高法院司法常务官核定上述酬金。

provision 还有另外的意思需要注意：

provision *v.t.* 为……提供配给品

provisions [prəˈviʒənz] *n.[pl]* 配给品，给养；准备金

provisional [prəˈviʒənəl] *adj.* 临时的；暂定的

provisional concluding observations 临时结论意见

provisionally [prəˈviʒənəli] *adv.*

purport

purport [pəˈpɔːt] *v.i.* to profess or claim, esp. falsely; to seem to be 表明，声称

n.[U] The idea or meaning that is conveyed or expressed, esp. by a formal document 主旨，意图

purported [pəˈpɔːtid] *adj.* reputed; rumored. 据说的，被认为的

例 1. Where the summons is served upon the defendant, his agent or pleader, an acknowledgment purporting to be signed by the defendant, the agent, the pleader or an endorsement by a postal employee that the defendant or the agent refused to take delivery may be deemed by the court issuing the summons to be prima facie proof of service. 传票送达被告、其诉讼代理人或辩护人的，被告、其诉讼代理人或辩护人声称签字的回执，或邮递员签署的被告或诉讼代理人拒绝接收传票的批注，应视为法院发出传票的初步送达回证。

例 2. No litigation: there is no claim, action, suit, proceeding, inquiry or investigation pending or, to the best of its knowledge threatened, against it before or by any governmental authority or regulatory body, which purports to affect the transactions contemplated hereby or would materially and adversely affect its ability to perform its obligations under this Agreement, nor, to the best of its knowledge, is there any reasonable basis for any such claim, action, suit, litigation, proceeding or investigation. 没有涉讼：不存在由他人在任何政府部门或管理机关针对该股东或由前述政府部门或管理机关针对该股东提起的任何尚未审结或者——就该股东所确知——表示将要提起的，表明影响本协议所筹划的交易或者将对该股东履行它在本协议之下义务的能力产生重大不利影响的索赔、诉讼、法律程序、询问或者调查，而且，就该股东所确知，亦不存在启动上述任何索赔、诉讼、法律程序或者调查的任何合理理由。

271

例 3. Consent is no defense to an offence under this Chapter where the person who is purported to have consented was incapable of giving consent by reason of mental incapacity or intoxication. 如看似同意了本节规定的犯罪的人由于无心智能力或昏醉而不能表示同意，对于该犯罪，同意不得作为抗辩理由。

例 4. The Agent may rely on any statement purportedly made by a director, authorised signatory or employee of any person regarding any matters which may reasonably be assumed to be within his knowledge or within his power to verify. 代理行可以信赖任何据称是由任何人的董事、授权签字人或雇员作出的声明，可以合理假定该董事、授权签字人或雇员知晓或有权核实前述声明所关涉的事项。

例 5. The Contractor shall not terminate or suspend or agree to the termination or suspension of any obligation under the Contract unless it has complied with its obligations under the Contract and, in the case of a purported termination, provided not less than 180 days prior written notice thereof to the Security Agent. 承包人不应终止或中止或者同意终止或中止合同项下任何义务，除非承包人已经遵守其在合同项下的义务，而且如果承包人表示终止该义务，须至少提前 180 日以书面形式将此意图通知担保代理人。

quorum & quota

(1)

quorum [ˈkwɔːrəm] *n.[C]* 法定人数
quorate [ˈkwɔːreit] *adj.* 达到法定人数的

例 1. Quorum. The President may declare a meeting open and permit the debate to proceed when at least one third of the members of the Council are present. The presence of a majority of the members shall be required for any decision to be taken. 法定人数。主席在至少有三分之一的理事会成员出席会议的情况下，可宣布会议开始并准许进行辩论。任何决定都要有过半数成员出席会议才能作出。

例 2. No business shall be transacted at any general meeting unless a quorum of members is present at the time when the meeting proceeds to business and continues to be present until the conclusion of the meeting; save as herein otherwise provided, if the Company has more than one member, two members present in person or by proxy shall be a quorum. If the Company has only one member, one member present in person or by proxy shall be a quorum of a general meeting. 除非在全体会议审议事务时，而且截至会议闭幕，出席全体会议的成员始终达到法定人数，不得在该次全体会议上审议任何事务；除本《公司章程》另有规定的以外，如果公司的成员在一人以上，两名成员亲自或通过代理人出席会议构成法定人数。如果公司仅有一名成员，该名成员亲自或通过代理人出席构成全体会议的法定人数。

例 3. An alternate Director shall not be counted in reckoning the maximum number of the Directors allowed by the *Articles of Association* for the time being. A Director acting as alternate shall have an additional vote at meetings of Directors for each

Director for whom he acts as alternate but he shall count as only one for the purpose of determining whether a quorum be present. 计算《公司章程》允许的董事人数上限，候补董事暂不计入。候补董事在董事会会议上为他所代理的每一位董事享有一个额外的表决权，但是在确定出席会议的人是否达到法定人数时，候补董事仅算作一人。

例 4. Where a minimum of two Directors are appointed to the Board, a quorum for the transaction of any and all such business at a meeting of the Directors of the Company shall be two Directors physically present. In counting a quorum, an alternate Director present shall be counted as part of the quorum, but only in the absence of his appointor. Whenever the number of appointed Directors is no greater than one, then a sole Director shall be empowered to exercise all and any such powers of the Company deemed to be vested in the Board of Directors of the Company. Clause 89 of Table A shall be modified accordingly. 倘若被任命为董事会成员的董事最低人数为二人，两名亲自到场的董事即构成在本公司董事会议上处理各种事务的法定人数。在计算法定人数时，应当将到场的候补董事计算在内，但是只有在任命该候补董事的人不在场时该候补董事方可计入法定人数。当被任命董事的人数不超过一人时，那么应当授权唯一的一名董事行使被视为赋予本公司董事会的本公司的一切权力。甲表第 89 条应作相应修改。

(2)

quota [ˈkwəʊtə] *n.[C]* 限额，配额，定额

例 5. The Committee also recommends that the State party further utilize temporary special measures, in accordance with Article 4, Paragraph 1, of the *Convention* and general recommendations 25, on temporary special measures, and 23, on women in public life, including establishment of benchmarks, quotas, numerical goals and timetables, to accelerate women's full and equal participation in elected and appointed bodies. 委员会还建议缔约国依照《公约》第 4 条第 1 款以及委员会关于暂行特别措施的第 25 号一般性建议和关于妇女参与公共生活的第 23 号一般性建议，

进一步利用暂行特别措施，包括设立基准、配额、数字目标和时间表，使妇女更快地充分和平等加入民选机构和任命机构。

例 6. The agreement reached at the Sixth World Trade Organization Ministerial Conference, held in Hong Kong, China, to provide duty-free and quota-free market access for LDCs should be respected and implemented. 在中国香港举行的世贸组织第六次部长会议达成的给予最不发达国家免关税和免配额的市场准入协议，应得到遵守并付诸执行。

例 7. The State Party takes note of General Recommendation No. 5 adopted at the Seventh Session in 1988 urging state parties to make use of temporary special measures such as positive action, preferential treatment or quota systems to advance women's integration into education, the economy, politics and employment. 缔约国注意到1988 年第七届会议通过的第 5 号一般性建议，建议敦促缔约国利用积极行动、优惠待遇、配额制度等暂行特别措施，推动妇女进入教育、经济、政治和就业领域。

例 8. No gender quota was set in the Government's Action Programme of 1998. Instead there was only a general statement that it was to be the aim of all the ministries to work towards equal representation on all public boards and committees. 1998 年的政府行动纲领中没有男女的数额限制。只在一份综述中提到，各部的目标是努力使各公共委员会和部门中的男女代表比例相同。

例 9. The amendment of the *Organic Law of the Villagers' Committees* in 2010 stipulates a quota for women's participation in the villagers' committee and its representatives' conferences. 2010 年修订的《村民委员会组织法》规定了参加村民委员会和村民代表会议的妇女名额。

random & ransom

(1)

random [ˈrændəm] *adj.* 任意的；随机的

例 1. The report is based on a random sample of 1,000 patients. 这份报告是以随机挑选的一千名患者为根据编写的。

例 2. The masked man fired a few random shots before he fled. 蒙面人胡乱开了几枪，然后逃走了。

at random 随意，随机

例 3. Some thriller buffs said that, Hitchcock's films, even selected at random, would be a masterpiece. 有些爱看惊悚片的人说过，希区柯克的电影，随便挑一部，都是杰作。

randomly [ˈrændəmli] *adv.*

例 4. The shop shall hand out giveaways to twelve randomly chosen customers. 这家商店将给 12 名被随机选中的顾客分发赠品。

randomize [ˈrændəmaiz] *v.t.* 随机排列，随机处理
注意：randomize 是术语。

(2)

ransom [ˈrænsəm] *n.[C]* 赎金；*v.t.* 赎回

例 5. Charles Lindbergh, famous American aviator, paid the $50,000 ransom demanded by the kidnappers, but sadly his infant son's dead body was found in the nearby woods weeks later. 著名的美国飞行员查尔斯·林德伯格支付了绑匪索要的五万美元赎金，可是很遗憾，几周以后，人们在附近的树林里发现了他的幼儿的尸体。

hold sb./sth. for ransom（美式英语），hold sb./sth. to random（英式英语）为索取赎金而扣押

例 6. This painting had been stolen from a museum and held for ransom, however, thanks to relentless efforts by police, it was recovered safe and sound. 盗贼曾经将这幅画作从博物馆盗走并索要赎金，多亏警方的不懈追查，这幅画作完璧归赵。

hold sb. to ransom（英式英语）要挟

例 7. It is known that politicians with an ulterior motive tend to hold their government to ransom by posting unconfirmed shocking photos. 人们知道，别有用心的政客会发布未经证实的触目惊心的照片，逼本国政府就范。

recant & decant

(1)

recant [ri'kænt] *v.t. & v.i.* ① to say publicly that you no longer have a political or religious belief that you had before 公开宣布放弃以前的政治或宗教信仰；② to withdraw or renounce prior statements or testimony formally or publicly （正式或公开地）撤回（先前的声明或证言）

recantation [ˌriːkænˈteiʃn] *n.[C,U]* 公开正式撤回证词

翻译法律文件，尤其是诉讼文书的时候，经常用到 recant 的第二个义项。

例 1. The prosecution hoped the eyewitness wouldn't recant her corroborating testimony on the stand. 检方希望证人在出庭作证的时候不要撤回作为佐证的证言。

例 2. Under grueling cross-examination, the witness recanted. 证人顶不过难以承受的交叉询问，撤回了证言。

(2)

decant [di'kænt] *v.t.* to pour liquid, especially wine, from one container into another 把液体（尤其是酒）倾入 / 倒入 / 注入

例 3. The best way to store your sake is to decant it into a small container and keep it in a cool dry place. 存放清酒的最好办法是把清酒注入一个小容器，然后搁在凉爽、干燥的地方。

decanter [di'kæntə] *n.[C]* 醒酒器

recourse & resort

(1)

recourse [riˈkɔːs] *n.[singular, U] (formal)* ① the act of seeking help or advice; ② enforcement of, or a method for enforcing, a right; ③ the right of a holder of a negotiable instrument to demand payment from the drawer or indorser if the instrument is dishonored; ④ the right to repayment of a loan from the borrower's personal assets, not just from the collateral that secured the loan

我们可以把 recourse 的意思归纳为两方面：一是借助，依靠，凭借，诉诸；二是追索权，也就是债权人在主债务人不履行债务时，要求保证人履行债务的权利；票据持有人在票据被拒绝承兑或拒付时对开票人或背书人的求偿权。

例 1. A brilliant and considerate lawyer, when addressing such issues, tends to make every effort to find an amicable solution, without recourse to litigation. 手段高明也替客户着想的律师处理这类问题的时候会想方设法达成和解，尽量不对簿公堂。

例 2. This law has played a critical role in protecting consumers from being defrauded and ensuring that victims of fraudulent misrepresentations have an adequate and prompt legal recourse. 在保护消费者免受欺诈，确保因欺诈性不实陈述而受骗的人获得妥善及时的法律救助方面，这部法律发挥了关键作用。

例 3. That intrinsic relationship has been fully recognized by Member States since the adoption of the *Universal Declaration of Human Rights*, in which it is stated that it is essential, "if man is not to be compelled to have recourse, as a last resort, to rebellion against tyranny and oppression, that human rights should be protected by the rule of law". 自从通过《世界人权宣言》以后，这种固有的关系已经得到各会员国充分认可，《世界人权宣言》规定"为使人类不致迫不得已铤而走险对暴政和压迫进行反叛，有必要使人权受法治的保护"。

例 4. The guarantor shall pay the First Party, without recourse, up to the sum of USD upon receipt of the written claim from the First Party stating the amount and nature of claim. 担保人应当在收到甲方提出的书面赔偿请求后向甲方支付以美元计算的款项，担保人不享有追索权，甲方的书面赔偿请求应当指明赔偿请求的金额和性质。

例 5. "Senior Term Loan Agreement" means the term loan agreement dated [M/D/Y] entered into between the Company as borrower, the Finance Parties as lender and the Security Agent as facility agent in relation to the limited recourse financing of the development and construction of the Works and the Project. "优先定期贷款协议"是指由公司、融资当事人和担保代理人于xxxx年xx月xx日订立的，关于为工程和项目的开发和建设提供有限追索融资的定期贷款协议，其中，公司作为借款人，融资当事人作为贷款人，担保代理人作为贷款代理人。

例 6. Immediate recourse

The Company waives any right it may have of first requiring any Secured Party to proceed against or enforce any other rights or security or claim payment from any Relevant Person or any other person before enforcing the security constituted under this Agreement.

直接追索

公司放弃自己可能享有的，在执行本协议构成的担保之前，首先要求有担保债权人起诉相关人或其他任何人，或者要求有担保债权人执行其他权利或担保，或者要求有担保债权人责令相关人或其他任何人偿还的权利。

(2)

resort [ri'zɔ:t] ① *n.[C]* a place where people go for recreation, especially one with facilities such as lodgings, entertainment, and a relaxing environment ② *n.[U]* something that one turns to for aid or refuge 凭借，采取，诉诸

大家对名词 resort 的第一个义项非常熟悉，例如：seaside resort 海滨度假胜地；Colorado offers such world-renowned ski resorts as Vail and Aspen.

名词 resort 的第二个义项，与 recourse 的第一个义项相同，后面也搭配介词 to。

resort 也可以作为动词：resort to sth./doing sth.。

大家还要注意 resort 的一个重要短语：one's last resort，意思是最后的出路 / 办法 / 希望等。

例如：I wouldn't recommend filing a suit, unless it is your last resort. 我不建议你起诉，除非你没有别的办法。

大家体会下面的例句：

例 7. Article 33 of the *Charter* is critical for the prevention of conflict and the peaceful settlement of disputes. Parties to an international dispute have access to diverse measures and mechanisms for dispute resolution, including negotiation, enquiry, mediation, conciliation, arbitration, judicial settlement and resort to regional agencies or arrangements. 《联合国宪章》第 33 条对于预防冲突及和平解决争端至关重要。国际争端的当事方可以采用多种争端解决措施和机制，包括谈判、调查、调停、和解、公断、司法解决以及利用区域机关或区域办法。

例 8. Eighteen universal instruments (14 conventions and 4 protocols) against international terrorism, including the relevant Security Council resolutions, have been elaborated within the framework of the United Nations relating to specific terrorist activities. The Special Rapporteur on the promotion and protection of human rights and fundamental freedoms while countering terrorism emphasizes that counter-terrorism measures that are compliant with human rights help to prevent the recruitment of individuals to commit acts of terrorism and that human rights abuses have all too often contributed to the grievances which cause people to make the wrong choices and to resort to terrorism. 在联合国抵制特定恐怖主义活动的框架内，已经精心制订了 18

个打击国际恐怖主义的普遍性文书（14个公约和4个议定书），其中包括安全理事会的相关决议。在打击恐怖主义的同时促进和保护人权和基本自由问题特别报告员强调：尊重人权的反恐措施有助于防止人们被招引从事恐怖主义活动；侵犯人权行为时常使冤情加重，进而导致人们作出错误选择而依靠恐怖主义。

例 9. Institutional care should be a last resort and alternative care and accommodation arrangements should be made available, including specialist foster or kinship care or semi-independent living, for children who cannot or do not want to return to their families. 对于那些不能或不想返回家庭的儿童来说，机构照管应当是最后的办法，应当为他们提供替代照顾和住宿安排，比如委托专业人员寄养或亲属照管或半独立生活。

例 10. If an Event of Default as outlined in Article 14.1.1 has occurred and at any time thereafter shall be continuing, the Provider of Facility may call the Payment Guarantee for the amount then due and unpaid, and if the Guarantor does not indemnify the Provider of Facility, the Provider of Facility may, by giving written notice to the relevant Bank, resort to any of the measures outlined in Articles 14.2.1 through 14.2.4. below. 如果上文第 14.1.1 条扼要说明的违约事件已经发生，而且在发生之后仍旧持续，贷款提供人可以实施付款保证催告，要求偿还届时到期但尚未偿付的款项，如果担保人没有向贷款提供人给予赔偿，贷款提供人可以给予相关银行书面通知，采取下文第 14.2.1 条至第 14.2.4 条所概述的措施。

例 11. A communication related to a violation of human rights and fundamental freedoms, for the purpose of this procedure, shall be admissible, provided that
…

(d) It is submitted by a person or a group of persons claiming to be the victims of violations of human rights and fundamental freedoms, or by any person or group of persons, including nongovernmental organizations, acting in good faith in accordance with the principles of human rights, not resorting to politically motivated stands contrary to the provisions of the *Charter of the United Nations* and claiming to have direct and reliable knowledge of the violations concerned. Nonetheless, reliably attested communications shall not be inadmissible solely because the knowledge of the individual authors is second-hand, provided that they are accompanied by clear evidence;

就本程序的目的而言，述及侵犯人权和基本自由问题的来文可以受理的条件是：

......

（d）是由声称自己是侵犯人权和基本自由行为受害人的一个人或一批人提出的，或是由真诚本着人权原则行事、不采取含有政治动机并有违《联合国宪章》规定的立场的、声称直接并可靠了解有关侵犯人权情况的任何个人或一批人，包括非政府组织在内提交的。然而，如果来文得到可靠证实，只要提供的证据清楚，便不得仅仅因为具体提交人对情况的了解是第二手的而不予受理；

recuse & rescue

(1)

recuse [riˈkjuːz] *v.t. & v.i.* ① to remove oneself as a judge in a particular case because of prejudice or a conflict of interest 回避；② to challenge or object to a judge as being disqualified from hearing a case because of prejudice or a conflict of interest 申请……回避。也就是说，recuse 是指因法官与案件有利害关系或对案件持有偏见、成见，当事人申请其（或法官主动）不参与案件审理的程序。

recusal [riˈkjuːzəl] *n.[C,U]* 回避

例 1. The judge recused himself from that case, citing a possible conflict of interest. 法官以自己可能与案件存在利害冲突为理由，回避了这起案件。

例 2. The defendant filed a motion to recuse the trial judge on the grounds that the judge's wife was the plaintiff's in-house counsel. 被告递交了申请庭审法官回避的动议，理由是这位法官的妻子是原告的企业法律顾问。

例 3. Art. 12. —Recusal of Judges.

(1) Upon motion by any party involved in the case, or upon his own motion, any judge scheduled to hear matters at the pre-trial, trial or appeal stages of a case shall recuse himself from participation in any proceedings in which:

(a) he has a personal interest;

(b) he is a relative of any person involved;

(c) he has had prior substantial involvement in the case; or

(d) for any other reason his impartiality in the proceeding might reasonably be called into question.

(2) If a judge decides not to recuse himself in accordance with this Article, that decision is subject to immediate appeal, before the continuation of the proceedings, to the Court which would hear the appeal of the case after judgment. In the case where the judge is a Justice of the Supreme Court, the appeal shall be heard by other Justices of the Supreme Court.

第 12 条 法官回避

（1）经案件的任何当事人提出申请，或经预定在案件的审前、庭审或上诉阶段聆讯事宜的法官主动申请，该法官应当回避，不再参加有下列情形的程序：

（a）他具有个人利害关系；

（b）他是涉案人员的亲属；

（c）他先前实质性介入该案；或者

（d）按理可以对他在该程序中的公正性产生质疑的任何其他因由。

（2）如果法官决定不根据本条作出回避，继续进行程序之前，可就其决定向法院立即提出上诉，法院将在判决之后审理案件的上诉事宜。如果该法官是最高法院大法官，上诉由最高法院其他大法官审理。

(2)

rescue ['rɛskjuː] *v.t. & n.[C,U]* 救援，援助，援救，解救，搭救，营救

例 4. Several firefighters dissembled the iron window shutters in an attempt to rescue people trapped in the inferno. 几位消防员拆掉了铁窗栈，试图营救被困在火海里的人。

例 5. Two medical helicopters were immediately dispatched to rescue the survivors from the sinking vessel. 马上派遣了两架医用直升机，将幸存者从正在下沉的船上救起。

例 6. The board of directors has resolved to rescue the company from hostile takeover. 董事会已经决定要对这家公司施以援手，防止它被恶意收购。

注意：动词 rescue 常用的搭配是 rescue sb./sth. from sb./sth.。

名词 rescue 常用的搭配是 come to the rescue 或 come to sb's rescue，意思是援助某人脱离危险境况或摆脱某种麻烦。

例 7. Sherpas came to their rescue when those climbers were in a critical condition of starvation and exhaustion. 这伙登山者饥肠辘辘、筋疲力尽，危急关头，夏尔巴人救了他们。

例 8. The considerate hostess came to the rescue by introducing this timid girl to a few people. 女主人做事周到，过来给这个腼腆的姑娘解了围，介绍她认识几位客人。

reimburse & disburse

reimburse 和 disburse 的区别是意思不同：reimburse 意思是偿付，尤其是偿付他人代付的费用；disburse 通常是指从某项基金中划出，以清偿债务或填补费用支出的货币支付行为。

(1)

disburse [disˈbɜːs] *v.t.* to pay out money, commonly from a fund or in settlement of a debt or account payable 支付，拨付

disbursement [disˈbɜːsmənt] *n.[C,U]* the act of paying out money, commonly from a fund or in settlement of a debt or account payable

例 1. FESCO is responsible for the detailed service executions, e.g. salary package calculation, payoff, risk fee collection and disbursement, and dispatched employee master file management. FESCO 负责详尽地履行服务，例如薪资福利的计算、员工工资表、风险金的收取和支出以及派遣雇员主体档案管理。

例 2. Compensation payment should be fully disbursed to dispatched employees in maternity leaves. 对于休产假的派遣雇员应当足额支付工资。

例 3. The aforementioned fees are exclusive of VAT and any expenses associated with our services. In this respect, we charge (indiscriminately) a fixed amount for office disbursements at a rate of 6% of the total amount of fees invoiced. Non-office expenses, such as travel, translation and courier expenses, are invoiced as they are incurred (with VAT if applicable). 前述收费不含增值税以及与本所提供的服务有关的任何费用。在这个问题上，本所按照发票所列律师费总金额的 6%（不加区别

地）收取一笔固定金额的垫付办公费用。本所按照实际垫付的非办公费用（如差旅费、翻译费和信使费）开具发票（如需缴纳增值税，则连同增值税一并开具发票）。

例 4. Lack of legal agreements to regulate the risk fee payments and lack of clear criteria of risk fee compensation coverage may lead to disputes on the amounts of the risk fees billed by FESCO to the Company, as well as disagreements regarding the area of disbursements of collected risk fees from FESCO to dispatched staff. 缺乏规管风险金支付的法定协议，而且缺乏风险金补偿内容的明确标准，可能导致对 FESCO 向公司收取的风险金的数额产生纠纷，并且对于 FESCO 从已经收取的风险金中向派遣员工支付多少款项发生争议。

(2)

reimbursement [ˌriːimˈbɜːsmənt] *n. [C, U]* 偿还

reimburse [ˌriːimˈbɜːs] *v.t.* 付还；补偿；偿付

例 5. CCC is entitled to reimburse reasonable out-of-pocket and incidental expenses. CCC 有权报销合理的实付费用和杂费。

例 6. Each Party to the *Contract* hereby waives any of its claims, in particular for compensation and/or reimbursement, and any and all other rights under that *Contract*. 《合同》的每一方当事人特此放弃它根据《合同》享有的任何请求权，尤其是要求获得赔偿和 / 或偿付的请求权，以及根据《合同》享有的任何和所有其他权利。

例 7. The Parties hereby agree that the payment of the amount of CNY 52,844,000.00 to be made by the Tenant as set out in Clause 3 of the *Letter Agreement* (the "Fee Payment") has been made and the Parent has been fully reimbursed for all USD-nominated funds already paid in accordance with the IA as set out in Paragraph 2 of Clause 2 of the *Letter Agreement*. 三方当事人特此约定，承租人已经支付按照

《书面协议》第 3 条的规定其应当支付的人民币 52844000.00 元（"费用"），母公司依照 IA 已经支付的所有采用美元标价的资金已经按照《书面协议》第 2 条第 2 款得到充分偿付。

例 8. If at any time the Company fails to perform any of its obligations under Clause 9.1, and the Onshore Security Agent chooses to indemnify the Affected Person concerned against any loss which it incurs as a result of such failure, the Company agrees on demand to reimburse the Onshore Security Agent for any amount paid by it pursuant to this Clause 9.2 together with interest thereon from the date of such demand until reimbursement at a rate equal to that payable (if it were treated as an unpaid sum) from time to time on sums due (but unpaid) by the Company under Clause 10 (Default Interest and Indemnity) of the *Term Loan Facility Agreement*. 如果公司在任何时候不能履行其依据上文第 9.1 条承担的义务，而且国内担保代理人决定向有关受影响者给予赔偿，使有关受影响者豁免由于公司不能履行上述义务致使有关受影响者遭受的损失，公司同意根据要求向国内担保代理人偿还国内担保代理人依照本《协议》第 9.2 条支付的款项，以及从国内担保代理人提出上述要求之日起至公司向国内担保代理人偿还之日为止，上述款项所孳生的利息，利息的利率等于公司根据《定期贷款协议》第 10 条（违约和赔偿）对于到期（但尚未支付的）款项（假若国内担保代理人依照本《协议》第 9.2 条支付的款项被视为尚未偿还款项）不时应当支付的利息。

relieve

relieve [riˈliːv] *v.t.* ① 减轻，缓解，使宽慰；② 接班，接替；③ 宽免，免除；④ 解围

翻译法律文件的时候，relieve 的第三个义项最常见。

例 1. Irrespective as to which remedy is chosen by Ordering Entity, XYZ shall not be relieved of its obligation under this Agreement and shall in particular be obligated to deliver any Product ordered by Ordering Entity in accordance with this Agreement unless XYZ has proven to Ordering Entity that XYZ's compliance with Articles 16.4.1 and 16.4.2 results in severe economical harm for XYZ which would put its corporate existence at risk. In this case, XYZ's obligations to indemnify shall remain unaffected. 无论订货实体选择何种救济方式，XYZ 均不得免除其在本协议下的义务，特别是，XYZ 有义务依照本协议交付订货实体订购的产品，除非 XYZ 已经向订货实体证明，XYZ 遵守第 16.4.1 条和第 16.4.2 条的规定，给 XYZ 造成严重的经济损失，将会使 XYZ 遭受破产的危险。在此情况下，XYZ 仍然应当履行赔偿义务。

例 2. Delaying Causes. Subject to the provisions of this Section, Supplier will not be liable for any delay in performance under this Agreement caused by any "Act of God" or other cause beyond Supplier's control and without Supplier's fault or negligence (a "delaying cause"). Notwithstanding the above, Supplier will not be relieved of any liability for any delay or failure to perform its defense obligations with respect to third party Intellectual Property rights or furnish remedies for Infringing Products as described in Section 17.3. 延误事由。根据本条的规定，对于由"天灾"或其他超出供货商控制的事由（"延误事由"）造成的供货商延误履行本协议，但供货商不存在过错或过失，供货商不承担责任。虽然存在上述规定，供货商不得免除延误或不履行供货商对于第三人知识产权提出抗辩的责任或者对于第 17.3 条

所述的侵权产品提供救济的责任。

例 3. Force Majeure. Notwithstanding anything herein to the contrary, the Parties hereto shall not be deemed in default as a result of any non-performance of any of the terms, covenants and conditions of this Agreement, to the extent such non-performance shall be due to any strike, lockout. civil commotion, invasion rebellion, hostilities, sabotage, governmental regulations or controls. Acts of God, or any other cause beyond the reasonable control of the Party in question (a "Force Majeure"): provided, however, that the above shall not relieve any party from its obligations to perform its part of this Agreement at such time and to such extent as may be possible subsequent to the Force Majeure and under no circumstances is any party relieved from its obligations to make any payments due hereunder due to the occurrence of a Force Majeure. 不可抗力。无论本协议作出何种相反的规定，如果由于罢工、封闭工厂、平民骚乱、侵略、叛乱、敌对行为、蓄意破坏、政府管制或监管、天灾或者有关当事人无法合理控制的任何其他事由（"不可抗力"），以致本协议的双方当事人无法履行本协议的任何条件、条款和约定，那么双方当事人不应被视为违约；但是，前述规定不应免除任何一方当事人在不可抗力终止后的可能时间和可能范围内履行本协议的义务，不论在何种情形下任何一方当事人均不得由于发生某种不可抗力而免除其在本协议之下的付款义务。

注意区分 relive 与 relieve：

relive [riːˈliv] v.t. 重温，回味

例 4. Whenever he heard the lovely melody, he relived the brilliant performance given by the pianist. 一听到那动人的旋律，他就回想起那位钢琴演奏家的精彩演出。

remit

remit [ri'mit] *v.t.* ① 汇款；② 将……移交；③ 减刑；['ri:mit] *n.[C]* 权限

remittance [ri'mitəns] *n.[C,U]* 汇款

remission [ri'miʃən] *n.[U]*（疾病）减轻；（刑罚）减轻；宽恕（罪责）

例 1. The New Lender shall pay to the Agent (for its own account) a fee of US$2,000 (the "Transfer Fee"). The Transfer Fee shall be remitted to an account designated by the Agent on the date on which the *Transfer Certificate* is delivered to the Agent pursuant to Clause 21.5(a) (Procedure for transfer). 新贷款人应当付给代理行一笔金额为 2000 美元的费用（"转让费"）（新贷款人自行负担该笔费用）。转让费应当在依照第 21.5（a）条（让与程序）将《转让证明》交给代理行之日汇入由代理行指定的一个账户。

例 2. XYZ sought an order that this court should determine the purchase price of its one share in the Company on the correct basis with no order for damages, alternatively that the valuation of the Company be remitted to another judge for re-trial. XYZ 请求法院颁下命令，饬令本庭根据正确的办法裁定它对 XX 公司拥有的一个股份的购买价格，并且不作出支付损害赔偿金的法官命令；或者将 XX 公司评估事宜移交另一位法官重新审理。

例 3. At KKK's request, CCC shall process remittance in timely manner of the principal of QFII investment quota or the after-tax returns from investment in Securities, subject to compliance with Applicable Laws and this Agreement. CCC 应当按照 KKK 的要求，及时汇兑合格境外机构投资者投资份额的本金或者源于证券投资的税后收入，CCC 办理上述汇款业务应当遵守适用法律和本协议。

例 4. The exchange rate used for the remittance mentioned above shall be the exchange rate agreed by both Parties in writing, or, where there is no such agreement, the basic exchange rate published by the People's Bank of China on the date of remittance. 前款所称办理汇款的汇率应当是双方当事人书面约定的汇率，或者，如果双方当事人没有达成书面协议，应当是中国人民银行在汇款日公布的基准汇率。

例 5. CCC shall keep or cause to be kept the books, records, reports and other relevant materials regarding transaction, remittance, exchange, receipt, payment, and transfers of funds. CEB shall provide KKK or any other authorized person with information as agreed by the Parties. CCC 应当保存与资金的交易、汇款、兑换、收款、支付和转移有关的账簿、记录、报告和其他相关资料，或促使其得到保存。CCC 应当向 KKK 或者其他得到授权的人提供双方当事人约定的信息。

例 6. Remittances have become significant private financial resources for households in countries of origin of migration. Remittances cannot be considered as a substitute for FDI, ODA, debt relief or other public sources of finance development. They are typically wages transferred to families mainly to meet part of the needs of the recipient households. The manner of their disposal or deployment is an individual choice. A large proportion of migrants' incomes is spent in destination countries and constitutes an important stimulus to domestic demand in their economies. 侨汇已成为外劳原籍国社区的重要私人资金来源。不应将侨汇视为可替代官方发展援助、减免债务、外国直接投资或其他公共的发展资金来源。侨汇是汇给家人的所得工资，主要用于消费。如何利用和安排这类钱完全是个人选择。

例 7. Remit of UNODC Secretariat 联合国毒品和犯罪问题办事处（UNODC）秘书处的职权范围

The secretariat should be responsible for managing the timescales of the review process. It should be actively involved in facilitation of meetings and discussions between the reviewed state and reviewers. It shall assist in the collation of the reports into a summary for use by the Conference. The option for the UNODC to attend country visits should be available where it is clear that on a cost/benefit analysis such attendance will add value to the process. 秘书处应当负责管理审查过程的时间安排。秘书处应当积极参与筹备受审查国家与审查人员之间的会议和讨论。秘书处将协助将报告整理成供缔约国会议使用的概要。如果对于联合国毒品和犯罪问题办事处（UNODC）而言，根据成本／收益分析，参与国家巡查将增加审查过程的价值，那么它应当有权选择参加国家巡查。

例 8. Remit of reviewers

The reviewers shall act as independent experts under the *Convention* regardless of the State which provides them. They shall review any state in accordance with the express aims set out in the finalised terms of reference and in particular paying close attention to the resolutions passed by Conference on the aim and scope of the review and Article 1 of the *Convention*. They shall carry their function in a fair and objective manner with a view to devising constructive dialogue for developing a states practice and implementation of the *Convention*. Any information provided to reviewers shall be considered confidential.

审查人员的职权范围

审查人员不论是由哪个国家／地区派遣的，都应当根据《公约》充当独立专家。他们应当根据最终商定的职权范围中阐述的明确目标，对任何国家进行审查，他们尤其应当密切关注缔约国会议通过的关于审查目的和审查范围的决议，以及《公约》第 1 条的规定。他们应当公平、客观地履行职责，以便为拟定某种做法和实施《公约》构思建设性对话。向审查人员提供的信息均被视为机密信息。

render & surrender

(1)

render ['rɛndə] *v.t.* ① to cause someone or something to be in a particular state 使……变得 / 处于某种状态；② 翻译；③ 给予，提供，表演

例 1. The *Companies Act 1985*, Section 310 renders void any provision (whether contained in the company's articles or otherwise) exempting or indemnifying any officer of the company from liability for negligence, default, breach of duty or breach of trust. 《1985 年公司法》第 310 条规定，对于公司任何高级职员的疏忽、失责、违反职责或违背信托行为，免除其责任或对其进行赔偿的条款（无论是否在公司章程中记载）均属无效。

例 2. There has been some academic debate concerning the possible civil law consequences of failure to disclose an interest under Section 317. Some commentators suggest that failure to comply with the section renders the contract voidable. 关于不根据第 317 条披露利益可能导致的民事法律后果，发生了一些学术辩论。有些评论人士建议，不遵守该条的规定会使合同无效。

例 3. The Company never disclosed the true source of its elevated profit margins and the true nature of the tax-related risks to which it was exposed, as particularized above. This omission rendered each of the following statements a misrepresentation. 上文已经详细说明，公司从未披露它的利润率提高的真实原因和它所承担的涉税风险的真实性质。遗漏这方面的内容使得下列每一项陈述成为虚假陈述。

例 4. Wang Ch'ung-hui (1881−1958), a prominent Chinese jurist, diplomat and politician, rendered the *German Civil Code* into English from its German version. 中国杰出的法学家、外交家和政治家王宠惠（1881—1958）曾将《德国民法典》从德文译成英文。

例 5. The Parties hereby agree that any arbitration award rendered in accordance with the provisions of this Clause shall be final and binding upon the Parties concerned, and the Parties further agree that such award may be enforced by any court having jurisdiction over the Party against which the award has been rendered or the assets of such Party, wherever the same may be located. 双方现约定，根据本条的规定作出的任何仲裁裁决即为终局裁决，且对关涉各方具有约束力。双方进一步约定，凡对于已作出的仲裁裁决所针对的当事方或对于该当事方的资产（无论该资产位于何处）具有管辖权的法院可以强制执行该裁决。

例 6. The sole ground on which it was sought to render them accountable was that, being directors of the plaintiff company and therefore in a fiduciary relation to it, they entered in the course of their management into a transaction in which they utilised the position and knowledge possessed by them in virtue of their office as directors, and that the transaction resulted in a profit to themselves. 试图使他们承担责任的唯一理由是，他们担任原告公司的董事，因此与该公司存在信托关系，而他们在管理过程中订立了一项交易，在这项交易中，他们利用了因担任董事职务所拥有的地位和知悉的情况，并且这项交易为他们本人带来了好处。

(2)

surrender [səˈrɛndə] ① *v.i. & n.[C,U]* 投降

例 7. There are several factors that will likely impede the ability of LARs to operate according to these rules in this regard, including the technological inadequacy of existing sensors, a robot's inability to understand context, and the difficulty of applying of IHL language in defining non-combatant status in practice, which must be translated into a computer programme. It would be difficult for robots to establish, for example, whether someone is wounded and hors de combat, and also whether soldiers are in the process of surrendering. 有几个因素有可能妨碍自主机器人杀手依照这些规则行动的能力，包括现有传感器的技术不够充分，机器人没有能力理解环境，实践中在界定非战斗人员身份时很难采用国际人道主义法律的语言而必须将其转化为电脑程序。例如，很难让机器人确定某人已经受伤处于非战斗状态，或确定士兵正在示意投降。

② v.t & *v.i.* surrender to sth./surrender oneself to sb. 屈服

例 8. According to police report, these investors, owing to paucity of expertise and attaching no importance to wise counsel, surrendered to temptation and became the latest victims of this Ponzi scheme. 据警方通报，这些投资者由于缺乏专门知识，对明智的忠告没有给予应有重视，抵挡不住诱惑，成了这宗庞氏骗局的最新受害者。

③ *v.t.* 交出，放弃

例 9. An exchange of letters between the chairman and the plaintiff's principal shareholder and director conveyed the false impression that the offshore company was an independent market operator, which had earlier acquired the market rights and which was willing to surrender these rights in return for payment. 董事长与原告主要股东和董事之间的函件往来表现出一种假象，也就是该离岸公司是一个独立市场经营者，该公司先前获得了市场权利，并且愿意为了获得付款而放弃这些权利。

例 10. Oil sands leases may also be surrendered at any time by the lease holder on notification to the provincial Crown, and the Minister of Energy may also cancel any oil sands agreement if the terms have been breached or if the agreement holder has not responded to notices or complied with the *Mines and Minerals Act* (Alberta) or applicable regulations. 租约持有人经通知省政府，也可以随时放弃油砂租约。如果承

租人违反油砂协议载明的条件或协议持有人对通知未作答复或未遵守《矿藏和矿物法》（阿尔伯塔省）或者相关条例，省能源部部长也可以撤销油砂协议。

例 11. The obligations of the Defaulting Investor and the rights of the non-defaulting Investors shall survive the surrender of the *Agreement*, abandonment of Operations and termination of this *Investors Agreement*. 违约投资人的义务和非违约投资人的权利，应当在退出《协议》、放弃作业活动和终止本《投资协议》之后继续有效。

repudiate

repudiate [riˈpjuːdieit] *v.t.* to reject or renounce (a duty or obligation); esp., indicate an intention
   not to perform (a contract) 拒绝履行（义务），尤其指不履行契约

repudiation [riˌpjuːdiˈeiʃən] *n.[C,U]* a contracting party's words or actions that indicate an intention not to perform the contract in the future; a threatened breach of contract 悔约

repudiator [riˈpjuːdiˌeitə] one who repudiates; esp., a party who repudiates a contract 悔约人

repudiatee a party to a contract that has been repudiated by the other party 被悔约人

例 1. Each of the events or circumstances set out in the following sub-clauses of
this Clause is an Event of Default:

   (f) Repudiation

The Borrower repudiates a Finance Document or evidences an intention to repudiate a Finance Document.

本条以下各款所规定的每一项事件或每一种情况均属于违约事件：

   （f）拒绝履行义务

借款人拒绝履行某一份融资文件或者表明其拒绝履行某一份融资文件的
意图。

例 2. 3. A material breach of a treaty, for the purposes of this article, consists in:

   (a) a repudiation of the treaty not sanctioned by the present Convention; or

   (b) the violation of a provision essential to the accomplishment of the object or
purpose of the treaty.

   三、就适用本条而言，重大违约系指：

   （a）废弃条约，而此种废弃非本公约所准许者；或

   （b）违反条约规定，而此项规定为达成条约目的或宗旨所必要者。

result in & result from

这两个短语在法律文件中使用频率非常高，很容易混淆，可以这样大致区分它们：result in 这个短语，是原因在前，结果在后。result from 这个短语，是结果在前，原因在后。下面我们结合例句体会这两个短语的用法。

(1)

result in sth./doing sth. 导致

例 1. As a Developer and Realtor for the Company, Mr. W has developed, marketed and sold numerous developments resulting in sales well over $200 million over the past 10 years. 作为公司的一位开发商和房地产经纪人，W 先生在以往十年里开发、营销和出售了大量地产项目，使销售额大大超过两亿美元。

例 2. As the Hong Kong court has no control over the conduct of the case by the plaintiffs in the Mainland proceedings, it may result in grave injustice to the plaintiff here if the court were to stay the Hong Kong proceedings. 由于香港法院无法掌控内地诉讼程序的各该原告人处理案件的做法，假如本庭中止香港诉讼程序，就可能给本案原告人造成严重不公正。

例 3. Additionally, PHEVs provide households with greater travel flexibility due to the ability to utilize current refueling infrastructure. This allows consumers to become familiar with vehicle battery charging, which we expect to result in increased BEV adoption in the future. 另外，插电式混合动力汽车能够利用现有的燃料补给基础设施，从而使家庭可以更灵活地出行。这使消费者能够熟悉如何给汽车电池充电，我们预计这样就会促使消费者今后更多地采用纯电动车。

例 4. Application for membership shall be made in such form as the Board may from time to time determine. Every application for admission shall be considered by the Board and may be acceded to or refused at its absolute discretion, provided always that no person shall be admitted to membership if such admission would result in the number of Members exceeding the maximum number of Members for the time being authorized. 凡申请成为基金会的会员，应当按照理事会不时决定的方式提出申请。理事会将审议每一份入会申请，并且自行酌情应允或者拒绝申请，但是需要始终遵守的条件是，如果接纳某人入会有可能导致会员人数超过当时核定的会员最高人数，则理事会不接纳此人入会。

(2)

result from sth. 因……发生，由于……导致

例 5. It may just be a desperate effort to protect "stated-owned assets", which is exactly the phrase used in the *Civil Complaint*, resulting from the lack of commercial prudence on the part of the two Companies in protecting their own interest. 在《民事起诉书》中使用的说法正是"国有资产"，内地诉讼程序中的上述举动也许正是孤注一掷地设法保护"国有资产"，而之所以采取上述举动，乃是这两家公司保护自身利益时在商业上不够慎重所致。

例 6. Where the Court makes an order under Subsection (4), it may make such further order as it thinks fit with respect to any additional costs of the arbitration resulting from its order. 凡高等法院根据本条第（4）款发布命名，对于因该命令产生的额外仲裁费用，高等法院可以签发它认为合适的进一步的命令。

例 7. Subject to the provisions of the *Ordinance*, if any prosecution, action or suit at law be commenced against any member or members of the Board or any officer, servant or agent of the Foundation for anything done by them in the proper or reasonable discharge of their duties, such person or persons shall be defended and indemnified by and at the cost of the Foundation from all damages, costs and expenses which may be incidental to or result from such prosecution, action or suit at law and the property and funds of the Foundation may be applied for such purpose as may be directed by the Board from time to time provided, however, that none of such funds shall be applied either directly or indirectly in payment of the whole or part of any fine or penalty imposed upon any person by sentence or order of a Court. 在不违反《条例》的规定的情况下，如果理事会的任何一位或多位成员或者基金会的任何高级管理人员、雇员或代理人，由于他们在适当或者合理地履行其职责过程中所作的事情而被提起刑事诉讼或者受到普通法起诉，基金会应当自行负担费用为上述人员辩护并且给予他们赔偿，使他们免于承受此类刑事诉讼或普通法诉讼可能附带产生的或者由此类刑事诉讼或普通法诉讼引起的所有损害、支出和费用，基金会的财产和资金可以用于理事会不时指定的目的，但是，上述资金不得直接或者间接用于支付由法院针对任何人判决或者裁定的全部或者部分罚款或者罚金。

sanction & sanctity

(1)

在法律文件中，sanction 作为名词和动词，有两个相去甚远的意思：制裁／处罚和批准。

具体是哪个意思，要结合语境判断。我们首先看一看《布莱克法律词典》给出的定义：

sanction [ˈsæŋkʃən] ① *n.[U]* official approval or authorization 批准；② *n.[C]* a penalty or coercive measure that results from failure to comply with a law, rule, or order 处罚；③ *n.[C]* an economic or military coercive measure taken by one or more countries toward another to force it to comply with international law 制裁

v.t. ① to approve, authorize, or support 批准，认可；② to penalize by imposing a sanction 制裁，处罚

注意：实施制裁 impose sanctions on；解除制裁 lift sanctions。

关于"制裁或处罚"这个义项：

例 1. The Romanian Parliament adopted the Law No. 197 from November 13, 2000, for the amendment of some provisions of the *Penal Code*. For the first time in the Romanian legislation express provisions related to the sanction of family violence acts were sanctioned. 罗马尼亚议会从 2000 年 11 月 13 日起通过了第 197 号法律，该法对《刑法典》的部分条文作了修订。罗马尼亚立法关于惩治家庭暴力行为的明文规定得到批准，这还是第一次。

在例 1 中同时使用了 sanction 的两个义项。

例 2. Each State Party shall, in particular, ensure that legal persons held liable in accordance with this article are subject to effective, proportionate and dissuasive criminal or non-criminal sanctions, including monetary sanctions. 各缔约国均应当特别确

保使依照本条应当承担责任的法人受到有效、适度而且具有警戒性的刑事或者非刑事制裁，包括金钱制裁。

例 3. The Committee urges the State Party to take effective measures to accelerate and increase the representation of women in elected and appointed bodies, including through a possible change in the election law or the use of incentives or sanctions for fulfilment of the obligation of local and central public authorities to reach "equitable and balanced representation of women and men" as proclaimed in the Law on Equal Opportunities Between Women and Men. 委员会敦促该缔约国采取有效措施，增加妇女在民选机构和任命机构的任职人数，并加快这方面的步伐，其中包括采取可能修改选举法或使用奖励或处罚等手段来促进实现男女机会均等法所宣布在地方或中央政府当局"男女任职人数必须公平均衡"目标。

例 4. The State Party continues to adopt legislative and administrative measures including laws, sanctions and policies that prohibit discrimination against women. Fair and protective procedures for hearing complaints and imposing appropriate sanctions on health care professionals guilty of improprieties including sexual abuse of women patients have been undertaken. 缔约国继续采取禁止歧视妇女的立法和行政措施，其中包括法律、制裁措施和政策。已经实施了公允而且有保护作用的程序，用以审理投诉，并对犯有不正当行为（包括对女患者实施性虐待）的保健专业人员予以适当处罚。

例 5. Pharmacovigilance and, more generally, market surveillance and sanctions in the event of failure to comply with the provisions should be stepped up. In the field of pharmacovigilance, account should be taken of the facilities offered by new information technologies to improve exchanges between Member States. 如果有关规定没有得到遵守，则应当扩大药物预警，更具有普遍意义的是，应当增进市场监察和处罚。在药物预警领域，应当考虑到新的信息技术为改善成员国之间的交流所提供的诸多便利。

例 6. For so long as The Hongkong and Shanghai Banking Corporation Limited or any of its Affiliates is the Agent, the Agent may take and instruct any delegate to take any action which it in its sole discretion considers appropriate so as to comply with any applicable law, regulation, request of a public or regulatory authority or any HSBC Group policy which relates to the prevention of fraud, money laundering, terrorism or other criminal activities or the provision of financial and other services to sanctioned persons or entities. 只要香港上海汇丰银行有限公司或者它的任何关联公司担任代理行，代理行即可自由决定采取它认为合适的行动并且指令任何代表采取这样的行动，以便遵守任何可以适用的与防止欺诈、洗钱、恐怖主义或其他犯罪活动或者防止向受制裁的人或实体提供金融服务或其他服务有关的法律、规章、公共当局或监管当局的要求或者汇丰集团政策。

关于"批准"这个义项：

例 7. Visits from parents and friends from the student's home country (and from relatives and friends in the U.S.) can be extremely detrimental to the student's adjustment process and language learning. Therefore visits from parents are not sanctioned by the Company until after the Christmas holiday or preferably at the end of the program. All visits must be in agreement with the host family. 学生家长与学生在母国的朋友（以及学生在美国的亲属和朋友）的探视对于学生的适应过程和语言学习极为不利。因此，圣诞节假日过后，本公司方批准学生家长探视，学生家长最好在项目结束以后安排探视。所有探视活动必须征得接待家庭的同意。

例 8. If at any time the share capital is divided into different classes of shares, the rights attached to any class may, whether or not the Company is being wound up, be varied with the consent in writing of the holders of three-fourths in nominal value of the issued shares of that class, or with the sanction of a special resolution passed at a separate general meeting of the holders of the shares of that class. 如果在任何时候，股本被划分为不同类别的股份，无论本公司是否正在停业清理，经该类别已经发行股份四分之三面值的持有人书面同意，或者经该类别股份的持有人在单独

的全体会议上通过的特别决议批准，可以变更附属于任何类别股份的权利。

例 9. If a majority of number representing three fourths in value of the creditors or class of creditors, and/or of the stockholders or class of stockholders of the Corporation, as the case may be, agree to any compromise or arrangement and to any reorganization of the Corporation as a consequence of such compromise or arrangement, the said compromise or arrangement and the said reorganization shall, if sanctioned by the court to which the said application has been made, be binding on all the creditors or class of creditors, and/or on all the stockholders, or class of stockholders, of the Corporation, as the case may be, and also on this Corporation. 如果根据具体情况，在本公司债权人（或某一类债权人）和／或股东（或某一类股东）所持有的四分之三价值之中有半数以上赞成和解或安排并且赞成由于和解或安排而对本公司进行重组，那么上述和解或安排以及重组经上面提到的当事人向其提出上述申请的法院批准，根据具体情况，不仅对本公司的全体债权人（或该类债权人）和／或全体股东（或该类股东）具有约束力，对本公司亦具有约束力。

例 10. If the Company shall be wound up, the liquidator may, with the sanction of a special resolution of the Company and any other sanction required by the *Ordinance*, divide amongst the members in specie or kind the whole or any part of the assets of the Company (whether they shall consist of property of the same kind or not) and may, for such purpose, set such value as he deems fair upon any property to be divided as aforesaid and may determine how such division shall be carried out as between the members or different classes of members. The liquidator may, with the like sanction, vest the whole or any part of such assets in trustees upon such trusts for the benefit of the contributories as the liquidator, with the like sanction, shall think fit, but so that no member shall be compelled to accept any shares or other securities whereon there is any liability. 如果本公司需要停业清理，清算人可以经过本公司特别决议批准和《条例》要求的其他批准，在成员之间以实物形式分配本公司的全部或者部分资产（无论它们是否由同类资产构成），而且可以为此目的，为按照上述方式分配的资产确定清算人认为公平的价值，清算人可以确定如何在成员之间或者

不同类别成员之间实施分配。清算人可以根据类似批准，根据清算人经类似批准认为适当的信托，为清算出资人的利益，将上述全部或者部分资产授予受托人，但是任何成员不得被强迫接受存在债务的股份或者其他证券。

(2)

sanctity ['sæŋktəti] *n.[U]* 神圣

例 11. The sanctity of contract is the principle that the Parties to a contract, having duly entered into it, must honor their obligations under it. 契约神圣是一项原则，规定契约的各方正式订立该契约后必须履行其根据该契约承担的各项义务。

specialize & specify

(1)

specialize [ˈspɛʃəlaiz] *v.i.* 专门从事，经营，研究

注意：specialize 是不及物动词，后面搭配的介词是 in。

specialization [ˌspɛʃəlaiˈzeiʃən̩] *n.[C, U]*

specialized [ˈspɛʃəlaizd] *adj.* 专门的；专业化的

例 1. For the solid wastes occurring during normal, abnormal and accidental operation, it is necessary to identify specialized service providers needed, their treatment methodology, licensing requirements and likely disposal locations. 对于正常、异常及意外作业过程中产生的固体废物，必须辨明所需要的专门服务提供者、处理方法、特许要求以及可能的处理地点。

例 2. A definition of fissile materials is contained in Article XX of the *Statute of the International Atomic Energy Agency (IAEA).* So there is scope for negotiation and for expert input from IAEA and other institutions specialized in inorganic chemistry and nuclear physics. 《国际原子能机构（原子能机构）规约》第 20 条载有裂变材料的定义。因此，原子能机构和其他专门研究无机化学和核物理的机构有开展谈判和提供专家意见的余地。

例 3. ISA interrogators are taught in detail about the relevant human rights conventions, including their direct implications in the unique Israeli context. This is done through specialized seminars, both during preliminary and ongoing ISA training, which aim to instill the importance of principles of human dignity and fundamental human rights, together with the upholding of the rule of law and practices stipulated by the courts. 以色列安全局向本局的审讯人员详细讲解相关的人权公约，包括公约在以色列独特的背景下产生的直接影响。这项任务是在以色列安全局的初步培训和不间断培训期间通过专门研讨会完成的，其目的是逐渐灌输人类尊严和基本人权原则以及维护法治和法院规定的惯例的重要意义。

例 4. This kind of complexity and knowledge requirement puts tremendous strain on both the tax authorities and the taxpayers, especially in developing countries where resources tend to be scarce and the appropriate training in such a specialized area is not readily available. 这种复杂性和知识要求给税务机关和纳税人都造成了巨大压力，特别是在发展中国家，那里往往资源很缺，而且在这样一个专业性领域不容易获得适当的培训。

例 5. From the early 1990s, MNEs began restructuring to specialize in the areas in which they had competitive advantages, such as unique firm-specific assets, in particular high value intangible assets, and the capabilities that provided the firms with their market position and competitive edge. 从 20 世纪 90 年代初开始，跨国公司开始进行重组，以便专门拓展其具有竞争优势的领域，如独特的企业专有资产，特别是高价值无形资产。跨国企业在这些领域也具有为企业提供市场地位和竞争优势的能力。

例 6. Knowledge of international taxation and good judgement is required to select the right areas to focus on and the right cases for an audit, as some transactions are more tax-driven than others. Staff with a background in accounting have, for example, often been regarded as easy to train in this area as they are often enthusiastic about specializing in this field, but similar enthusiasm can be found in those with other skill sets. Others, such as lawyers and economists have special skills in dealing with the often complex law and economics of transfer pricing cases, and one of the challenges in this area is having all those skills working together effectively. 由于某些交易比其他交易更受税收驱动，因此要想选择正确的审计重点领域和正确的审计案例，就得了解国际税收并具备良好判断力。比方说，具有会计背景的工作人员往往被

认为在这方面容易培养，因为他们往往热衷于钻研这一领域，但在掌握其他技能组合的人员身上也能找到类似的热情。律师和经济学家等其他人士具备特殊才能，可以处理转让定价案件中通常错综复杂的法律和经济问题，而这方面的挑战之一就是要让掌握所有这些技能的人有效地协同工作。

例 7. There are sometimes questions as to whether a group with a specific professional specialization, such as economists, should be distributed within other teams or should comprise, at least in the start-up phase, a separate unit. 有时候会产生这样的疑虑：是否应当在其他团队中安排一个具有特定职业专长的群体，如经济学家，或者至少在创业阶段，是否应该让这样的群体组成一个独立单位。

(2)

specify ['spɛsifai] *v.t.* 指明，明确规定，具体说明

specified ['spɛsifaid] *adj.* 指明的

specification [ˌspɛsifi'keiʃən] *n.[C,U]*

specification 有两个义项，一是 the act of specifying，另一个义项更常用，意思是规格、规范。

例 8. Vendor agrees to perform the Vendor Services in accordance with the performance metrics specified herein. 销售商同意按照本协议中指明的绩效衡量指标履行销售商服务。

例 9. There are no conditions, understandings, agreements, representations, or warranties, expressed or implied, which are not specified herein. 任何条件、谅解、协议、声明或保证，不论其为明示抑或默示，凡本协议中未作明确规定，则不属于本协议所规定之内容。

例 10. The Client agrees to pay the fee specified in *Attachment E* in connection with the Consultant's provision of the Legal Services as to evidence gathering and document drafting. 对于顾问提供的证据采集和文书起草法律服务，客户同意支付

《附件戊》中规定的酬金。

例 11. Contractor will supply Services specified in any P.O. in a timely manner and to the satisfaction of the issuing Nortel entity (e.g., Subsidiary or Affiliate). 承包商将及时提供任何采购订单中指明的服务，并达到令签发订单的实体（如子公司或关联公司）满意的程度。

例 12. End-products must be manufactured or produced in the United States, subject to a number of specified exceptions. 最终产品必须在美国制造或生产，但明确规定的例外情况除外。

例 13. The general notice must state that he or she is to be regarded as interested in contracts of any description that may subsequently be made by the company by reason of the facts specified in the notice. 一般通知必须说明，由于通知中叙明的事实，他或她将被视为对公司随后可能订立的任何类型的合同具有利害关系。

例 14. Selection of businesses for the 8(a) program is conducted by the SBA, in accordance with specified criteria. 小企业管理局按照规定的标准遴选承办 8（a）计划的企业。

例 15. If the arbitral tribunal makes an award under this section, it shall specify in its award, the issue, or claim or part of a claim, which is the subject-matter of the award. 如果仲裁庭根据本条作出裁决，应当在裁决中具体说明构成仲裁裁决标的的争议点或权利请求或权利请求的组成部分。

例 16. Where any provision of this Act requires an application or appeal to be made to the Court within a specified time, the *Rules of Court* relating to the reckoning of periods, the extending or abridging of periods, and the consequences of not taking a step within the period prescribed by the *Rules*, shall apply in relation to that requirement. 凡本法的条文要求在规定时间内向高等法院提出申请或提起上诉，《法院

规则》中关于计算期间、延长或缩短期间，以及不在《法院规则》规定的期间采取行动所产生的后果的相关规定应当适用于本法的上述要求。

例 17. Where the act is required to be done, a specified number of clear days after a specified date, at least that number of days shall intervene between the day on which the act is done and that date. 凡需要在某一指定日期之后利用规定数目的整日完成某一行为，期限是指完成该行为的日期与上述指定日期之间至少等于规定天数的期间。

例 18. The defendant failed to provide the Plaintiff with all customer product literature and technical specifications on each licensed product. 被告未向原告提供每个许可产品的所有客户产品资料和技术规格。

例 19. AAA warrants to DISTRIBUTOR that during the Warranty Period, AAA will, at its option, repair or replace Products which fail to function substantially in accordance with the Specifications or refund to DISTRIBUTOR the price paid by DISTRIBUTOR therefor (the "Warranty"). AAA 向经销商保证：在质量保证期内，AAA 将自行选择维修或更换未充分按照规格说明运行的产品，或向经销商退还经销商为此支付的价款（"质量保证"）。

spouse & espouse

(1)

espouse [i'spauz] *v.t.* 赞成，拥护

espousal [i'spauzəl] *n.[singular, U]*

例 1. Legal realism is the theory that law is based, not on formal rules or principles, but instead on judicial decisions that should derive from social interests and public policy. American legal realism, which flourished in the early 20th century, was espoused by such scholars as John Chipman Gray, Oliver Wendell Holmes, and Karl Llewellyn. 现实主义法学是一种思潮，认为法律应当源自社会利益和公共政策的司法裁决，而非形式上的规则或原则。美国的现实主义法学在 20 世纪初蓬勃发展，得到了约翰·齐普曼·格雷、奥利弗·温代尔·霍姆斯、卡尔·卢埃林等学者拥趸。

例 2. No member State of the Conference genuinely espousing the twin goals of nuclear disarmament and non-proliferation has questioned the necessity of controlling fissile material for weapons purposes. 真心拥护核裁军与核不扩散这两项目标的大会成员国均未质疑控制用于武器的易裂变材料的必要性。

(2)

spouse [spaus] *n.[C]* 配偶（指丈夫或妻子）

spousal ['spauzəl] *adj.* 配偶的

例 3. According to the statements from female drug users themselves, they have become addicted to illicit substances because of the influence of their spouses. 据吸毒妇女本人的陈述，她们因受配偶影响而对非法药物上瘾。

例 4. That Article 1494 of the *Civil Code* stipulates that a man can remarry 180 days after divorce or the death of a spouse, while a woman who is divorced or widowed has to wait 300 days. 《民法典》第 1494 条规定：男性在离婚后或配偶死亡后经过 180 天即可再婚，而离异或守寡的妇女必须等待 300 天方可再婚。

例 5. The legal protection against domestic violence had not been de facto available to former spouses or long-term partners that did not share a common household. 并未共同居住的前配偶或长期伴侣在事实上不能获得抵制家庭暴力的法律保护。

例 6. Giving up one's economic independence when starting a family with a spouse or registered partner can mean that a woman remains financially dependent on her ex-partner if the relationship ends, often living in poverty and reliant on benefits. 与配偶或登记伴侣成立家庭的时候放弃自己的经济独立会意味着如果家庭关系终止，妇女就要在经济上仰仗自己的前伴侣，以致她往往生活贫困，依赖救济。

例 7. Under article 317, paragraph 1 of the current *Penal Code*, if the victim of domestic abuse falls within the definition of the abuser's spouse, the law treats this as an aggravating factor. 根据现行《刑法典》第 317 条第 1 款，如果家庭虐待的受害者按照定义属于施虐者的"配偶"，法律将这种情形视为加重情节。

statue, stature & statute

(1)

statue [ˈstætʃuː] *n.[C]* 雕像，塑像

例 1. Hachik Statue, which was erected in memory of a legendary dog in front of Shibuya Station, has become a landmark ever since. 忠犬八公像是为了纪念一条有传奇色彩的小狗而在涩谷站前树立的，它从此成了一座地标。

statuary [ˈstætʃʊəri] *n.[U]* 雕像，塑像（总称）

statuette [ˌstætʃuˈɛt] *n.[C]* 小雕像，小塑像。例如：the Oscar statuette 奥斯卡金像

statuesque [ˌstætʃuˈɛsk] *adj.* large and beautiful in an impressive way, like a statue

(2)

stature [ˈstætʃə] *n.[U]* ① the degree to which someone is admired or regarded as important 声誉，名望；② someone's height or size 身高，身材

例 2. Taj Mahal is a tourist destination of international stature. 泰姬陵是蜚声国际的旅游胜地。

例 3. If this university continues to grow in stature as a foreigner-friendly place, it will attract the necessary financial resources. 如果这所大学继续扩大适合留学生的名气，就会吸引到必要的资金。

注意：stature 是书面语词汇。

(3)

statute ['stætʃuːt] *n.[C,U]* ① a law passed by a legislative body; specifically, legislation enacted by any lawmaking body, including legislatures, administrative boards, and municipal
courts. The term act is interchangeable as a synonym 制定法，成文法规。在英美法中，
statute 专指由立法机关所制定的法律，表现为正式的法律文件，其制定机关不一定
为议会或国会，例如在美国，联邦、州、市或县的立法机关均可制定。该词在使用
时专指以立法的形式创设的法律，故与由法院判决所形成的判例法相对。 ② 规约。
关于机构设置及其权限范围的国际性文件，例如：Statute of the International Court of
Justice《国际法院规约》。

结合《布莱克法律词典》和《元照英美法词典》的解释，区分下面两个重要术语：

statute of limitations *n.[C]* ① a law that bars claims after a specified period; specifically, a
statute establishing a time limit for suing in a civil case, based on the date when the claim
accrued (as when the injury occurred or was discovered); the purpose of such a statute is to
require diligent prosecution of known claims, thereby providing finality and predictability
in legal affairs and ensuring that claims will be resolved while evidence is reasonably available and fresh 诉讼时效法。它以诉因形成（例如损害的发生或被发现）的日期为起
点，确定当事人可以提起民事诉讼的时间期限。该制定法的目的在于要求当事人对
已知的诉讼请求积极主张权利，从而为法律行为提供确定性和可预测性，并确保
在证据尚未湮灭时能解决争议。 ② a statute establishing a time limit for prosecuting a
crime, based on the date when the offense occurred 追诉时效法。它以犯罪行为实施之日
为基础，确定可以对某一犯罪行为提出指控的时间期限。

statute of repose *n[C]* a statute barring any suit that is brought after a specified time since the
defendant acted (such as by designing or manufacturing a product), even if this period ends
before the plaintiff has suffered a resulting injury 除诉期间法。诉讼时效法（statute of
limitation）本身即是除诉期间法，它们的目的均在于阻止当事人对失效请求权（stale
claim）提出主张。除诉期间是一种比较少见的美国法律用语，其与通常的诉讼时效
期间的区别在于：除诉期间与诉因的形成无关，其从某一特定事件的发生之日起计
算，而不管诉因是否已经发生或是否已造成损害，例如规定自被告实施某一特定行
为（例如制造产品或完成工作）之日起若干年后不得再行提起诉讼，即使原告的损
害发生于该期限届满之后。诉讼时效期间则以诉因形成之日起计算，例如规定自原

316

告遭受损害之日起经由某一特定时期而原告未起诉的，则不得再行起诉。

statutory [ˈstætʃʊtəri] *adj.* 与制定法相关的；法定的；符合制定法规定的；合法的

例 4. According to *Compulsory Education Law of the People's Republic of China*, the statutory age of primary school attendance is six. 根据《中华人民共和国义务教育法》的规定，法定小学入学年龄为六周岁。

subjugate, subrogate, supplicate & surrogate

(1)

subjugate [ˈsʌbdʒugeit] *v.t.* 征服，使……屈服，使……臣服

subjugation [ˌsʌbdʒuˈgeiʃən] *n.[U]*

例 1. After the Peloponnesian War, Athenians, whose city used to be a beacon of hope for the whole Greece during the Greco-Persian Wars, became a subjugated people. 雅典人的城邦在希波战争期间曾经是全希腊的希望灯塔，伯罗奔尼撒战争过后，他们却成了臣服于人的民族。

例 2. During the Second Punic War, the Carthaginian soldiers led by Hannibal fought bravely against the subjugation by the Romans, but ultimately they were outwitted and outfought by the Roman army under the command of Scipio. 第二次布匿战争期间，汉尼拔率领的迦太基军队英勇抗击罗马人的征服企图，可是最终他们敌不过西庇阿指挥的罗马军队。

subjugate sb./sth. to sth. 使……服从于……

例 3. Parents have subjugated themselves to the urgent needs of their children—to buy a decent dwelling unit in this notoriously unlivable city. 父母克制自己，满足子女的迫切需求——在这座出了名的不宜居的城市买一套像样的住房。

(2)

subrogate [ˈsʌbrəˌgeit] *v.t.* to substitute (a person) for another regarding a legal right or claim 取代，代位

subrogation [ˌsʌbrəˈgeiʃən] *n.[U]* 代位。指由一人取代另一人的地位而对第三人依法请求给

付或主张权利、要求补救或担保等。在债权债务关系中，若某人代为偿付债务，则其取代债权人的地位，可以对债务人行使债权人的一切权利，与其未代为偿付时原债权人对债务人的权利相同。代位通常发生于建筑合同、保险合同、保证以及流通票据法中。保险中的代位，如某人已投保的船舶因他人过错而致撞毁，则其可从保险人处取得保险金而恢复船舶价值，从而由保险人代位行使船舶所有权人的权利，以向造成船舶毁损者提起诉讼。代位是衡平法上的一种制度设计，以使债或义务能最终清偿，而又使偿付债务者不致显失公平。代位分为两种，即协商代位（或称合同代位）（conventional subrogation）与法定代位（legal subrogation），前者是通过债权人与第三人的行为而明示的代位，后者则是由于法律实施而产生的代位或默示的代位，例如保证人的代位。（《元照英美法词典》）

subrogee [ˌsʌbrəˈdʒiː] 代位人；代位权人。指因代位而获得他人权利之人。例如，保险人在支付保险赔偿金后通常就成为代位人，从而有权对侵权人提起诉讼。又如保证人在向债权人清偿债务后亦成为代位人，取代债权人得以向债务人主张权利。

subrogor [ˌsʌbrəˈɡɔː] 被代位人。与代位人相对，指因代位而致其自身的权利被他人获得的人。例如，保证合同中的债权人。

例 4. The policy will be endorsed to waive the insurer's subrogation rights against AAA. 通过签发保险单批单，放弃针对 AAA 的保险人代位求偿权。

例 5. Unless otherwise agreed by the Bank in writing, the Provider of Facility may only assign its rights under this *Individual Letter Agreement* to (insert name of relevant Export Credit Agency). Following such assignment Export Credit Agency will be subrogated to the Provider of Facility and will have the same rights towards the Bank as if Export Credit Agency was the Provider of Facility. 除非银行以书面形式另行同意，贷款提供人只能将自己在本《单项信用证协议》项下的权利转让给（填入相关出口信贷机构的名称）。在转让之后，出口信贷机构将取代贷款提供人并对银行享有相同的权利，犹如出口信贷机构就是贷款提供人。

例 6. Until all the Liabilities have been irrevocably paid in full and all facilities which might give rise to Liabilities have terminated and unless the Lender otherwise directs, the Mortgagor will not exercise any rights which it may have by reason of performance by it of its obligations under the Finance Documents:

(a) to take the benefit (in whole or in part and whether by way of subrogation or otherwise) of any rights of the Lender under the Finance Documents or of any guarantee or other security taken pursuant to, or in connection with, the Finance Documents.

直至所有债务均已不可撤销地足额偿还，所有可能产生债务的贷款已经终止，而且除非贷款人另有指示，抵押人不得行使抵押人通过履行融资文件所规定的义务而享有的任何下列权利：

（a）受益于（全部或部分，无论以代位抑或其他方式）贷款人依据融资文件所享有的权利或者依据融资文件设定的保证或者其他担保。

例 7. If such Party obtains other insurance, such insurance shall contain a waiver of subrogation in favor of all the other Participating Investors and/or ABC, as the case may be, Operator and their insurers but only in respect of their interests under the *Association Agreement* and this *Operating Agreement*. 如果非分红当事人获得其他保险，该保险应当包含有利于所有其他分红投资人和 / 或 ABC，而且根据具体情况，有利于运营人和它们的保险人的放弃代位求偿权证明，但是放弃代位求偿权证明仅关涉它们在《联营协议》和本《运营协议》项下的权益。

(3)

supplicate ['sʌplikeit] *v.t.* 哀求，恳求；祈求

supplication [ˌsʌpli'keiʃən] *n.[U]* (literary)

supplicant ['sʌplikənt] *n.[C]* 哀求；恳求别人；祈求神灵的人

(4)

surrogate ['sʌrəgeit] *adj. & n.[C]* 作为替代的（人或物）

surrogate mother 代孕母亲。该妇女接受另一妇女的丈夫的精子进行人工授精、怀孕、生产，并且在产后即将其亲权转移给孩子的生父和其妻子。

surrogate parenting agreement 代孕生子合同。根据该合同，由一妇女接受另一妇女丈夫的精子进行人工授精、怀孕、生产，并且在产后即将其亲权转移给孩子的生父和其妻

子。合同的目的是使孩子与其生母永远分离，而由孩子的生父与其妻子成为该孩子的完全父母。如果某一妇女为获利而担任代理母亲并在生产后转让其对孩子的亲权，那么，为此而订立的合同则是非法和无效的。（《元照英美法词典》）

substantial & substantive

(1)

substantial [səbˈstænʃəl] *adj.* ① large in size, value or importance 重大的，可观的；② 基本上的，大体上的

substantially [səbˈstænʃəli] *adv.* ① to a large degree 在很大程度上；② 基本上，大体上

例 1. In order to fulfill its customers' needs, the Company must place orders with suppliers over ten months before the season begins, and to start to take delivery of products, as early as May, for the upcoming season. Any disruption in this schedule places the Company, its retailers, and its customers at a substantial risk that the Company will be hindered from meeting customer demands and performance requirements during the upcoming season. 为了满足客户的需求，本公司必须在赛季开始之前的 10 个月就向供货商订货，而且早在五月份，就必须开始为即将到来的赛季接收产品。扰乱上述时间安排将使本公司、本公司的零售商以及本公司的客户承担巨大的风险，即本公司可能无法在即将到来的赛季满足客户的需求和实现绩效要求。

例 2. The Court shall not make an order under this section unless it is satisfied that substantial injustice would otherwise be done. 除非高等法院确信如不根据本条签发命令将会造成严重不公正，否则高等法院不会签发该命令。

例 3. The judge was satisfied some substantial loss had been incurred, and did the best he could to assess damages on the available evidence. 原审法官确信 XXX 蒙受了某些重大损失，竭尽全力根据已有证据估定损害赔偿金。

例 4. In addition, while the Manufacturer did manufacture and ship products pursuant to the Company's purchase order, from almost at the beginning of the term of this Agreement, the Manufacturer's conduct caused the Company to have substantial concerns about its financial viability and its ability to meet the Company's needs. 此外，虽然几乎从本协议的期限开始，制造商确实依据公司的采购订单生产和装运产品，但是制造商的所作所为使公司对于它的财务能力和满足公司需要的能力产生了严重忧虑。

例 5. Unless otherwise agreed by the Parties, the Court may, on the application of a Party to the arbitral proceedings who has given notice to the other parties, determine any question of law arising in the course of the proceedings which the Court is satisfied substantially affects the rights of one or more of the parties. 除非双方当事人另有约定，经仲裁程序的一方当事人（该当事人已经通知其他当事人）申请，高等法院可以查明在仲裁程序中发生的高等法院确信对一方或多方当事人的权利有重大影响的任何法律问题。

例 6. Buyer and Each Founder shall enter into an Assignment and Assumption Agreement substantially in the form attached hereto as Exhibit A (the "Assignment Agreement"). 买方与每一位创始人须大致按照本协议附件 A 的格式订立一项转让和责任义务承担协议（"转让协议"）。

例 7. The Fund anticipates that substantially all of its assets will be invested in the form of loans to the Developer, bearing interest at 5% per annum, secured by real and personal property held by the Developer. 预计本基金大体上全部资产将采取对开发商提供贷款的形式进行投资，贷款按照每年 5% 的利率计收利息，由开发商拥有的不动产和动产作为担保。

(2)

substantive [səbˈstæntiv] *adj.* 实质性的，实体的

例 8. The arbitrators shall decide the dispute according to Luxembourg substantive law and pursuant to the rules of procedure applied by the *Rules of the Chamber of Commerce and Industry of Geneva.* 合议仲裁员应当根据卢森堡实体法，并依照《日内瓦工商会规章》所适用的程序裁决纠纷。

例 9. I see no basis to set aside item (c) and Mr. B had not advanced any substantive reason for doing so. That leaves item (b), which is yet another new point not taken below. 我认为没有理由撤销（丙）项，而且 B 先生也没有提出任何实质理由来支持撤销该项。剩下的（乙）项仍然是下文没有处理的另一个新要点。

例 10. The topical headings used in this Operating Agreement are for convenience only and shall not be construed as having any substantive significance or as indicating that all of the provisions of this Operating Agreement relating to any topic are to be found in any particular Article. 本运营协议中使用的标题仅为行文便利的需要，不应被解释为具有任何实质意义或表明须在特定条款下查阅本运营协议关于任何主题的所有规定。

therefor & therefore

therefor 和 therefore 是同音词（homophone），而且都是副词，拼写仅差一个字母，意思却有很大差别。

(1)

therefor [ðɛəˈfɔː] *adv.* for it or them; for that thing or action; for those things or actions 因此，为此

例 1. The paramount purpose of such an investigation is to determine the circumstances and causes of the accident or occurrence with a view to avoiding similar accidents or occurrences in the future, rather than to ascribe blame therefor to any person. 此项调查的首要目的，是确定意外或事故的情况及起因，以避免日后发生相似的意外或事故，而非将责任归咎于任何人。

例 2. We do not consider either the outcome or reasons therefor as enunciated by Smart AJ in Mandagi have any relevance to or effect upon our approach to our determination of the present applications for leave. 我们认为上诉法院法官斯马特在曼达吉一案中为此阐述的结果或理由与我们如何裁定本案上诉许可申请没有任何关联和影响。

例 3. The Founders have timely paid all Taxes that will have been required to be paid on or prior to the date hereof, the non-payment of which would result in a Lien on any Purchased Assets or would result in Buyer becoming liable or responsible therefor. 创办人已及时缴纳了在本协议订立日或该日期之前本应缴纳的所有税款，不缴纳这些税款可能导致已购得资产被设定留置权或导致买方须负缴纳该税款的义

务或责任。

例 4. If any such liens attach, or charges or claims therefor are made, Contractor will at its own cost cause such lien to be discharged within five (5) days from recordation of the lien. 如果在本公司的地产上附着此类留置权，或对该地产设定担保或对该地产提出请求权，承包商将自行承担费用在上述留置权登记之日起五（5）日内促使解除该留置权。

例 5. References to any agreement or document herein shall be a reference to the same as from time to time varied in any manner whatsoever and any other agreements or documents from time to time executed supplemental or in addition thereto or in substitution therefor unless the context otherwise requires. 除非本协议的上下文语境另有规定，本协议中所称之协议或者文件应当指随时以各种方式变更的协议或者文件以及随时签署的补充、附加或者替代协议或者文件。

(2)

therefore [ˈðɛəfɔː] *adv.* for that reason; on that ground or those grounds 因此，所以

例 6. The United States therefore requests that automakers have the option to optimize their production plans over time, which would include the ability to address NEV deficits in one year by applying the NEV credits earned in previous (carry-forward) or future (carry-back) years. 因此，美国要求汽车制造商有权选择经过一段时间优化其生产计划，包括能够利用在先前年份（结转）或将来年份（抵前）赚取的积分来解决新能源汽车亏损。

例 7. Therefore, Mr. C had profited from his position as director. The court held that is was appropriate to appoint a receiver in view of the considerable danger in dissipating the assets of the company, on condition that the plaintiff undertook to use its best endeavours to ensure that the audited accounts were completed by the due date. 因此，C 先生从其担任的董事职务中获利。考虑到这家公司的资产有被耗散的重

大风险，法院裁定任命破产管理人是妥当的办法，条件是原告承诺尽最大努力确保在到期日之前完成经过审计的账目。

例 8. The application therefore turns on a narrow issue: has the defendant discharged the burden of establishing a triable issue as to fraud? 因此，有关简易判决的申请就取决于一个具体的问题：被告人是否履行了证明成立有关欺诈的应审判争点的义务？

例 9. NOW, THEREFORE, in consideration of the foregoing and the mutual covenants contained herein, and other good and valuable consideration, the receipt and sufficiency of which is hereby acknowledged, the Parties agree as follows: ... 因此，鉴于前述内容及本协议载明的相互契诺，以及其他有效且有值对价，双方当事人现确认已收到该对价并确认该对价之充分性，双方当事人现达成如下协议：……

unconscionable & unconscious

(1)

unconscionable [ʌnˈkɔnʃənəbl] *adj.(formal)* 过分的；不合情理的

unconscionability 显失公平；显失公平原则

参看《元照英美法词典》的解释：

法院根据该原则可以以合同缔结中的程序滥用或以与合同内容相关的实体滥用为由拒绝
强制执行不公平或压迫性合同，任何一种滥用都是以显失公平为基础的。对合同是否
显失公平的基本检验标准是，根据缔约时的环境和通常的商业背景以及特定交易的商
业要求，确定合同条款是否不合理地使一方当事人受益，从而压迫另一方当事人或
对另一方当事人不公平。如果一方当事人未能对合同内容作出有实质意义的选择却
使另一方不合理地受益，则属于显失公平。美国《统一商法典》（*U.C.C.*）第 2–302
条规定：1．如果法院作为法律问题发现合同或合同的任何条款在缔约时显失公平，
法院可以拒绝强制执行，或仅执行显失公平以外的其他条款，或限制显失公平条款
的适用以避免显失公平的后果。2．由于一方当事人主张或法院认为合同或合同的任
何条款有可能属于显失公平时，应给予另一方当事人合理的机会提供证据，证明缔
约的商业背景、合同的目的和效果，以帮助法院作出决定。美国《第二次合同法重
述》（*Restatement of Contracts, Second*）第 208 条亦有相同规定。在英国，它是衡平
法中的传统术语，与公平（good conscience）相反，衡平法院通常对显失公平的交易
不予认可。

例 1. Unconscionability involves a court's refusal to enforce a contract or part of
a contract that is unfair and unreasonable, or where a court changes such a contract.
Case law tends to deem contracts unconscionable where there is manifest inequality
between the parties and where one side is taking advantage of the other on account of
this inequality. The *Unconscionable Contracts Ordinance* (Chapter 458, Laws of Hong

Kong) essentially provides the same, although only in contracts where a consumer is one of the parties. Both the legislation and the case law provide a limited role for unconscionability in order to minimise interference with the commercial certainty that should naturally flow from contracts. 不合情理涉及法院拒绝执行不公平和不合理的合同或合同的一部分，或者法院更改此类合同。如果当事双方之间存在明显的不平等，并且一方由于这种不平等而利用了另一方的利益，那么判例法往往认为合同不合情理。《不合情理合约条例》（香港法例第 458 章）实质上提供了相同的规定，尽管仅在消费者为当事方之一的合约中。立法和判例法都为不合情理性提供了有限的作用，以最大程度地减少对自然应该来自合同的商业确定性的干扰。

(2)

unconscious [ʌnˈkɒnʃəs] *adj.* 失去知觉的；无意识的

例 2. Art. 304 —Aggravated Sexual Assault.

A person who, in committing a sexual assault:

(a) carries, uses or threatens to use a weapon or otherwise uses violence, intimidation or coercion or in any other way renders the victim incapable of resisting;

(b) threatens to cause bodily injury to a person other than the person assaulted;

(c) wounds, maims, disfigures or otherwise causes bodily injury to the assaulted person, or transmits a communicable human disease to the person assaulted or exposes him to the same, regardless whether such disease is treatable or is a public health problem, provided that if the person assaulted dies as a direct effect of the disease, the offender is guilty of murder, punishable under Article 275;

(d) is fifteen or older and assaults a person under the age of fifteen;

(e) abuses a position of trust, power or authority (pupil, apprentice, school boarder, domestic servant, adopted child, prisoner, patients);

(f) endangers the life of the person assaulted or if the assaulted person, due to sadism of or transmission of diseases from the assailant, commits suicide from distress or despair;

(g) is a party to the offence with any other person;

(h) performs such act on an unconscious or deluded person or old people;

(i) performs such act by misrepresentation; or

(j) performs such act as a member of a group,

is guilty of aggravated sexual assault, a Class 8 serious offence, punishable with a definite term of imprisonment of not less than 3 years and not more than 5 years.

第 304 条　严重性侵犯罪

行为人在实施性侵犯罪时有下列情形，即构成严重性侵犯罪，本罪属于第八级重罪，应当对犯罪人处以不少于三年，不超过五年的定期监禁：

（a）携带、使用或威胁使用武器，或另外使用暴力、恐吓或胁迫，或以任何其他方式使受害人不能反抗；

（b）威胁给受性侵犯者以外的人造成身体伤害；

（c）使受性侵犯者受伤、残疾、毁容或以其他方式对其造成身体伤害，或者向受性侵犯者传播人类传染病或使其遭受罹患该病的威胁，不论该病能否治疗或者是否成为公共卫生问题，但是，如果作为该病的直接后果，受性侵犯者死亡，犯罪人即构成谋杀罪，应当根据第 275 条的规定对其予以处罚；

（d）行为人年满 15 岁或 15 岁以上，侵犯不满 15 岁的人；

（e）滥用信任、权力或职权地位（学生、学徒、学校寄宿生、家庭佣工、养子女、囚犯、病人）；

（f）危及受性侵犯者的生命，或者倘若由于行凶者施虐或传播疾病，受性侵犯者因痛苦或绝望而自杀；

（g）与任何其他人一起是性侵犯罪的一方；

（h）对失去知觉或受骗的人或者对老人实施性侵犯；

（i）借助失实的陈述实施性侵犯；或者

（j）作为团伙的成员实施性侵犯。

underlie & underline

(1)

underlie [ˌʌndəˈlai] *v.t.* to serve as a basis of or to be a hidden cause of 构成······ 的基础，

　是······的深层原因

underlie 是不规则动词，它的过去式和过去分词分别是：underlay, underlain

注意动词 underlie 的现在分词和它的同源形容词是 underlying。

underlying [ˌʌndəˈlaiiŋ] *adj.*

例 1. The principles underlying the procurement system of the Government of the Hong Kong Special Administrative Region are consistent with the spirit and objectives of the *WTO GPA*. 香港特别行政区政府采购制度所蕴含的原则符合《世贸组织政府采购协议》的精神和目标。

例 2. Public policies should address the underlying causes of poverty and marginalization that indigenous peoples suffer as a result of the denial of their rights. 公共政策应当消除土著人民因其权利被否定而遭受贫困和边缘化的潜在原因。

例 3. It seems to us that the purpose or object underlying Section 21E is, notwithstanding the manifest deficiencies in the drafting of the section, clear. The purpose or object is that an offender who fails to co-operate in accordance with a relevant promise in that regard, is not to have his sentence of imprisonment increased unless, in fact, the failure to co-operate is "without reasonable excuse". 在我们看来，虽然第 21E 条的起草有种种明显的不足，不过该条隐含的目的或宗旨却一目了然。它的目的或宗旨就是：如果犯罪分子没有按照相关承诺配合调查，除非事实上其不配合调查行为"没有合理辩解"，否则不得增加其监禁刑期。

例 4. The Company failed to use best efforts to ensure that its sales force was fully trained in the use, advantages and technical competence underlying the System. 公司没有尽最大努力确保其销售队伍在系统的使用、优势和技术能力方面得到充分培训。

例 5. However, since fraud is recognized as a possible defence to a claim on performance bond and there is evidence of fraud in relation to the underlying contract, Mr. M submits that it is not appropriate for the court to grant summary judgment here. 但是，由于欺诈被认为是一项可以对抗履约保函赔偿请求的抗辩理由，又有基础合同存在欺诈的证据，M 先生认为本庭在本案中作出简易判决并不适当。

例 6. The concept of continuing fiduciary duty is now well established. It is, in my view simply an application of the underlying principle that what a person, who was previously in a fiduciary position, can and cannot subsequently do is governed by good conscience. 持续受托责任的概念现在已经深入人心。在我看来，这不过是应用如下基本原则，也就是先前处于受托人地位的人以后能做什么和不能做什么取决于良知。

(2)

underline ['ʌndə‚lain] *v.t.* ① 在……下面划线；② = emphasize 强调，使……突出

例 7. For the purposes of being conspicuous, all the terms and clauses as to the seller's liability in this Agreement have been underlined in red. 为醒目起见，本协议中关乎卖方责任的所有条款和文句下面都划了红线。

例 8. In her report of 2013 to the Human Rights Council, the Special Rapporteur underlined that the quality of legal aid depends first and foremost on the qualifications and training of legal aid providers, who include lawyers and paralegals. 特别报告员在她提交人权理事会的 2013 年报告中强调，法律援助的质量首先取决于法律援助

提供者——包括律师和律师助理——的资质及所受训练。

例 9. The *ISS Intergovernmental Agreement* provides that ISS shall be developed, operated and utilized in accordance with international law, including four of the United Nations treaties on outer space (Article 2.1). With respect to a specific principle, e.g., non-appropriation of outer space is reconfirmed [Article 2.2 (c)] and the establishment of ISS for peaceful purposes is underlined (Article. 1.1). 《国际空间站政府间协定》规定，国际空间站的开发、运转和利用，应当依照包括四个联合国外层空间条约在内的国际法为之（第 2.1 条）。关于具体的原则，例如，再次确认不占有外层空间［第 2.2（c）条］和强调设立国际空间站用于和平目的（第 1.1 条）。

例 10. The *Declaration* contains a set of collective rights that are fundamental for the survival of indigenous peoples as distinct peoples, as underlined by international, regional and national law and jurisprudence. These are their right to self-determination and the related rights over their lands, territories and natural resources, on which the enjoyment of the whole panoply of their human rights depends. 《宣言》载有一组集体权利，对于土著人民以独特民族身份生存极为重要，国际、区域和国家的法律和判例也强调了这一点。这就是土著人民的自决权和对他们的土地、领土和自然资源享有的关联权利，他们享受种类繁多的所有人权取决于这些权利。

例 11. The parties to the *Memorandum* underlined the important role played by the Central Asian Regional Information and Coordination Centre (CARICC) in strengthening regional cooperation on drug control, including by facilitating intelligence-sharing and joint operational activities to address drug trafficking. 《备忘录》的缔约方强调中亚区域信息和协调中心（CARICC）借由促进情报交流和打击贩毒的联合行动等措施，在加强药物管制区域合作方面发挥了重要作用。

up to

我们可以把 up to 这个短语大致归纳为下面四个义项：

(1)

up to 将近，最多。表示至多可以达到某一数额、程度、水平。

例 1. This Agreement sets out the terms and conditions upon which the Lender will make available to the Borrower a loan facility of up to USD 710,000 (the "Facility"). The Facility shall be applied towards general corporate purposes. 本协议列明多项条款及条件，贷款人将据此向借款人提供一笔最高额度为 710000 美元的贷款（"约定贷款"）。约定贷款应当被用于实现一般公司目的。

例 2. Conventional oil royalties in Alberta are set by a single sliding rate formula containing separate elements that account for oil price and well production, with royalty rates ranging up to 50% and with rates capped when oil prices reach C\$120 per barrel. 阿尔伯塔省的常规石油使用费按照一个单一浮动费率公式确定，这个公式含有不同的要素，分别代表石油的价格和油井的产量；使用费的费率最高可达 50%，当石油价格上涨到每桶 120 加元时，就要限定费率的上限。

例 3. The provision gives victims undoubtedly increased protection since the police are able to arrest the offender right away in the beginning of the case and hold him for up to 24 hours or until formal decision has been made on an exclusion order and the ejection of the offender from the home. 上述规定无疑给予受害人更大保护，因为警察可以在案件发生伊始立即拘捕犯罪者，将其拘留最多 24 小时或者拘留到作出驱逐令的正式决定并将其逐出家宅为止。

例 4. If AAA is in material breach of any term of this letter agreement (including, for the avoidance of doubt, its obligations set out in Paragraphs 8 and 9), then HRL may withdraw up to the entire amount deposited by a member of the HRL Group in the New Account (including any interest accrued on that amount). 如果 AAA 严重违反本协议的任何条款（为免生疑问，包括第 8 款和第 9 款中列明的义务），则 BBB 最多可以提取 BBB 集团的成员存入新账户的全部金额（包括该金额产生的任何利息）。

(2)

up to 意思相当于 until，表示直到、截至。

例 5. On the facts as found by the judge, AAA firm had access to the Company's records including its accounting records through Mr. BBB up to the end of 2004 and through Mr. CCC until mid 2008. 根据 XXX 法官查明的事实，AAA 事务所有权通过 BBB 先生（截至 2004 年年底）和 CCC 先生（截至 2008 年中旬）查阅包括会计账簿在内的公司记录。

例 6. The ambassador also discussed the work in progress on Iceland's family policy for the period up to 2020 and the difficulty of finding a way to increase men's participation in the social discussion. 大使还讨论了到 2020 年为止的这段时间，正在进行的关于冰岛家庭政策的工作，以及在找到某种办法提高男子参与社会讨论方面所存在的困难。

(3)

it is up to sb. to do sth. 表示做某事是某人的职责。it 作为形式主语，后面的不定式是真正的主语。

例 7. A takeover bid is an offer to acquire the shares of a company's members. It is up to the members, therefore, to decide whether or not to accept. 收购要约是旨在

取得公司成员的股份的要约。因此，须由公司的成员决定是否接受。

(4)

be up to something 搞鬼，捣乱，耍花招，使坏

例 8. You ought to be careful. People might think you're up to something. 你最好小心点，否则别人会认为你在捣鬼。

up to no good 不干好事

例 9. I solemnly swear that I am up to no good. 我庄严宣誓我不干好事。

waiver & waver

　　waiver 和 waver 是同音词，拼写相近，但意思不同，waver 是准备雅思和托福考试时会用到的词汇，而 waiver 和它的同源动词 waive 是法律文件，尤其是协议中出现频率非常高的重点词汇，所以我们要格外注意。

(1)

waiver ['weivə] *n.[C]* ① the voluntary relinquishment or abandonment—express or implied—of a legal right or advantage; forfeiture. The party alleged to have waived a right must have had both knowledge of the existing right and the intention of forgoing it. ② the instrument by which a person relinquishes or abandons a legal right or advantage.

waive ['weiv] *v.t.* ① to abandon, renounce, or surrender (a claim, privilege, right, etc.); to give up (a right or claim) voluntarily. Ordinarily, to waive a right one must do it knowingly—with knowledge of the relevant facts. ② to refrain from insisting on (a strict rule, formality, etc.); to forgo.

上面是《布莱克法律词典》的解释，再来看看《元照英美法词典》对它们的解释：

waive 放弃；放弃权利；弃权

waiver （1）放弃；权利放弃；弃权。指故意或自愿抛弃其明知的权利，或实施可以推定其抛弃该等权利的行为，或放弃其有权要求实施的行为，或者其在享有法律规定或合同约定的权利并明知相关的重大事实时，作为或不作为与其权利要求相矛盾的行为。诸如对请求权、权利、特权的放弃，或者在受到他人的侵权或伤害后未对之提起请求，即是对法律规定的侵权行为补救权的放弃。放弃可以是明示的，也可以默示方式为之。例如，一承租人实施了违反租赁合同的行为，则依照法律规定出租人可以解除租赁，但出租人亦可以在明知违约事实后，通过明确承诺不行使解除权的方式或以接受租金的方式放弃其解除权。前一种方式即为明示的权利放弃；后一种则为默示的权利放弃。权利放弃是建立在衡平法原则之上的，但亦为普通法法院所承认。在本质上，权利放弃是一种单方行为，仅需一方当事人的行为即可完成并产生法律效力，而无需因之受益的相对方的任何行为。权利放弃与"不容否认"（estoppel）并非同义语，前者是指对明知权利的自愿或故意放弃；后者则是基于这样的原理：当某人实施某一行为或作出某一陈述后，他人对该行为或声明产生信赖并因之而实施行为，则公平和诚信原则要求该方当事人不得否认该行为或收回该声明。但有时这两者的区别又是模糊的。例如，在保险法中，不容否认的范围比权利放弃的范围要广，在某些情况下，甚至包括了权利放弃。如保险人放弃权利的，则根据不容否认原则，其不得在此后又主张该权利。权利放弃亦存在于其他法律中。例如，刑法中经常用于当事人对取得律师帮助权（right to counsel）的放弃〔如，"米兰达警告"（Miranda warning）〕或对刑事司法程序中的某一步骤的放弃，其核心在于每一当事人的自愿同意。在国际法中，经常用于对外交豁免权（diplomatic immunity）的放弃，该种放弃须以明示方式为之，并须经有关使团首脑的批准。各种权利放弃的具体内容参见各相关词条。

（2）弃权证书；权利放弃证明。指某人据以放弃其法律权利或利益的书面文件。

在翻译法律文件，尤其是协议文本的时候，要结合具体语境传达出 waive 和 waiver 的意思，不以词害意。

例 1. No waiver or amendment of any *Proposed Terms* shall be effective unless it is in writing and signed by the Borrower and the Coordinating Arranger. 对于《拟议条款》的放弃或者修正，须经借款人和协调安排人以书面形式签字确认，方可发生效力。

例 2. Each Party irrevocably and unconditionally waives all claims, rights and remedies which but for this Clause it might otherwise have had in relation to any of the foregoing. 各方不可撤销和无条件地放弃若非因本条则其原本可以对前述任何一项享有的一切请求权、权利和救济。

例 3. Each party irrevocably waives any right it has to object to any legal process being brought in those courts including any claim that the process has been brought in an inconvenient forum or that those courts do not have jurisdiction. 各方不可撤销地放弃其享有的对在该等法院提起的法律程序表示异议的权利，包括放弃声言该

法律程序是在不方便法院提起或者该法院无管辖权的任何主张。

例 4. The waiver by any Party to this Agreement of any breach of any term, covenant or condition herein contained shall not be deemed to be a waiver of such term, covenant or condition or any subsequent breach of the same or any other term, covenant or condition herein contained. 本协议的任何当事人对于违反本协议载有的任何条款、契诺或条件的行为放弃追究，不应被视为放弃该条款、契诺或条件，也不应被视为对于此后违反本协议载有的相同条款、契诺或条件或者任何其他条款、契诺或条件的行为放弃追究。

例 5. No failure to exercise, nor any delay in exercising, on the part of any party hereto, any right or remedy under this Agreement shall operate as a waiver hereof, nor shall any single or partial exercise of any right or remedy prevent any further or other exercise hereof or the exercise of any other right or remedy. 本协议任何一方当事人未行使或者延误行使本协议项下任何权利或救济，不应作为放弃该权利或救济；单独行使或部分行使任何权利或救济，不妨碍进一步或者以其他方式行使该权利或救济，亦不妨碍行使其他权利或救济。

例 6. Any term or provision of this Agreement may be waived, or the time for its performance may be extended, by the person or parties entitled to the benefit thereof. Any such waiver shall be validly and sufficiently given for the purposes of this Agreement if, as to any person, it is in writing signed by such person or an authorized representative of such person. The failure of any person hereto to enforce at any time any provision of this Agreement shall not be construed to be a waiver of such provision, nor in any way to affect the validity of this Agreement or any part hereof or the right of any person thereafter to enforce each and every such provision. No waiver of any breach of this Agreement shall be held to constitute a waiver of any other or subsequent breach. 凡有权获得本协议规定的利益的人或当事人，可以放弃本协议载明的条件或条文，或者可以延长履行本协议的时间。不论何人放弃上述条件或条文，如果采取书面形式并经此人或此人授权的代表签字，就本协议而言，才能

有效而且充分完成对上述条件或条文的放弃。本协议的任何当事人在任何时候未执行本协议的任何条文，不应被解释为放弃该条文，也不会以任何方式影响到本协议或本协议任何部分的有效性，任何人此后执行本协议各该条文的权利亦不会因之受到影响。对违反本协议的行为不予追究，不应被认为构成对其他违约行为或后续违约行为不予追究。

(2)

waver ['weivə] *v.i.* ① to become weaker or less certain 动摇

例 7. One hour had passed before the students' concentration began to waver. 过了一小时，学生们的注意力开始下降。

例 8. Dr. Watson never wavered in his loyalty to Sherlock Holmes. 华生医生对夏洛克·福尔摩斯忠心耿耿，从未动摇。

② to not make a decision because you have doubts 踌躇，犹豫
waver between sth. and sth.

例 9. I'm wavering between la choucroute and le cassoulet for dinner. 我拿不定主意，晚餐吃酸菜好，还是吃豆焖肉好。

例 10. The government is wavering between taking tougher measures to combat drugs and decriminalizing marijuana. 采取更严厉的缉毒措施，还是把大麻合法化，政府首鼠两端，不知如何是好。

③ to move gently in several different directions 摇摆

例 11. The fireplace flame wavered, throwing shadows on the wall. 炉火跳动，在墙壁上投下影子。

例 12. The branches of the weeping willow wavered in the breeze. 垂柳的枝条在轻风中摇曳。

wavering [ʌnˈweivəriŋ] *adj.* 犹豫不决的

unwavering [ʌnˈweivəriŋ] *adj.* 毫不动摇的

withstand & notwithstanding

(1)

withstand [wɪðˈstænd] *v.t.* (withstood, withstood) 经受住，抵御住

例 1. Timber frame builders have responded to modern concerns by investing considerable effort in professional engineering and design to ensure that their frames will meet today's needs and standards and will withstand the test of time. 木框架制造商在专业工程和设计上投入大量精力，消除现代人的顾虑，确保生产的木制框架能够满足当今的需求，符合当今的标准，经得起时间的考验。

例 2. The Seller shall have the Goods strongly packed and shall take measures to protect the Goods from moisture, rain, rust, corrosion and shock, etc. according to their different shapes and special features so as to withstand numerous handling, loading and unloading as well as long-distance transportation to ensure the Goods' safe arrival at the Site without any damage or corrosion. 卖方应当按照货物的不同形状和独特属性，牢固地包装货物，并采取措施防止货物受潮、遭雨淋、生锈、受腐蚀和震动等，以便确保货物经受多次搬运、装卸和长途运输之后可以不受损毁或者侵蚀地平安抵达现场。

例 3. The Technical Documentation provided by the Seller shall be properly packed to make them withstand numerous handling, long-distance transportation and to be protected against damages from moisture and rain. 应当妥善包装卖方提供的技术资料，使其能够经受多次搬运、长途运输，不会因潮湿和雨淋而受损。

例 4. All the Contract Equipment shall be packed in accordance with the normal

international standards in new and strong wooden cases or containers and necessary protective measures shall be taken to prevent the Contract Equipment from moisture, rain, rust, corrosion, shock and damages so as to make the Contract Equipment withstand numerous handling, loading and unloading as well as long distance ocean and inland transportation. 所有合同设备均应按照通常国际标准采用新的坚固木质容器或者集装箱进行包装，而且应当采取必要的保护手段防止合同设备受潮、遭受雨淋、生锈、遭到腐蚀、震荡和毁损，以便使合同设备能够经受多次搬运、装载、卸货以及长途海运和内陆运输。

(2)

notwithstanding [ˌnɔtwiθˈstændiŋ] *adv. & prep. (formal)*

例 5. Notwithstanding the foregoing, and with respect to any item of Disclosed Technology, the license granted in this Section 2.1 is subject to the limitations, if any, set out in Exhibit A with respect to that item. 虽然存在前述规定，如果附录 A 对于公开技术的任何项目作出限制规定，第 2.1 条授予的许可应遵守附录 A 对于该项目的限制规定。

例 6. Notwithstanding Clause 4.2, a financial institution providing the debt financing for the Project (the "Senior Lender") and its legal successor shall have the option to assume any and all rights and obligations under this Contract (the "Step-in Right"). 尽管有第 4.2 条的规定，为项目提供债务融资的金融机构（"高级贷款人"）及其合法继任者有权选择取得本合同之下的一切权利和义务（"介入权"）。

例 7. The obligations of both Parties as to disclosure and confidentiality shall continue in force for a period of at least 10 years from the date of disclosure notwithstanding the termination of this Contract for whatever reason. 不论本合同因何种原因而终止，双方当事人应当在从披露之日起的至少 10 年期间内继续承担披露和保密义务。

例 8. Upon termination of this Agreement, notwithstanding anything to the contrary in this Agreement, the Representative / Distributor shall be entitled to the payment of commissions under this Agreement only with respect to purchase orders placed with the Company by the Representative / Distributor prior to the termination of this Agreement resulting in the shipment of Products so ordered no later than 12 months after the termination of this Agreement, but in no event shall the Representative / Distributor be entitled to the payment of any commissions with respect to shipments of Products occurring more than twelve months after termination of this Agreement. 在本协议终止后，即便本协议存在相反的规定，对于代理人 / 经销商在本协议终止之前向公司发出的订货单，仅在所订购产品在本协议终止之后不迟于 12 个月装运时，代理人 / 经销商方可享受本协议所规定的佣金，但是对于本协议终止后 12 个月之后装运的产品，代理人 / 经销商无权享受佣金。

例 9. Notwithstanding subsection (1), the parties may agree to exclude the jurisdiction of the Court under this section and an agreement to dispense with reasons for the arbitral tribunal's award shall be treated as an agreement to exclude the jurisdiction of the Court under this section. 不论本条第（1）款作出怎样的规定，双方当事人可以约定排除高等法院根据本条享有的管辖权。双方当事人可以约定，凡协议规定无须说明仲裁庭作出仲裁裁决的理由，该协议应被视为一项排除高等法院根据本条享有的管辖权的协议。